"This wonderful book explains how a new 1
tion is revolutionizing our culture, and how Christians can and must
use the new media properly to spread the good news."
  —PHILLIP E. JOHNSON, Professor of Law
    (emeritus, University of California, Berkeley);
    author of *Darwin on Trial*

"*The New Media Frontier* is a much needed book that looks at the
historical, philosophical, and biblical why's behind the rising communication forms of blogging, vlogging, and podcasting. These are powerful opinion expressions and tools that can be used for good, bad, and
ugly purposes. So we'd better be prayerfully and intelligently thinking
about the words we type or say. All persons with a computer, whether
living in a major city or in an unpopulated rural area, now all have
the same instant ability and potential to build, encourage, challenge,
or tear down others to an unlimited audience on the Internet. You will
not look at blogging, vlogging, or podcasting the same way again after
reading this book."
  —DAN KIMBALL, author of *They Like Jesus but Not*
    the Church

"*The New Media Frontier* provides us with expert insight into the new
media revolution transforming our lives and today's culture and how it
can be used as an effective communication tool for advancing the love
and truth of God's Kingdom."
  —ANDREW JACKSON, blogger, SmartChristian.com;
    author of *Mormonism Explained: What Latter-Day Saints*
    Teach and Practice

"Can't tell a URL from and MP3? Here's a place to start."
  —MARVIN OLASKY, Provost, The King's College,
    New York City; Editor-in-Chief, *World* magazine

THE
NEW MEDIA
FRONTIER

BLOGGING, VLOGGING, AND PODCASTING FOR CHRIST

EDITED BY
JOHN MARK REYNOLDS & ROGER OVERTON
FOREWORD BY HUGH HEWITT

CROSSWAY BOOKS
WHEATON, ILLINOIS

Library of Congress Cataloging-in-Publication Data
The new media frontier : blogging, vlogging, and podcasting for
Christ / John Mark Reynolds and Roger Overton, editors.
   p. cm.
   Based on the 1st annual GodBlogCon held in Oct. 2005 at Biola
University.
   Includes bibliographical references.
   ISBN 978-1-4335-0211-8 (tpb)
   1. Mass media in religion—United States. 2. Mass media—Religious
aspects—Christianity. I. Reynolds, John Mark, 1963–   . II. Overton,
Roger, 1982–   . III. GodBlogCon (1st : 2005 : Biola University)
BV652.97.U6N49   2008
261.5'2—dc22   2008004193

VP		17	16	15	14	13	12	11	10	09	08
15	14	13	12	11	10	9	8	7	6	5	4	3	2	1

To
HUGH HEWITT,
our inspiration for exploring the frontier.

CONTENTS

FOREWORD

IT IS THE BEST OF TIMES. It is the worst of times. Some even believe it is the end of times.

I don't know about the latter, but I am certain about the former two observations.

These years wherein the full reach of instant and global communication was unleashed on the world, along with access to anyone with an Internet connection, will be studied for centuries, provided we retain the civilization that allows such study and the power generation to provide it.

And among church historians, the pioneers of Christian missional effort in the virtual world will receive quite a lot of attention for all that they did right, all that they did wrong, and all that they failed to see coming. Many of the pioneers of that effort are here in these pages. As we approach the 500th anniversary of Luther's nailing of his theses to the Wittenberg castle door, we are reminded of the immense numbers of years since then and his undeniable impact on the people of God, no matter what one's Christian denomination is. Luther was among the first to launch the enormous change brought about by a technology jump—the printing press—and just like Luther and those who followed him on both sides of the Reformation disputes, this first generation of Christian bloggers and virtual missionaries are laying down precedents and carving paths through dense woods. We have to hope they are the right ones.

Even as Christian new media launch, we have to see the virtual world for what it is—a deeply degraded place, even a dangerous one.

At this writing the world of commercial pornography is under assault, its sales and thus its profits plummeting, but this is no cause to cheer wholeheartedly. The revenues are plummeting because a slew of new free porn sites are exploding on the virtual scene, offering thousands of hours of the hardest-core porn for free, adopting the model of YouTube and flooding the Web every few weeks with what certainly must be more (and more distinctively bizarre) porn than the entire world had ever produced in its collective history prior to 1900, and perhaps even later.

An academic elite on edge over minute changes in global temperature is wholly indifferent to this tidal wave of porn. Global porning gets zero headlines even as global warming triggers conference after conference, film after film, award after award.

What if, as Christians suspect, porn scars the soul and disfigures the mind? What if, as experts in the field say, it can addict a young teenage boy in a very, very short time?

Then the years since the arrival of the Internet will have been the triumph of that particular evil, and the modest success of Christian blogging should not obscure that awful fact.

I have a friend who remarked to me long ago that Satan arranged for the demise of the Berlin Wall because he was doing better on our side. Would you be surprised to see the Web celebrated by Screwtape if Lewis were still writing today?

Then there is that small problem of the global jihadist virtual network, a universe of web sites peddling hate and intolerance, with many even encouraging the worst forms of extremism—the suicide murder of innocents. "The Terror Web," as Pulitzer Prize-winning *New Yorker* writer Lawrence Wright calls it, is empowering the worst of the Islamist extremists behind the 9/11 attacks and hundreds of other outrages.

The new media also comprise a force for polarization in Western politics, for crude and vulgar political speech, and for anonymous cruelty and quick-tempered vitriol.

And, yes, the doctrinal disputes that have long riven the body of Christ have moved online, adding velocity and ferocity to a half-century of clashes over the meaning of Christ's message and life.

In other words, the virtual world is a distorted mirror of the real world, which is itself a distorted and deeply broken version of the original model.

And it is exactly where Christ calls his best and brightest to be— among the pornographers and their victims, alongside the jihadists and their targets, side by side with the casualties of the new incivility in politics and theology.

This book brings together the thoughtful observations of the first wave of Christian new media activists and contributors, and they are an astonishingly talented group. As a Christian, I am grateful for their labors. As a broadcast journalist, I am humbled by their deep talent with communication skills. As a believer in the Western ideal, I hope for their success.

"How many divisions has the Pope?" Stalin once contemptuously asked.

"What chances have the Christians on the new media terrain?" postmodern skeptics might well pose as a successive question.

Be sure to revisit that question after you have read this volume.

Hugh Hewitt

INTRODUCTION

WHAT HAS BEEN IS WHAT WILL BE, and what has been done is what will be done, and there is nothing new under the sun" (Ecclesiastes 1:9).

This may seem like an odd quote with which to begin a book on new media. Certainly I could have chosen something more inspiring, like the Great Commission (Matthew 28:18–20) or "How beautiful are the feet of those who preach the good news!" (Romans 10:15). While the contributors to this book do hope to inspire, we hope to inspire in the right way, and to do so we must start by understanding that the new media are not all that new.

New media are nothing more than means of communication, which we've been doing for a very long time. All that is new is the form and availability of communication. Instead of writing to a local paper hoping to get an opinion published, many people have turned to publishing their thoughts on the Internet (primarily on blogs). Internet technology has enhanced textual communication by allowing anyone to publish their opinions. Likewise, YouTube is online television, podcasting is online radio, and Facebook and MySpace are online networks of mailing lists, but they are all democratized. With the click of a few buttons, each of us may add our voice to the media.

In the world of the Internet anyone with access can produce and publish information that is viewable by millions of people around the globe. Today we have direct access to eyewitnesses of news events worldwide, the speculations of scholars, and daily mood updates of old friends from high school (at least, we think that's how we know them). But not only do we have access to such things, we can also respond to this information and repackage it in our own distinctive ways.

Certainly this democratized technology has its benefits. Most obviously, we can note that any one person can preach the gospel throughout the world via the new media. We can more easily stay in touch with relatives and people within our own church communities. We can receive updates more regularly from missionaries who are in need of our spiritual and financial support. The opportunities to use new media to advance and demonstrate the Kingdom of God are significant, and we'll discuss many of them in this book.

If we were simply to leave it at that, though, we would be uncritical stewards of this new technology. It is far too easy to embrace the intended benefits of new technology without noticing the unintended consequences. One such consequence is that frequent readers of blogs become accustomed to brief, cursory thoughts and lose their appetite for longer, deeper commentaries. We might expect, then, that in the long run people will generally have a lower tolerance for complex lines of argument and will only give ear to pithy sound bites.

Through social networks like Facebook and MySpace we can easily keep in touch with hundreds of friends and family members. But such platforms make it easier to neglect spending time with people face-to-face. We are exchanging live human interaction for artificial Internet relationships. While the new media merely give us a new way of doing something we've done before, they establish both new opportunities and new consequences.

What are Christians to make of these changes in media? Should we dive in immediately and use every sort of media to the fullest extent for the sake of the gospel? Or should we wait and see what the consequences of new media might be before considering our participation? Since what we call "new" is inherently tied to the past, it will be helpful for us to reflect on a similar situation in church history to help formulate answers for today.

Perhaps the most notable advances in textual communication were those by Johannes Gutenberg in the mid-1400s. When the name Gutenberg comes up, most people tend to think of the printing press, a device that enabled pressmen to print up to 250 sheets per hour. Using his skills as a goldsmith, Gutenberg also developed the first hand molds used for creating the movable type needed in large quantities for the printing press. Additionally, he has been attributed with producing an oil-based ink more suitable for the press.

The most obvious benefits (from a Christian perspective) of these inventions took form shortly after a Roman Catholic monk, Martin Luther, nailed an academic complaint to a church door in 1517. Since his article was written in Latin, only scholars would have been able to read and respond to the document. But a new era of textual communication had emerged, and due to the work of an unknown translator and a printing press, copies of Luther's Ninety-Five Theses could be found throughout Europe within a month.

Textual information had once only been the domain of scholars and was also time-consuming and costly to produce. However, the advent of the printing press meant that the same information was now available to anyone who could read (a demographic that was growing dramatically), and more quickly and cheaply than ever before. Once Luther translated the Bible into German, common people could judge for themselves whether Luther's criticisms of the Church were accurate.

A longer list of benefits provided by Gutenberg's printing press could be provided, but it's important also to reflect on some of the unintended consequences. Many of the consequences were beneficial. Features such as page numbers and indexes began to be added to books since texts were becoming standardized. Gutenberg's movable type led to the creation of various fonts, and when thinner fonts were developed, that meant that books could be printed on fewer pages, again saving time and cost.

However, the ability to widely distribute ideas meant that harmful ideas could spread as quickly as helpful ones. Many people credit Martin Luther with many great writings that challenged Roman Catholic authority with sound doctrine. But not all of his contributions were praiseworthy. One of his books was titled *On the Jews and their Lies*, a book that encouraged hatred and violence against Jewish people. Just as the printing press helped spread knowledge of the Bible to popular society, so too did it help spread anti-Semitism across Germany.[1]

As it was during the time of the Reformation, the democratization

---

[1]There is some debate among historians as to just how much influence Luther had on anti-Semitism throughout German history since the Reformation. For more on this, see Johannes Wallmann, "The Reception of Luther's Writings on the Jews from the Reformation to the End of the 19th Century," *Lutheran Quarterly* (Spring 1987).

of information through technology will bring about both good and harm. Such lessons from the past are available for our instruction, and we would be unwise to ignore them as they can help guide us today.

Hugh Hewitt drew the connection well: "What is really going on is an information reformation similar in consequence to the Reformation that split Christianity in the sixteenth century. The key to that Reformation was the wide dissemination of Scripture among an increasingly literate laity. Today we do not have a canon, but we do have an appetite for information, the arrival of a new technology of distribution, and a million willing content providers."[2]

If we are going to seek God's glory during the dawn of this new technology, we cannot use it uncritically. God's people must be astute observers, seeking to keep in mind not only the benefits of our new abilities to communicate, but also what consequences we might not intend to bring about by their use. Yet in our critical stance, we cannot stand aside to wait and see what happens. If Christians are not on the forefront of this new technology to advance God's Kingdom, some other kingdom will be advanced through it. We must go forward thoughtfully, seeking to use whatever new technology is developed for God's glory.

It is to this end that we seek to inspire you in the right way. We'd like to offer some direction for how Christians can use the new media with discernment and grace. Part One of the book will further explain new media in general. Dr. John Mark Reynolds begins with a chapter examining the history of human communication in order to provide a fresh perspective on what *new media* really means. In the second chapter John Mark looks to the future of new media and stresses the urgency for Christian involvement before the opportunities vanish.

Matthew Anderson contributes our third chapter by looking at what dangers new media pose for those who uncritically dive into it. His chapter advocates the careful use of wisdom in consuming and creating digital content. With the foundation laid by these first three chapters, the next two chapters spell out exactly how consumers can become creators in the new media. Joe Carter explains how to blog in Chapter 4, and in Chapter 5 Matthew Eppinette and Terence Armentano explain how to podcast and vlog.

---

[2]Hugh Hewitt, *Blog* (Nashville: Thomas Nelson, 2005), xvii.

Part Two of the book looks to specific areas in which Christians can utilize new media more thoroughly and specifically. These areas include theology (David Wayne), community (Tod Bolsinger), pastoral ministry (Mark D. Roberts), youth ministry (Rhett Smith), evangelism and apologetics (Roger Overton), academics (Fred Sanders), education (Jason D. Baker), politics (Scott Ott), bioethics (Joe Carter and Matthew Eppinette), and social justice (Stephen Shields).

While these brief explorations of each topic will in no way say everything that could or should be said, we do hope they can help start a process of critical assessment so that when Christians use new media they will do so in a manner consistent with the character and quality of Christ.

This book has its roots in a conference that took place October 2005 at Biola University. That conference was the first annual GodBlogCon, hosted by the Torrey Honors Institute and administered by Matthew Anderson (MereOrthodoxy.com). The subsequent annual conferences were just as important to the progress of this project, and they were administered by Dustin Steeve (RightHouse.blogspot.com). These two men are on the front lines of new media ministry, and they have earned our deepest respect and gratitude. We are in debt to the many wonderful people at Crossway who helped this project come to print, including: Justin Taylor, Allan Fisher, Jill Carter, and Ted Griffin. We would also like to thank Joe Carter (EvangelicalOutpost.com) for his help in preparing the Glossary.

Roger Overton

PART ONE

THE LANDSCAPE
OF
NEW MEDIA

1

THE NEW MEDIA: FIRST THOUGHTS

John Mark Reynolds

www.ScriptoriumDaily.com

WHAT IS THE NEW MEDIA REVOLUTION? IS IT JUST HYPE?

The world of communication is changing quickly. Nobody disputes that. When I started graduate school in the late eighties, I was still using a Commodore 64 with 32K of usable memory. While my students point out that this simply means I am old, it also demonstrates that just twenty-five years ago education was very different from what it is today.

Not much e-mail existed back in the late eighties. By the early nineties e-mail had produced the friendship that would lead to my founding the Torrey Honors Institute at Biola University.

Not much information was easily available online. I taught an early introduction to philosophy on Q-Link, which used the massive installed base of Commodore computers to form an early network. A good class might include as many as ten or eleven students. This network (but sadly not the class!) evolved into America Online (AOL). Online philosophy is now extensive, and the dialogue is vast.

Not much Greek text was available in my field of ancient philosophy outside of expensive books. Now I use Perseus to research text every week for free.[1]

---

[1] See www.Perseus.tufts.edu.

Of course, the changes due to new media are not limited to philosophy, a field hardly at the cutting edge of technology. Some of these changes are not earth-shattering but still make life more pleasant. My computer just informed me of the weather forecast for tomorrow through a pop-up window, and the days of waiting in agony for Packer scores is over.

There are two reactions to this kind of change. The first is to dismiss it as unimportant, and the second is to proclaim that it is the beginning of a new age. The dismissive attitude always sounds wiser, while the optimist sounds as if he is trying to sell something.

The problem for the new media pessimist is that he is probably complaining about the new media from his Internet-based journal or on a television show that will be aired on the Net within minutes of his appearance. If he is giving a lecture on the unimportance of the new media revolution, clips from his talk can (and often will) be posted while he is speaking.

Information is so easy to get that anyone under forty is frustrated when it takes more than a few minutes to discover even a relatively obscure fact. When my wife claimed Gwyneth Paltrow was less than forty years of age, I could confirm the claim after the movie using my cell phone and the Internet. That is trivial, but it was not so trivial when I could easily compare local banks' home appraisals while talking to them on the phone.

This change in the availability of information and the ease of communication is real. In fact, it is so pervasive and has so quickly replaced the world that came before it that it is easy to forget how massive a change it is. The information and communication revolution is changing everything, from how one lives daily life to how one writes an airport novel.

Don't believe me? Watch reruns of detective shows from before the eighties (pre-cellular phones), and notice how many plot points would be ruined if the detective or victim had access to a cell phone.

Imagine a world where a few reporters can kill a story that does not fit their definition of news and where it is relatively easy for "stars" and personalities to massage their image.

Now recall that Dan Rather could report a story in 2004 about President Bush, but citizens of the new media, many with expertise that

CBS did not have, were able to expose the documents that were the basis of the Rather report as almost certain forgeries.

Get used to citizens with video cameras so cheap and small that opposition candidates can afford to shadow their opponents with devices to catch them in a career-ending gaffe like the infamous "macaca" incident that helped end George Allen's political career.

Hugh Hewitt, professor, lawyer, and talk radio star, wrote a book in 2006 whose title sums up the case for the optimists: *Blog: Understanding the Information Reformation That's Changing Your World*.

Hewitt focused on the web log (or blog for short), a kind of online journal that anyone can set up for free. He was right to do so since the rise of the blog meant that any person could set up his own opinion journal with theoretic access to millions. Of course, most blogs are not worth reading, but many provide up-to-the-second eyewitness testimony about the conduct of war, Christian apologetics, and informed pastoral reflections. In the 2008 presidential elections, both parties, but especially the Democrats, found themselves forced to deal with the power of the "net roots."

Of course, the new media are not limited to printed text. Ask the music industry, which is still trying to come to terms with the digital revolution. In the Torrey class of 2008, few if any students had purchased any music anyplace other than from their computers.

My students spend more time on YouTube than with the dying "major" networks. Consumers can easily become producers in this environment. One of my former students, Josh Sikora, creates high-demand content for YouTube from his modest apartment that can compete online with George Lucas.

The revolution is here, and it is real, but what does it mean? What will the implications be for Christendom[2] and for the church?

Philosophers like to ask big questions.

We also like to make sense of changes and suggest what these changes mean. At this stage of the development of new media, all thinking must be a sort of playful philosophizing because the change is so new and so little hard research has been done. But it is my belief that

---

[2]By Christendom I mean the Christian culture and polity that naturally flows in this present life from the normal life of the citizen of the City of God before the Second Coming.

while technology changes, the essence of men does not. The past can be of some help in speculating about what the future may hold, and even speculation might help start the discussion that this topic needs within Christendom.

WHAT DO WE MEAN BY NEW MEDIA?

You can know something without defining it.[3] I know that my old vinyl Amy Grant album is not part of the new media revolution but that my *Badly Drawn Boy* download for my iPod is. My new Madden 2008 Wii game is new media, but the Sorry board game we just played is not.

Definitions can help us think about a thing with more precision. "The new media revolution" is a catchphrase, perhaps a dated one, but it is the best available. It covers a wide range of activities from my ten-year-old playing Runescape to my sixteen-year-old listening to Fred Sanders's lecture on the Trinity online.

Let me propose a definition of new media that will capture video games, downloaded music, and TiVo.

> *New media*: any material presented to a person in a digital format that can be cheaply and easily accessed, distributed, stored in a variety of ways, manipulated, and consumed by an average person.

New media are digital.
New media are cheap.
New media are easy to access.
New media are almost too easily distributed and are easy to store.

New media can be transformed by the "consumer." In fact, the new media allow any consumer to quickly become a producer.

It will someday be possible for consumers to easily manipulate their favorite "shows." Imagine the ability (if you dare) to create new episodes of long-dead TVLand staples such as *Green Acres* or *Star Trek*. There will be no reason for a virtual William Shatner to ever

---

[3]The opposite belief, that you must define a thing in order to know what it is, is sometimes called the Socratic Fallacy after the mistaken notion that Socrates thought this way. He did not, and we should not. You can put the walrus on display in the zoo without being able to define it with precision, a task that cost the great J. R. R. Tolkien a great deal of labor.

stop "playing" Captain Kirk as fans manipulate his image and voice to produce new episodes of *Star Trek* featuring his character.

These are trivial (and even somewhat frightening!) examples, but the same power will allow the creation of new drama, music, and art forms that cannot even be imagined today. Most of it will be of poor quality (of course, most of the old media was of poor quality too), but nearly universal opportunity to produce will lead to greater chances for greatness.

This much we know. The old media produced *My Mother the Car* and gave a variety show to Sonny and Cher. Broader access seems unlikely to do much worse in entertainment.

For the serious-minded the new media revolution is a paradise. Cut from the need to produce a mass audience, it is now possible to "publish" as much as one wants on Shakespeare or even Sheldon Vanauken. My piano-playing fifteen-year-old daughter downloads reams of sheet music every week that would have been unavailable to her before the new media revolution. The sounds coming from her analog piano are made richer by the digital revolution.

The ability to "transform" new media content has come with a radical lowering of costs in producing high-quality materials compared to the past.

When I went to high school, the school sent home dittos made on ancient mimeograph machines. These dittos were painstakingly produced by secretaries creating stencils on manual or primitive electric typewriters. The stencils were placed on drums of ink that whirled out copies that were often smudged and hard to read. But since the stencils were hard to make and the job was a daily one, a certain amount of errors were tolerated. This is no longer the case. The reports from my children's school are stunningly professional compared to the old dittos.

New media are radically democratic, at least for now.

THE LONG TENSION BETWEEN LIVE AND PRESERVED PERFORMANCES

The new media are very important to Western culture because they promise to correct an imbalance between "live" and "preserved" performance. Early in human history almost all performance was live. A performance is live if you experience it while it is being produced, and in ancient times that was the way most people experienced music, storytelling, and education. If you wanted to hear music, you needed a musician. If you wanted to hear a good lecture on a topic, then you needed an expert present to give it.

The "old media" revolution changed this situation. With the rise of writing, painting, and other means of storing "performance" for later consumption, people were able (in some manner) to experience performances without being at the original performance. You did not need a rhapsode to recite the *Iliad* once Homer's work was written down in order to hear the poem. If you could read, then Homer could travel with you everywhere, as one copy of *The Iliad* did with Alexander the Great.

I love theater, and I love film. One art form is live, and the second is (mostly) preserved. Of course, theater might use some "preserved performance" (if it uses pre-recorded sound effects), and film has a live audience interacting with what is happening on the screen. Still, it is safe to say that theater is mostly live and film is mostly preserved performance.

But the example of theater and film also demonstrates the obvious truth that for some time in the West live performance has been declining relative to preserved performance. The situation from ancient times is reversed. Most of us hear almost all our music in a preserved form while hearing very little live. Many of us get most of our information from books and programs that preserve the information distribution of others.

There are advantages to both live and preserved performances. If this is so, then a loss of either would be harmful to society. It is my contention that the new media will correct the favoring of the preserved performance at the expense of the live. Old media was about preservation. The new media favor something very much like incarnation.

It is easy to forget that there are disadvantages to preserved performance. Even old technology, like this very book, has downsides for a culture or an individual. A seminal attack on preserved performance was written by the philosopher Plato who worried that philosophy in books lost something when compared to philosophy learned live in the marketplace with a teacher such as his own beloved Socrates. Plato said:

Take a man who thinks that a written discourse on any subject can only be a great amusement, that no discourse worth serious attention has ever been written in verse or prose, and that those that are recited in public without questioning and explanation, in the matter of the poets, are given only in order to produce conviction. He believes that at their very best these can only serve as reminders to those who already know.

And he also thinks that only what is said for the sake of understanding and learning, what is truly written in the soul concerning what is just, noble, and good can be clear, perfect, and worth serious attention: Such discourses he may have discovered already within himself and then its sons and brothers who may have grown naturally in other souls insofar as these are worthy; to the rest he turns his back. Such a man, Phaedrus, would be just what you and I both would pray to become.[4]

PLATO'S PROBLEM WITH PRESERVED PERFORMANCE

What is Plato arguing in this passage? It is very odd that a literary genius writing one of the greatest books, *Phaedrus*, would attack books in his book.

There is a silly opinion about Plato among artists, poets, and communicators that he didn't like art, poetry, and communication.[5] Plato worried about preserved discourse but went ahead creating it. He warned about the abuse of texts while creating them. One way he guarded against the dangers of static discourse was to write in the dialogue format. By building his conversations around conversations, Plato intentionally invited the reader to challenge his opinions. He tried to invite the reader into an active conversation with himself by paradoxes and puzzles.

Something more subtle than a rejection of preserved text is at play in *Phaedrus*. Plato is attacking written communication to argue that something is being lost when you preserve a performance.

First, preserved performance is static. It cannot change to suit the needs of the audience.

As a member of the audience, my interaction with a theater performance can change the play. A "hot audience" makes a play better, and a

---

[4]Plato, *Phaedrus*, 278.
[5]This is usually based on an unsubtle reading of Plato's criticism on some art in *The Republic*.

"cold audience" can do the reverse. Different responses draw attention to different aspects of the play often unseen by cast and crew.

Any actor knows this is the case. I once performed in a play held during a blizzard. Almost nobody showed up, and all the energy was drained from the cast or at least from me. It was the hardest performance of my life since getting three people to laugh is basically impossible, and when they do, solitary laughter in a great space is hard to tell from mockery.

Community is formed between actor and audience in live theater, music, or any other artistic performance. The audience is part of the event.

On the other hand, if I go to a film, whatever my response, the film just keeps rolling. I might be able to impact the viewing pleasure of fellow audience members but not the performers. Recently my wife and I had the misfortune of seeing a film in a theater full of junior high students. They ruined our evening, but they did not change the film. The actors and the production were not impacted by them. This is an important difference between the community formed between actor and audience in theater and the more distant relationship between film actor and filmgoer.

The community of audience and performers in a live performance is something that should not be missed, but our culture is making it ever easier to miss it. Music, for example, is now rarely experienced live, and this cheats us out of a deep musical experience that cannot be duplicated with even a perfect sound system.

When I married my classically trained musician wife, I thought the invention of the compact disc utterly exciting. With proper investment in a sound system, we could experience a performance of any composer—say, Bach—better than that heard in all but the finest concert halls. In my ignorance, musical paradise would dawn: the disc would never wear out, and we could purchase a "perfect" performance and repeat it whenever we wanted. Someday computers would execute the score perfectly, obviating the need for human musicians entirely.

It did not take long for my wife to demonstrate my folly. There is no such thing as a perfect performance of Bach. A score is not like a set of program instructions to be executed by the mechanical musician but a guide to be interpreted by the artist. One does not have to fall into postmodernism to say that authorial intent is not all there is inside a performance.

Most importantly, any canned music misses the interaction of the audience and performers. The response of the audience is *not* a distraction from hearing the music but is part of the concert. While a rude audience may ruin a concert by coughing or a ringing cell phone, a lively and well-informed audience helps create a unique experience for everyone in attendance.

Plato could point to a more serious problem: the fixity of the music is unfair to the musician. The musician cannot change the tone or color of the music to make it appropriate to her audience. The musician might wish to make her music fit my mood, but she cannot if it is recorded. Her interpretation of a piece might be cheerful when my mood is morose, but the musician cannot minister to my needs because she is caught in one musical mood eternally.

Even more potentially deadly to society is the fact that once fixed it is difficult for the author or artist to monitor the distribution of a performance (including books). This problem must be separated from any issues of government censorship. Whatever the means used to prevent it, most people understand that it is bad news when some people can access certain information.

A preserved performance is passive and waiting to be misused. The author can do little to prevent such a misuse.

Live discourse can be modified for the audience. An adult can change the topic when he sees a child walking into the room. A teacher can leave out key material in a lecture if she suspects that it might be misused by a student in the class. Meanwhile, the manual sits waiting for the terrorist to find information on weapons of mass destruction, and inappropriate entertainment waits for children to find it. There is no way for a book to monitor who picks it up.

A preserved text or performance simply cannot defend itself from misinterpretation or from vandalism. A lunatic attacked Michelangelo's stunning statue, *David*, in 1991 and chipped off part of a toe on the left foot. Michelangelo preserved his beautiful vision in a statue and placed it in public. With the glorious good came the opportunity for a great crime against art to be perpetrated by a madman.

Public displays of beauty allow for public profanation. The simple

lunatic can become a blasphemer against art and beauty. Even worse
is the simpleton who misunderstands the message of the preserved art,
so powerful that it commands his attention. In this way, the beauty
of the Bible can motivate horrific behavior when the simple-minded
misunderstand its message. The powerful work of the artist goes out so
that those who have ears to hear can blaspheme the message ignorantly
and inappropriately.

BOOKS CAN BE GOOD: THE BENEFITS OF PRESERVED DISCOURSE

I am writing a book chapter about the dangers of writing a book
chapter. Obviously I think the risk is worthwhile. The vast benefits of
preserved discourse to society far outweigh the liabilities. This is why,
despite the problems, nobody is going to quit painting, writing poetry,
publishing scientific articles, or sculpting.

The very permanence of preserved discourse allows an argument or
community to build knowledge over time. Science would be impossible
without preserved speech. Each generation can build on the discoveries
of the last. This is also true in theology and art. Old heresies need not
be fought in every generation if one attends to the old, preserved arguments. Beauty from one generation can grace the lives of succeeding
generations.

Preservation allows original arguments to be extended. There is
no need to begin each conversation at the very beginning, though one
can if it is helpful. Preservation allows the teacher or student to begin
where he or she wishes to begin.

The ability to preserve ideas and art allows a community to create
amazing works that are greater (potentially) than the sum of their parts.
A film is not just one preserved act of creation but the accumulated
contributions of many people. Any Hollywood movie must accumulate
small preserved actions in order to create the greater whole. A newspaper
is another example of preserved work composed of many smaller parts.
The whole paper can be greater than the sum of its parts.

In fact, in the light of these terrific benefits, it is easy to forget the
limitations of preserved media. Preserved discourse tempts humankind
to avoid community and become isolated from other living humans.
The pasty pale academic with no social skills is an obvious example of

this problem. Many of my students shun concerts and live in a world defined by the space between their iPod ear buds.

THE PRINTING PRESS TIPPED THE SCALE: THE IMPLICATIONS OF THE TRIUMPH OF PRESERVED MEDIA

For most of Western history, there was a place for both preserved and live encounters with ideas. Most music was heard live, and a lecture was a cheaper way to mass distribute ideas than costly hand-copied books. Isolation necessitated cultural ignorance.

Gutenberg changed all of that. The ability to produce books cheaply tipped the scale in favor of preserved media. Each technological advance, up to the creation of the personal computer, seemed to exacerbate this imbalance.

While the "new" technology allowed for cheaper end products (books and eventually records), producing and especially distributing them were still fairly expensive. Production and distribution came to be concentrated in the hands of a relatively small number of people. Access to certain ideas was much easier (a good thing), but the decision of which ideas or works of art would be preserved or distributed was in the hands of a few.

When books were hand-copied, anybody could produce a book if they had the time. There were fewer books, but there was bias toward copying only the best works. The slow distribution of books allowed for regional cultures to survive and even thrive. Folk ideas could survive in such a society. A local monastery with one copy of a regional book was not flooded by "imported" books.

When books were reproduced on expensive printing presses, there was a tendency toward uniformity. People could own more books, but they tended to be the same books as everyone else in their language group. Ancient libraries would often contain eccentric tomes (even the sole copies of an entire work), but the modern educated person's collection soon became much like his neighbor's.

There was a slow rise in power of the national over the local. This had many positive benefits, as anyone who has ever grown up in an inbred community knows, but something was lost as well. The regional or local can often serve as a breeding ground for new ideas. It can also serve as a conservative redoubt against a national madness such as fascism. Only a Germany where strong regional and local ties had been severely compromised could fall prey to a lunatic idea such as National Socialism.

In Christendom the authority of the university or seminary became dominant over the experiences of the local teacher or parish priest. The Grimm brothers gathered folk tales and preserved them for the future, but the very publication of their work tended to standardize the tales. In the age of Disney, there is no use asking what the children's tales of West Virginia are because they are the same as those of Los Angeles or New York City.

Slowly there developed an aristocracy of information and performance that began to stamp out competition. The local community theater could not compete with Hollywood. Even national filmmaking could not compete with the massive power of talent concentrated in Los Angeles making expensive films. The local paper could not easily compete with the national news service. Small regional colleges struggled to compete with giant state universities.

Homogeneity in speech and acceptable opinions resulted. Even regional accents could not survive the advent of television and movies, which tended to standardize speech patterns. Powerful media figures could marginalize or promote figures. Billy Graham could be puffed by William Hearst, developing an international ministry partially at the expense of regional ministries.

The dominance of preserved discourse eventually led to mass "orthodoxies." It was hard for small movements to compete with the power of those who had means to dominate a region with their preferred preserved discourse. Since power tended to be concentrated at national levels, bizarre and dangerous ideologies (such as Stalinism) could thrive by monopolizing the means of distribution of preserved discourse. A region could be neighbors with utterly different ideologies with little fear of "contamination" from the other ideas.

Even in Western nations that valued liberty and multiple opinions, expense in the production and distribution of preserved dialogue limited discourse. Options were criminally few in Stalin's Russia but, while crucially better, were still not broad by new media standards in Franklin Roosevelt's America. Fortunately, both World War II and the Cold War marked the triumph of more liberal societies over the possibility of an entire Western World held in thrall to one cruel ideology, whether fascism or communism.

Where there was a consensus about knowledge, stunning good and little harm was done by this situation. In engineering and the sciences, the vast wealth of the twentieth century was unlocked through the standardization and regularization of scientific methods and language.

It was also easy to develop a canon of "greats" in the arts and literature that did much to raise the tone of society. Shakespeare, the Book of Common Prayer, and the King James Bible could be read universally in the English-speaking world. This helped create a common cultural and linguistic framework that unified people groups in the Anglo-sphere.

There was remarkable growth in those areas best served by "preserved discourse" (science, "high" arts), but at a cost to those areas that need some "live" discourse such as the humanities. Folk art finds it difficult to flourish when it is forced into immediate competition with the establishment.

CHRISTIANS NEED LIVE AND PRESERVED PERFORMANCE

Christians do not choose between live and preserved discourse. One is not good and the other bad. Folk religions might denigrate the religion of books, but Christians do not. Some modern hedonists might want to cocoon away from the culture, but no Christians can and be true to the Faith.

Christians are inherently part of a community of believers, the gathering of his visible body on earth. This living body of Christ cannot be preserved in stone or writing but must be *experienced* in his church. If some Christians are called to a hermitage, they are the exception to emphasize the rule. As Hebrews 10:24–25 commands:

> *And let us consider how to stir up one another to love and good works, not neglecting to meet together, as is the habit of some, but encouraging one another, and all the more as you see the Day drawing near.*

The importance of living experience does not mean that Christians are hostile to preserved discourse. After all, Christians are also people of the Book, the Creeds, and centuries of literature, art, and music. Christians live together in a community informed by the preserved goodness, truth, and beauty of the past or other communities.

Because of this balance, Christian orthodoxy cannot survive without both the life of the Spirit and the Word. An overemphasis on texts and dogmas made possible by the rise of "old media" allowed the easy spread of "orthodox" teachings (at first a seeming advantage) but also made difficult any authentic community life within those teachings. By and large, those parts of the church based on personal experience began to suffer while "preserved" things prospered.

Even the so-called individualism of the modern church is not. Tales of conversion are published and religious experiences compared. This tempts churches and individuals to aspire to a standardized "personal" relationship with Jesus Christ. The advent of mass-marketed Christian books and other preserved media limited diversity.

Christian commitments to both "live" and "preserved" culture made it hard for the church to thrive in a culture that came to be overwhelmingly centered in "preserved" discourse. People spent far more time in front of their televisions or other forms of preserved discourse than in interacting with other humans. They did not just forsake the assembling of the brethren but nearly every other assembly.

IMPLICATIONS AS LIVE, OR ALMOST LIVE, DISCOURSE IS REVIVED

New media will rectify this old imbalance. They will empower live, or almost live, discourse. Why? New media put a premium on the reaction and creation of content and not just consumption. Due to the ease of production, they allow and even encourage conversations and not just presentations. This might seem counterintuitive since much of the media appear on screens, like much of the old media, but the ease of creating one's own content allows for immediate reaction to anything printed on the Internet.

As a result, new media encourage "conversations," whether on blogs or Facebook pages. If I like your web page, game, or blog, then I can recommend it quickly on my web page or blog. If I disagree with what you say, write, or produce, then I can review it quickly. After attending a local play, I am able to write a review that night that will be read by hundreds the following week. Someone who disagrees with my criticism of the play could respond just as easily. The comment sections of many blogs allow this to be done right on the original site.

These virtual conversations can lead to real conversations. People have bodies, and their physicality is an important part of who they are. As a result, the best and truest conversations will always be face-to-face. This book (an old media presentation on new media!) is the result of a group of new media writers (bloggers) who started meeting at a Godblog Convention for the past three years. These "live" meetings were invaluable, and we decided to preserve some of our conversations.

The reason for not merely preserving our thoughts in the new media (our blogs, podcasts, videos) points to the difference between old and new media. New media are vast and tend to be ephemeral. It is easy to create content, but the very ease weakens the demand for high quality, at least at this stage of the development of new media.

Books are, for the moment, more "serious" ventures. More time is spent on them since (unlike most new media) consumers will pay for the contents. As a result, there was still a role for "old media" in discussing the impact and future of "new media."

This book has probably already stimulated questions and disagreements in the minds of the reader. He may have underlined or written passionate marginalia disagreeing or agreeing with some points we are making. This marks a limitation to old media. If this book were online, the marginalia could be read by everyone who reads the main content. The reader could immediately ask the authors questions.

Unlike old media which were passive and required great effort to start a conversation, new media are preserved discourse that invite further conversation. In this way they are "preserved" discourse more like a Platonic dialogue than an Aristotelian thesis. Plato wrote in dialogues to provoke further dialogue. Aristotle wrote in arguments to transmit what he thought was knowledge to students. Since every web browser contains the ability to blog about any item viewed on the Web, Internet-based digital media in particular carry a Platonic invitation to challenge on every screen.

It is so easy to respond to the new media, to create, to modify, and to transform, that passivity is discouraged.

A good example is the web log or blog. Blogging is permanent but only to a point. The best blogs are sometimes worth keeping, but only if one kept the best of all the other blogs to which they respond. A blog is a living book.

New technology soon will allow for living film, art, and music. If a viewer does not like the ending of a new media "movie," he will be able to change it and post his new edit as a competitor. This discourse was impossible in the old theater system.

Particularly in the humanities and the arts, the new media will revolutionize those disciplines. They will be able to escape their science envy, the endless production of useless journal articles, in order to create human things.

Other areas that have flourished through the old media will not be harmed by the changes. They will continue to utilize the more hierarchical structures of old media appropriate to them. This includes fields such as the hard sciences and formal theology. These disciplines will be improved by new media by being exposed to lay criticism that can prevent "group think" from developing.

We can anticipate a decrease in respect for arguments based solely on positions of cultural authority but a simultaneous premium on trustworthy information sources. A professor can be criticized by a learned amateur and cannot escape that scrutiny by hiding behind his credentials in the new media world. People are going to be able to evaluate arguments by direct comparison. On the other hand, if the professor knows her stuff, she will soon be able to demonstrate it and has nothing to fear from comparison. Once she becomes a trusted information source, she will be a powerful player in the new media revolution.

Individuals will be their own brand instead of merely living off the reputations of the institutions that may pay their salaries.

THE NEW MEDIA REPRESENT A NEO-PLATONIC REVOLUTION

What will be the result of this revolution on education? We can anticipate educators shifting even more quickly from providing information (now easily available to anyone who wants it) to facilitating human development.

The kind of education that Plato encourages in his dialogues will flourish in this environment. Asking good questions will be paramount in the age of ever more sophisticated search engines. Learning to flourish as a human being will still require a teacher meeting with students. Humans have skin on and so will always learn how to be good humans best from other humans "live."

While there will always be an elite (at the very least based on intelligence), the new media do present opportunities for the rest of us to share some of their power. At least for the immediate future, many more people have access to means of global communication than ever before in history. As long as liberty prevails, a chance for more entrepreneurial activity in information distribution will exist.

The changing technology will also create new elites. This is true because some old institutions (such as universities) will not adapt quickly enough to the new way of doing things. Any institution that depends on a monopoly of information is doomed.

The new media will give power to people who lead with their whole souls within a community context. There will be no way to assert authority that is not historic or earned by excellence. The leader will have to be a servant of the servants of God. Churches and other institutions with power will not be able to bury or hide problems.

These are changing times, and it is sometimes fearful to live in such times. Fortunately, the church and Christendom survived many changes in the past. We have plenty of role models for courageously dealing with massive culture shifts.

The great Florentine poet Dante lived in times of even greater cultural change. Italy, the Empire, and the church were changing rapidly due to new ideas. Dante is a worthy guide to adapting the ancient message of the gospel to new times without trivializing it. He was part of a communication shift greater than that from old media to new as Dante wrote in Italian instead of the traditional Latin of the educated class. His use of vulgar language was never vulgar but united the vulgar and the aristocrat in admiration for his *Comedy*.

Dante demonstrated the power of Christendom to integrate ideas. His masterwork explored science, theology, philosophy, and poetry and was great art. He put it all together for his readers, bewildered by changing times.

Christianity retains the ability to unite the disparate elements of human culture. In a world where information overload may threaten to drown coherence in a sea of detail, the continued ability to integrate all parts of life into a worthy vessel will attract many to Christendom.

The good news is that for any group, propaganda will be harder to foist off on readers or viewers. Most people will have easy access to information from all points of view. Ideologies that depend on narrow outlooks and protection from dissent will wither. There will be an opportunity for open systems that can integrate without tyrannizing over the human mind.

Traditional Christianity is well suited for such a climate.

In the new media future it will be far harder to box off religion (or irreligion!) from the rest of life. Critics will be impossible to ignore, and any topic will be fair game. This can only strengthen the church. Basic understanding of apologetics will no longer be for a few but necessary for all Christians. If a group is willing to be modest about its claims and can defend the claims it makes, this will be a great environment for it.

More fringe groups like the Mormons will be able to survive only if they adopt defensible doctrinal positions. While new media make it possible for ideologically plausible groups to survive, even as tiny minorities, they make it harder for ideologically sketchy groups to flourish. Small religious groups will be able to publish but not to hide from scorching criticism.

The new technology also will revive the lure of the small town so loved by Burke and Tolkien.[6] The new media will allow small communities to be as in touch with the "great cultural conversation" as big cities. They will be able to compete more easily with those great centers as the cost of the creation and distribution of ideas continues to plummet.

Because traditional Christians must by nature embrace living and orthodox faith, they are uniquely placed to benefit from both live and preserved performances.

WHAT SHOULD BE DONE?

It might seem obvious, but the religion of the Incarnation cannot stop at blogging. God is not our "Facebook" friend. He is a person, and he has chosen in his sovereignty to reach out to humankind. For all the

---

[6]Ironically, Tolkien loathed much of modern technology.

benefits of new media, we are not yet in paradise. With great good will come great evil. Old institutions will be shaken, and much that has been taken for granted for hundreds of years will change. How should the Christian react?

"Be not afraid!" John Paul the Great would say.

Too much Christian discussion about the new media concentrates on what is wrong with them. It is true that new media have allowed bad ideas to find an audience and easier access to terrible things. Such a concentration on evil runs the risk of missing what the Holy Spirit is doing in new media. Charles Williams warns that fixating on the Devil's work often leads to acting like devils. Liberty is truth's best friend, while attempting to protect the truth out of fear often does more harm than good.

Christians should err on the side of liberty and embrace dialogue. Closed communities, such as Christian universities with strong statements of faith, allow for a home base where ideas can be safely generated, but Christians must move outside of those groups to broader communities. The new media provide an excellent opportunity to do so. I have been able to watch the reaction to my apologetic arguments on hostile web sites and tune them to make them more effective. I have had errors corrected and have learned from loving my ideological enemies enough to listen to them.

Christendom needs preserved discourse within a living community.

For the Christian, our motive must always be based in love. Love can be hinted at in books and art but can only be experienced between living beings. The best of Christian new media, like the best of old media, will move men to their own quest for God, powered by a love that drives us beyond words to a Word so true, beautiful, and good that it can only be lived and not spoken.

High phantasy lost power and here broke off
Yet, as a wheel moves smoothly, free from jars,
My will and my desire were turned by love,
The love that moves the sun and the other stars.

Paradise, XXXIII, 42.

2

THE FUTURE OF
NEW MEDIA

John Mark Reynolds

www.ScriptoriumDaily.com

THE PLACE OF TRADITIONAL CHRISTIANITY IN THE NEW MEDIA

Traditional Christianity will benefit from the new media revolution, but only if it acts quickly. The greatest impediments to action are fear and complacency. Christians are beginning to overcome their fear but still cling to old media paradigms or ways of doing things. Christians also run the risk of misunderstanding the change or misidentifying where we are in it.

Where are the new media headed? How should Christians strategize in this new technological world?

Anyone who claims to know the truth about these questions is either God or one of his prophets.

Anyone not named Jesus who also lacks a virginal mother is not God. I am neither a prophet nor the son of a prophet.

So instead of the truth, let me offer some suggestions designed to provoke thought by proposing tentative answers to these questions. The full story of the new media revolution is being blogged, captured on YouTube, and podcast as I write. In the months between my writing these words and your reading them, I am only certain of this: much will have changed.

Studies of the new media are of limited use. There is little precedent for a change in human behavior that is so rapid that many of us over forty know we lived in a time before e-mail, mobile phones, and the Web but still find it hard to believe it. Our lives now are so radically different that we cannot remember the time before the revolution.

I have discussed the new media revolution with hundreds of Christian bloggers, educators, leaders, and students. It seems safest to me to predict the future of the new media revolution by looking at other revolutions in human affairs and trying to find a pattern in them.

The new media revolution has not, after all, changed the essential nature of mankind.

My own educated guess about the future of new media is this: the days when it was easy to "buy into" the new media are either over or are ending now. Christians must act quickly while we still have any chance to capture the new media habits of this generation.

Humans can only consume a finite amount of media in a day and tend to be creatures of habit. Just as those who have hundreds of cable channels end up watching a small fraction of the total, so the coveted spots on the browser bars of the world are limited. There is no reason to think browsing habits will be any harder to shake once formed.

God bloggers still have a chance to shape a rapidly evolving new media world, but our opportunity is shrinking fast.

Definitions: God Bloggers and Traditional Christianity

Who is a God blogger? A God blogger is any person who uses the new media to discuss his religious faith.

In the United States most religious people are "Christians"; so the term has been dominantly applied to Christians writing about or expressing their Christian faith using new media. The first three Godblog Conventions (2005, 2006, and 2007) invited speakers and participants who affirmed traditional, creedal Christianity whether Protestant, Catholic, or Orthodox.[1]

The exclusive nature of the Godblog Convention was controversial to some non-Christians and a few Christians on the religious left who organized their own meetings as a result.

---

[1] I helped organize the first three Godblog conventions. C. S. Lewis's idea of a "mere Christianity" was a guide.

The 2007 Godblog Convention was held in Las Vegas in conjunction with the Blog World and New Media Expo, "the first and only industry-wide trade show."[2] The goal of this move was to provide traditional Christians in new media a "home base" within the broader industry convention. As we shall see, the existence of a God Blog Convention within a "mainstream" expo fits well with the best strategy for Christians as they approach the new media.

Current State of God Blogging

Blogging is easy to start but hard to continue. Five years ago it was easy to become overly enthusiastic about the immediate power of the new media. As people rushed to start blogs or to load family videos onto YouTube, it appeared the old media would be totally lost like Atlantis under a wave of homegrown content.

That did not happen. Most people discover that maintaining a blog is hard work. They actually have very little to say and only a small amount of expertise. Though the aggregate knowledge base of the new media world is huge, any individual blogger has only a minuscule slice of it. If oversold on their potential influence, the actual experience of writing and producing for a tiny audience can be discouraging to a new blogger.

Like everything else on the Internet, the speed at which the revolution would take place was vastly overestimated. This is a natural mistake. Because the Internet itself has vastly increased the speed of communication, it is easy to assume that it has increased the speed of everything else. Since it is now easy to donate money online to repair hurricane damage, Americans forget that moving steel and other building materials still takes place in the real world. Trucks do not move as quickly as money.

People do not change as quickly as Microsoft can produce system patches. Old habits die hard, and the older generation of consumers (thankfully) remains to buttress old media. A quick glance at commercial advertising on the evening news programs demonstrates that this can be a lucrative market. Old media are also very good at what they do. YouTube videos are entertaining for a while, but even the best of them cannot yet compete with the professional quality, coming from decades of experience, of the old media.

---

[2]See http://www.blogworldexpo.com.

All of this is discouraging to those who believed the revolution would immediately wash away every trace of the old media regime. However, this is never the way revolutions work. Even decades after the fall of the tsars in Russia there was evidence of Old Russia's sway in the hearts and minds of the Russian people. Even very rapid and aggressive changes, like the Revolution of 1917 in Russia, do not immediately change people's deep habits, dispositions, and customs.

The reaction to the hyperbole on the new media prophets has been a foolish confidence by the "counterrevolutionaries" of the old media that blogging and new media were just illusions all along. This is impossible to maintain when each year more Americans turn their attention away from old media to new. The process is not as immediate or as fast as some of the prophets of new technology predicted, but it is happening and at historically rapid rates.

The fad of God blogging is over, but the real culture influence is just beginning.

STAGES OF A REVOLUTION

There are many ways of thinking about the stages of a revolution. My own reading has concentrated on political revolutions. While an imperfect analogy for business or cultural change, such revolutions still can illuminate the stages of the process. Why? Humans are the common factor in both kinds of change. Political revolutions are changes in thought. They can occur very rapidly as one order is swept away by the new. They can be relatively benign (for example, the American Revolution) or horrific (for example, the Russian Revolution), but they tend to follow patterns.

The new media revolution is technological, but it is a technological change much more profound than the introduction of television or radio. Why? The new media make up a new delivery system and means of production for *every* form of indirect human communication. Printing changed libraries and information distribution. The invention of musical recording had a great impact on live bands. Movies changed drama, and television transformed movies. The new media change every medium simultaneously and make possible the communication of almost any message.

It is useful to compare earlier technological revolutions to this one.

The development of the printing press was seminal to all of the changes now occurring. But in many ways the very success of the earlier revolutions limits their usefulness. The earlier big changes in technology occurred very slowly relative to the changes taking place in the new media revolution today. This is natural since changes in technology rely and build on each other. One way to view the new media is as the natural outcome of centuries of technological progress. At this stage in development, however, the speed of progress has increased.

For this reason, *political* revolutions, which have taken place very quickly in the twentieth century, may be more useful for a perspective on how sudden changes shape and are shaped by their participants. Earlier, slower technological change was evolutionary more than revolutionary as the speed of impact on culture was often measured in centuries. These were slow-motion revolutions.

Like political revolutions, the new media changes are best measured in decades. This means that just as a young boy might have been born in pre-revolutionary Saint Petersburg, lived most of his adult life in Leningrad, and then died in a rechristened Saint Petersburg, so many of us will live through the birth, maturity, and perhaps even the senility of the new media revolution.

This was not true of earlier communication technological changes before the twentieth century.

Will the course of a political revolution act as a useful metaphor or guide for another kind of social change? At the very least, I think it serves as a story to illuminate the kind of change we have experienced and are about to experience in communication, entertainment, and education.

The most important revolution of the last century was the Russian Revolution of 1917. In many ways, most of the political history of the century was a reaction to it. The rise of fascism in Italy and Germany would have been very unlikely without the fear it engendered. The Cold War that dominated the end of the twentieth century spurred on many of the technological changes that created the new media, including the development of the Internet itself. The Russian Revolution was mostly harmful, but it need not have been. In many ways a relatively benign constitutional monarchy under a new tsar may have been as probable as the advent of the tiny Bolshevik party to power.

The Old Regime: Complacent but Unstable
Nicholas II ruled a Russian Empire that was rich, long-lasting, but ready for change.

The "old media" of the 1970s and 1980s failed to serve many communities well. This was especially true of minority groups, religious people, and social conservatives.

The Revolution: Chaos and Creativity
The fall of Tsarist Russia ended up being tragic, but it began with a more hopeful period of chaos and creativity. Early on Michael, the brother of the last tsar, might have been able to take power if he and other leaders in Saint Petersburg had possessed more nerve or foresight. Even more likely, the moderate socialists in the government might have been able to form a republic and avoid the tyranny of Lenin and Stalin.

Many relative unknowns had a chance at power, from generals like Kornilov on the right to socialists like Kerensky on the left. The first period of the revolution took unexpected turns and led to a feeling of extreme hope. Anything seemed possible.

Similarly, the pre-Internet of the BBS or "bulletin board system" was relatively unstructured. Almost anyone seemed capable of putting together a local system, linking several systems, and doing (relatively) amazing things. I signed on to a "town hall" BBS that allowed access to conservative punditry and discussion threads. It was a "closed world" with no access to any other system. At the same time, I could access Commodore 64 BBS systems that were filled with game tips, games, and even more discussion threads. But the two BBS systems could not talk to each other.

Biola University still retains a BUBBS system (Biola University Bulletin Board System) that functions more like the closed networks of the late eighties and early nineties. There is only clumsy access to the Internet from it.

Young men in their basements could often run "networks" that were better than those found at much richer companies. Some older ways of doing things survived, such as the QWERTY keyboard, when they might have changed. In the early days, the joke was that the desire of *Star Trek* fans to network created the Internet. The harmless desire to get *Star Trek* episode guides probably did drive the technology and motivate some early users, but so did the more pernicious desire for easy and private access to pornography.

This period of time ended when universities, major technology firms, and businesses began to settle on universal protocols and technology. The rapid rise of e-mail, which depended on the ability to get information from one computer to another, suggested that closed systems could not last. The guy in the basement could not compete with MIT, Microsoft, and Mosaic.

This period of a revolution is short and chaotic and is often looked back on with nostalgia after things have settled down.

The First Players: Promise and Peril

The first Russian governments after the Revolution against the tsar were very unstable. They contained men who appeared to be of enormous importance at the moment but who spent the rest of their lives writing books to remind folk that once they had been enormously important. Whether their names were Lvov or Kerensky, they made the first attempts to govern the new situation. Most of them failed, but their failure allows us to overlook an important fact: however brief their time in the sun, the Revolution allowed even that one moment of greatness.

Similarly, the nineties marked a period of time when it was possible for a local newspaper to have a deeper and better site than a major network. "The Nando Times"[3] was just one example that seemed to show that a small start-up could compete with much bigger players.

As early browsers and search engines developed, content providers who took risks could flourish. They also soaked up vast amounts of money on dubious projects. Oddly, the "Internet bubble" and the collapse of some of the sillier .coms is still the image that many people have of the Internet, especially among Christians with whom I speak.

They imagine the Internet as being a vast untamable wilderness of scams from Nigeria, dubious medicines, and even more disreputable web sites. More naively they imagine that one can still just throw up a church web site using free templates and that this will be acceptable or even make them "cutting-edge and cool."

---

[3]See http://en.wikipedia.org/wiki/Nando.

These same people get e-mail from their mother and sports scores from ESPN online and check the polling numbers of presidential candidates on Rasmussen Daily.[4] Such mainstream companies distribute vast amounts of data better than the old media, but this points to an important fact.

The world that allowed Matt Drudge to move from nobody to President Clinton's online tormentor is fading. Many of the first players are now forgotten or vastly richer since they now work for companies playing catch-up in the new media. Like tsarist generals fighting for the Bolsheviks in World War II, the more nimble old media companies were able to use their large resources to catch up. Microsoft itself initially missed or mishandled the Internet Revolution but was able to make up for it with the best protection against rapid change: cash.

Sadly, despite being warned, many churches, denominations, and individual Christians missed this stage of the revolution entirely. Even worse, as many are dimly becoming aware that the tsars in denominational headquarters can no longer control the conversations, they are producing new media content as if the revolution were still in the early stages.

Just being able to give a good speech made Kerensky a player in the early days of the Russian Revolution, but as the revolution matured, the need for an organized party with resources caught up with him. The price for success kept increasing, but Kerensky would not pay it. Lenin did, and so Lenin ended up running Moscow while Kerensky wrote whining books in exile.

Christians must distribute information and content in the new media, but the infrastructure required is now greater. Just as photocopiers upped the ante for the acceptable presentation level of the church bulletin or newsletter, so the maturing of the new media revolution is changing what is acceptable in the presentation of our ideas through the Internet.

The church runs the risk of failing to keep up and playing Kerensky to the secularist Lenins of the new media. After all, just because you are on the Internet does not mean anyone is paying attention. As new media make the Internet more crowded, quality will be the easiest way to get through the noise.

---

[4] See www.RasmussenReports.com.

Civil War and Consolidation

Sadly for Russia, the brief period of freedom ended in civil war, socialism, and Stalin. Power was consolidated, and new social, political, and cultural norms closed in on Russia until the late 1980s and 1990s.

Ironically, the thaw in Russian politics took place during the time of utmost flexibility in the new media revolution. Over the next decade, just as the promise of liberty in Russia receded, so competition began to weed out competitors in the new media. Not surprisingly, deep pockets of some competitors began to increase the cost of running a competitive site.

Revolutions die. The opportunities to control the direction of those revolutions can die more quickly. The revolutionaries of 1917 often died in the consolidation that followed. Those who did not die physically died spiritually as the temptations of power caused them to do great evil.

For good or bad, most societies are able to shake off the fever of revolution and establish a new "normal." Sometimes this is mostly good, as in the American Constitution of 1789 following the American Revolution, and sometimes it is horrific, as was the rule of Stalin in post-revolutionary Russia.

During the drunken days of revolutionary change, it is easy to imagine that such shifts are the permanent state of men. People begin to talk about "permanent revolution." This is nonsense, however. In fact, once a political revolution becomes that self-aware, it has generally ceased to be truly revolutionary and merely becomes political. The political man of affairs begins to replace the man of action at the center of things.

Just as the exciting, wicked, and daring revolutionaries of Russia became the tired old men mostly seen attending funerals for their fellows in the Reagan years, so the new media revolution will eventually taper out.

Some suggest that the very nature of the "new media" revolution means that it will not slow down. The Internet is, after all, not a person, so it cannot grow old.

The most important limit to the new media is the *time* and patience of the human consumer. The second limit is the price of *quality* as the industry matures. There may also be an absolute limit to the amount of available *talent* in a culture. It might be that most people want to be consumers and not creators or that many people simply lack the talent to be creators of quality content.

A new technology may widen the pool of those who get to write, but it cannot widen it past the point where everyone who can write well has the chance to do so. At that point the revolution stagnates due to the limited pool of potential new, talented revolutionaries.

A comparison with the history of the movie industry may make this point. We can easily forget that there is no theoretical limit to the number of movie companies that could exist. Early movie technology was relatively cheap, and many studios sprouted up all over the nation. In a relatively short time, however, most of those companies merged into the great studio systems.

Why? Early films were not very good. Very good films required the combined genius of many crafts. Technology was cheap and getting cheaper, but audiences began to demand higher quality. The higher quality tended to force up the human cost (always the greatest) of doing business. People still needed to get paid for making movies (if they were to be of high quality) as they had been paid to make theater.

People could only go to so many movies because they had only so much free time they wanted to spend on movies. The more entertainment options they had, the harder it was for studios to get an audience. Studios with the expertise and money to advertise or find other tricks to get an audience had an advantage.

Part-timers will always have some quality disadvantages when compared to full-timers. The movie industry could have been more diverse, but the three limiting factors (time, quality, and talent) kept it from being so.

There is every reason to think the new media revolution will end the same way. Many sites will feel the call to exist, but few will be chosen in browsers.

Americans will, after the first rush, have only limited free time that they will choose to spend on the new media. However high that number might be, it will still be finite. You might be able to browse billions of sites, but most people will choose to stick to a few comfortable favorites. They will choose to spend that time on higher quality sites.

(I do not mean by that the "best" sites. The best movie-makers did not end up running the biggest studios.)

Quality demands in new media are increasing. The cost of having a good web site is soaring. When I started, I could get readers by designing a site myself, but now Scriptorium Daily must hire web consultants to compete in order to maintain our relatively low market penetration. While new media will always be "cheap" compared to old media, the costs of looking good on the Internet are getting relatively higher.

The simple analogy with printing technology will show why this is so. When it was hard and costly for printed material to reach a certain standard, consumers were tolerant when reading matter scarcely made it. When new printers and software made it easy to achieve these levels, some assumed that productivity would increase, and costs would decrease. This did not always happen, however. Competition set a new standard of professionalism. If everyone could now easily meet the old standard, schools and businesses simply adopted a new more rigorous standard.

The same thing is happening on the Web. GE spends millions on the content and design of web sites, and the standard for an acceptable site increases. If a blog is interested only in getting family to view its content, then a lower standard is possible (though even there it is getting higher!). If a church wishes to get young adult eyes, they'd better seek professional new media help.

Finally, a quick scan of blogs indicates that most people simply cannot write well or do not wish to learn to write well. Giving more people access to writing technology may produce more opportunities to get a C. S. Lewis, but it has self-evidently not made me one.

There is a finite talent pool out there, and the higher the standard, the smaller the pool. There is an ocean of bad blogs, a great lake of decent ones, a pond of Lewis-level talent (if we are lucky), and each generation may produce a cup or two of genius.

The good thing about the new media is we will get more, but the bad thing about the new media is that we will get more. Most of the "more" will be bad (just as it was in the old media). Of course, the exciting thing is that there can be (due to easier access) more of the precious good content, but the talent pool is not infinite and almost certainly is not the same as the population of the world.

If the talent pool becomes dominated by secular thinking (as happened in the movie industry), there will be no way for Christians to "buy" their way into the game. You cannot hire twenty mediocrities to equal one genius, but when you have one genius you can hire twenty mediocrities to make his presentation better.

If they were wise, parachurch and church ministries would scan the revolutionary new media pool now, seek to mentor the best of them, and hire the talent long-term while they are still moldable, available, and cheap. The motivation for this must not be so we can win a culture war but for the sake of the souls of the talented and of the billions they will influence in the future.

WHAT SHOULD TRADITIONAL CHRISTIANS DO?

My students talked to scores of Christian workers in churches all over the western United States before the 2007 God Blog Convention. What we discovered was a shocking ignorance of trends already a decade old.

Christians are going to be locked out of the new media revolution if we do not know it has happened before it is over. Almost as bad is if we merely fear the changes and so carp about them like Russian reactionaries in exile in the 1920s longing for a tsarist restoration. We may still exist but will be marginalized at the edges of American culture.

Christians must not miss this biggest communication revolution the same way we missed or messed up our response to the smaller changes in radio, movies, or television.

First, Christians must recognize the opportunity and cost of the new media revolution. Having recognized the opportunity, Christians should check their motivations. Are we acting to serve Christ or to build personal kingdoms? Are we acting in love to help our fellow human beings or to win? We must pray, think, and then act on our opportunities. We must never fight a culture war for the sake of fighting but for the sake of a just peace that will follow victory.

Second, we must form Christian communities online for fellowship and the development of better content. Virtual reality allows for the creation of a Christian community, a virtual Christendom, in ways that would be much more difficult or dangerous in real-reality.

Some Christians have an immediate distaste for "Christian" anything. This is understandable as the experience of Christians retreating from the culture has not always been positive. When I was growing up, the phrase *Christian movie* meant a mediocre film. Christians do need mutual fellowship and encouragement, however, to act Christianly.

The experience of the monastic movement, which formed communities in order to impact culture, is a more positive example. Many people think of the medieval monastery as a retreat from the world, but that is not accurate. The best monastic communities were centers for broader cultural education and technological innovation, as well as being safe redoubts for Christendom. Many were centers for missionary work and cultural renewal because they were centers where Christian ideas could safely dominate.

The missionary monk with his world-class education and new technology moving out from his beautiful and safe home base is a lovely example for Christians confronting the barbarian world of cyberspace.

We do not need Christian new media but Christians in new media. That is easy to say but much harder to do. If Christians form a ghetto in communication, then quality and impact will suffer. Christian new media will have the impact of Christian television.

Total integration can be equally devastating. If most encounters in new media that a Christian has are secular and the demands for success are secular (mostly financial), then the soul and the product of that soul will tend to be shaped in a secular direction.

We have it on good authority that bad company does, after all, corrupt good morals (1 Corinthians 15:33).

New media, with their unlimited virtual space, allow for "porous borders." A Christian should network and work with Christians in a home base (a province of Christendom) that allows him a like-minded community in which to try out bold ideas while also being part of a bigger body so as to keep away from the errors of the culturally inbred. This broader community will allow him to remain a full citizen of Christ's bigger Kingdom. Equally, he can easily expand his network to include non-Christian friends and allies.

Christians should not totally retreat from open forums such as YouTube but should also not abandon building a parallel infrastructure of their own. I can take my children to play in my own backyard and to a public park. Caution must be exercised in both!

Most of all, Christians and Christian organizations must identify gifted souls and encourage them. These gifted souls should be taught to be servants to those less gifted and help them realize their potential in Christ. We must occupy the new media until King Jesus comes.

I am not, of course, suggesting any centralized command structure for Christian development of the new media. Individual Christians are free to develop social and business networks of like-minded people. These networks can and should be narrow (people who agree with me on most important things) but must also be broad when the churchman wishes to capture the attention of the American public. The limits of time, quality, and talent will necessitate broad alliances within virtual Christendom and outside it.

Christians should send "new media" ambassadors into hostile environments online. These representatives of the faith can serve to remind non-Christians of the existence of Christians and Christian ideas. Christians should allow friendly skeptics into their own communities as well.[5] Embassies work both ways!

Christianity has faced pagan persecution, barbarians, heresy, and the challenge of integrating the faith into nearly every culture in the world. The new media revolution is no greater challenge and is in some ways far less of a threat than any of these.

Blogs and the new media are not going away. It would not be desirable to go back to a time without e-mail or the easy distribution of information. Liberty is, after all, a blessing even in the fallen world.

The hype around the new media has diminished, but the serious work of developing new ways of delivering ideas, stories, and communication has just started. Christians will do this work best if they apply the same standards to it that should govern our work in every area. Christians will fail in virtual reality just as we have in plain-old-reality, but just as surely the Holy Spirit will overcome our weakness and will mercifully bring great good to the world through us.

The future is not fearful but is God's. As a result, powered by love, we can bring the Kingdom that is within us to the new media age.[6]

---

[5]Think of MacPhee at Saint Anne's in C. S. Lewis's book *That Hideous Strength*.
[6]Some material in this chapter appeared on my blog at Scriptorium Daily.

THREE CAUTIONS AMONG THE CHEERS: THE DANGERS OF UNCRITICALLY EMBRACING NEW MEDIA

Matthew Lee Anderson

www.MereOrthodoxy.com

IT IS RARE THAT I FIND MYSELF stuck in a discussion with high schoolers, so this was foreign territory. I was attempting to get a group of seventeen- and eighteen-year-olds to reflect on the societal changes that recent technological developments (iPods, cell phones, MySpace, etc.) have precipitated, and failing miserably. Rather than the enthusiastic, lively discussion I was expecting, I was greeted by skepticism and resistance.

Yet I found it an illuminating conversation all the same. As these Christian high school students talked, two themes emerged. First, the changes technology has wrought are mostly invisible to them. Just as most of us do not remember life before cars were ubiquitous, so these students could not conceive of a world without text messaging, cell phones, or iPods. Their cell phone, after all, has been affectionately stored in their purse since fifth grade. For them, the world was static—technology had no impact on their experience at all.

The second theme was closely related and far more prevalent: "It just depends on how you use it." Technology, they claimed, is a tool, and as such, its value is measured in strictly utilitarian terms. If

MySpace helps them "stay in touch" with friends better, then no further questions are worth thinking about (such as what they mean by "stay in touch" and "friends").

That young people would approach technology through strictly utilitarian categories is not surprising. But a corollary to this notion was far more interesting: everyone in the room agreed that if you didn't *want* the technology to affect you, it wouldn't. "We can choose," they fervently insisted, "whether we let ourselves be affected by technology. If we watch a movie and don't want it to change us, it won't."

There is clearly an element of truth to this notion. Humans will always preserve the freedom to respond to the world intentionally. But it also demonstrates a crucial naivete about the interaction between the world and us. While it is possible to live in a world without lightbulbs, their ubiquity makes it nearly unthinkable that anyone would, which consequently subtly moves the lightbulb into the "need" category for us. This shift in our attitude toward lightbulbs is imperceptible, at least until the power goes out and our normal habits and routines are disrupted. When this happens, we quickly discover that the lightbulb has shaped our experience of the world in ways far deeper than those of which we are aware.

In other words, we do not control how technology shapes our lives as much as we might think. The notion that technology is neutral is not quite accurate. It may open up new opportunities, but its development and implementation almost always comes with hidden costs. Technology, in other words, is a sword that cuts both ways. On the one hand, it can be used to help solve or reduce social problems. During the Virginia Tech massacre, students compensated for the slow official communication by searching for information online.[1] On the other hand, the implementation of new technologies raises new challenges and problems (the solving of which often leads to newer technologies). As Leon Kass points out in *Life, Liberty and the Defense of Dignity*, the introduction and widespread adoption of the automobile brought with it the need for roads, fuel, steel, factories, gas stations, garages, body shops, parking facilities, traffic laws, in addition to fumes, smog, auto graveyards, the insurance industry, and medical personnel. The

[1]Michelle Quinn and Alex Pham, "Students Trace a Tragedy Online," *Los Angeles Times*, April 17, 2007. Available in the latimes.com archives.

system of rules and services necessary for the production and operation of vehicles is extraordinary, and most of it wasn't conceived of when automobiles were being invented.[2] The automobile changed the fabric of American life, as anyone who has lived in Los Angeles—a city built around its freeways—understands.

The question of whether cars are an "improvement" over horses and buggies, of course, depends upon what values are in place, which is true of all technology. If we value mobility, speed, and comfort, cars are obviously superior to the horse. But if we value interaction with nature and patience, then the horse and buggy is clearly "better." This means, however, that the high schoolers' utilitarian approach to technology failed to recognize that some technologies are better suited for the reinforcing of some values than others. Technology is, in this crucial sense, not neutral.

Christians, then, must attempt to understand new media within the broader perspective of human goods. One obvious good of new technologies is that they force us to reevaluate our value structure as we seek to understand our new powers. While Facebook, for instance, allows us to see the events our friends self-report, its introduction can prompt us to reflect upon what is most important to us. But such a reflective period will only last so long. For most high schoolers, it has already passed, and these new technologies have been integrated into the fabric of their lives. Like the telephone or the lightbulb, new media will reach a point where their effects—both good and bad—will be hidden from view.

It is worth, then, sounding a cautionary note about the new technologies and media that are being widely distributed and adopted. But any such cautions necessarily suffer from two problems. First, as technology tends to exacerbate and reinforce existing human and cultural values, the problems that arise from technology are ultimately in our values, not in the technology itself. Our use of technology illuminates values already present within us. Second, the problems that technology poses to us often only arise when such technological developments are in their infancy. As the technologies mature, the problems associated with them are often remedied by new technologies or alterations. For

---

[2]Leon Kass, *Life, Liberty and the Defense of Dignity: The Challenge of Bioethics* (San Francisco: Encounter, 2002), 41.

instance, the debate over whether scientists should use embryonic stem cells—which involves the destruction of human life—or adult stem cells took a turn when researchers discovered a third way: amniotic fluid stem cells. According to *Newsweek*, such cells "rival embryonic stem cells in their ability to multiply and transform into many cell types," which makes them extremely effective for researching diseases.[3] This new development was hailed as potentially providing the benefits of embryonic stem cell research without being morally questionable. The point illustrates the fact that those who lament technological developments for their undesirable consequences and applications must also work to discover new technologies that avoid such problematic uses.

In other words, technology critics must also be technology fans. What's more, they must criticize the technological developments *because* they are fans of technology. People err both when they do not love technology enough and when they love it too much. The trick is to understand both its prospects *and* its limitations, to see its benefits *and* its drawbacks. In a world where technological developments are transforming public discourse and interpersonal communication, ignorance and apathy are not viable options for Christians.

Here, however, it is my job to play the critic of the new media. I accept the role with some trepidation. Such criticism is easy to write off, as new media are so sprawling, so diverse, and so new that it is extraordinarily difficult to attain a level of precision and universality so as to be helpful. Ironically, the very ubiquity of new media and the immense amount of information has made some critiques so prevalent as to render them uninteresting (for example, the lack of constraints and editing in blogging can result in terrible content). Yet such criticisms are still necessary to have a responsible and moderate view of the role of new media in our lives and communities. We should be wary of drinking too deeply at the well without at some point examining the water.

In what follows, then, I offer three critical explorations on the role of new media in our lives, explorations that are based on my own experience as both a consumer and creator of new media. I use "explorations" carefully, as the open nature of new media means that

---

[3]Mary Carmichael, "A New Era Begins," *Newsweek*, January 7, 2007. Available at http://www.newsweek.com/id/37906.

today's vice may be overcome by tomorrow's new development. The last word on this subject is a long way off, and it will doubtlessly be spoken by someone else.

THE PROBLEM OF DESENSITIZATION

Those who spend any amount of time absorbing new media quickly discover their subtly addictive nature. Clicking through to the next page takes no effort, and the fact that a real person has deemed whatever lies on that page as worthy of a link provides a real incentive to follow. It is like a perpetual treasure hunt, except without a fixed end and with all the obstacles minimized. The nature of the environment is such that people can spend enormous amounts of time reading and listening and writing.

The problem of time management online is fairly obvious. Far more subtle, and hence more problematic, is the potential for desensitization to the information we consume. And nearly all creators of new media are, to some extent, consumers of new media. One key aspect that establishes the new media as new is their conversational and communal nature. It is user-generated, blurring the lines between consumers and producers. But it is this ease and fragmented nature of consumption and production that critics of new media point to as so destructive. Douglas Groothuis writes:

> Cyberspace offers the promise of a kind of cognitive ubiquity—the world at our keyboard and screen—at the cost of depth. This encourages one to become a cognitive tourist, who visits many sites on the Net, downloads and combines many bits of data, but understands very little . . . the cognitive tourist of cyberspace may easily visit (and possibly record) information without digesting it.[4]

Groothuis's critique is poignant but doesn't go far enough. The prevalence of information potentially has a numbing effect on the reader and can engender a curiosity in things otherwise considered trivial. The popular web site Fark.com has developed a following by finding the most obscure, weird, and otherwise forgettable stories, attaching witty commentary, and providing a community of would-be comics a space

---

[4]Douglas Groothuis, *The Soul in Cyberspace* (Eugene: Wipf and Stock, 1997), 73–74.

to ply their trade. It is an amusing site, but it thrives on the thirst for the odd and unique that the plentitude of information has exacerbated.

This numbing effect of information is one of the most significant challenges that users of new media face. The inability to think deeply, to integrate what we are experiencing into ourselves, ultimately stifles creativity. The twentieth-century apologist, novelist, and aesthetician Dorothy Sayers once described the task of the poet as expressing in words the events that happen to him. According to Sayers:

> A poet is a man who not only suffers the impact of external events but also experiences them. He puts the experience into words in his own mind, and in so doing recognizes the experience for what it is. To the extent that we do that, we are all poets. A poet so-called is simply a man like ourselves with an exceptional power of revealing his experience by expressing it, so that not only he, but we ourselves, recognize that experience as our own. . . . By thus recognizing [the event] in its expression, [the poet] makes it his own—integrates it into himself. He no longer feels himself battered passively by the impact of external events; it is no longer something happening to him, but something happening in him.[5]

The distinction between the event and the experience is helpful for illustrating the effect of consuming too much media. In the hours after the news of the Virginia Tech tragedy, I found myself scouring the Web to find articles and news stories with interesting angles. Each story that I read was, in Sayersian language, an event—it was new information from outside of me that hit my eyes. As such, it needed to be considered carefully and eventually expressed in language of my own—if, that is, I wanted to *experience* the world and not simply be a passive recipient of the world. But the speed and ease of finding more "events"—more information, more externalized facts—overcame my need to digest, effectually numbing me to the effect of the information and the ability to wrestle deeply with it.

G. K. Chesterton, one of Christianity's most prolific writers in the twentieth century, corroborates the point. In a speech in the 1930s, Chesterton offered this prophetic analysis:

---

[5]Dorothy Sayers, "Toward a Christian Aesthetic," in *Letters to a Diminished Church* (Nashville: W Publishing Group, 2004), 162–163.

The coming peril is the intellectual, educational, psychological and artistic overproduction, which, equally with economic overproduction, threatens the wellbeing of contemporary civilisation. People are inundated, blinded, deafened, and mentally paralysed by a flood of vulgar and tasteless externals, leaving them no time for leisure, thought, or creation from within themselves.[6]

Chesterton's language indicates that overstimulation prevents people from interacting with the world around them. They are "blinded, deafened, mentally paralysed." In Sayers's language, the inundation of "events" happening around us prevents us from reflecting appropriately upon them, which ultimately stifles our ability to understand and express them in language that is distinctly ours. For the creator of new media who wants to be a relevant voice, all analysis is time-sensitive. This premium upon speed threatens to short-circuit the creative process of fitting the right words to our thoughts and reflections.

The chief danger of new media, then, is that our souls will die for want of silence, solitude, and reflection. The world of new media is short on Dorothy Sayers's poets, and if Christians are to make a significant impact through this technology, we must cultivate more of them. To do so, however, entails setting aside the need for more information and reflecting on the world in a way that ensures that our commentary is insightful and powerful. It means ensuring that as creators of new media, we recognize the danger inherent in *over*production—that we will impoverish our own souls and contribute to an ultimately meaningless and powerless chatter. We must be poets and prophets who speak powerfully, which means that we must be discerning consumers and patient, conscientious creators.

THE DEFICIENCIES AND DANGERS OF ONLINE COMMUNICATION

One of the chief reasons I began blogging, and why most people began blogging, was because it increased my opportunities to "connect" with like-minded people. Suddenly people across the world with unique interests could "communicate" with each other. The quotes are crucial,

---

[6]Stratford Caldecott, "Chesterton Alive Today: Reviving the Moral and Social Imagination for a Re-Evangelisation of Culture"; http://www.secondspring.co.uk/spring/beaconsfield.htm.

because the communal nature of new media raises serious questions about what it means to communicate online.

In his widely read and extremely wise book *Habits of the High-Tech Heart*, Quentin Schultze makes the following observation:

> Such brevity [of information] may be a virtue if the purpose of communication is purely instrumental, such as conveying information about stock market conditions, baseball scores, and weather forecasts. But what if our purpose is noninstrumental and intrinsically moral—such as becoming genuinely intimate with a person or community, conversing about life, sharing in the fellowship of kindred spirits, mentoring colleagues, and nurturing children? Cyberspace is then at best an ancillary messaging medium rather than a prime location for cultivating shared knowing and moral wisdom. The real value of online communication, then, is largely instrumental—such as getting information, sending a message, setting up appointments, and making contact.[7]

The reduction of online communication to purely *instrumental* means is interesting. It is also that limitation that new media are attempting to overcome. Through blogs, videocasts, and social networking sites, individuals are ceasing to view the Internet as ancillary to their messaging ends but as a useful tool for communicating in *every* way (hence mortuaries are starting to offer "funeral webcasting" services to families).[8]

It is not clear, however, *why* Schultze relegates the Internet to the category of "instrumental." The obvious and apparently presumed answer is that the Internet facilitates communication that is nonphysical. But the obvious answer only hides more questions. It is, after all, not entirely clear what the physical body adds to interpersonal communication, such that it can't be accomplished through videochatting. Why *is* shared space important for noninstrumental interaction?

For one, in the "noninstrumental and . . . moral" communication that Schultze highlights, an enormous amount of content is transmitted nonverbally. A stern frown, a hand on a shoulder, a sly grin—these are the sorts of nuances to human communication that "speak" volumes.

---

[7]Quentin Schultze, *Habits of the High-Tech Heart* (Grand Rapids, MI: Baker Academic, 2004), 65. I am thankful to Keith Plummer of christianmind.blogspot.com for highlighting this passage from Schultze.
[8]See, for instance, FuneralOne.com.

On a broader scale, a live basketball game, a live concert, a live sermon all carry with them a power available only in the performance, and not in the digitized replication (as anyone who has been in the audience of a live sporting contest automatically understands). This power depends upon more than the words that are being communicated. It is a fusion of the physical presence of the performer or speaker—which is why public speakers use gestures to emphasize their points—and the response of the audience or listener.

In online and digital communication, however, this dynamic is lost. In concerts or sermons or plays, the exchange between the actor and the audience is unconscious, just as most of what individuals communicate when they gather together as friends is unconscious. There is no need to *intentionally pursue* this shared energy—it is present already. The transaction between audience and performer, speaker and listener exists by virtue of their being in the same space at the same time. If nothing else, their souls are in the same room, giving their communication an added dimension and power that they are not necessarily able to control.

But in online communication, the only "presence" someone is able to have is when they act intentionally in some way. There is no "presence by default." A silent audience at a concert is still very "present," just as Job's friends made their compassion known before they spoke. But here online communication seems fundamentally deficient. The ability to effect change can only be gained through intentional, active communication—through writing comments or linking or posting a video response. We cannot simply *be* online and influence others like we can *be* in a concert hall or with a friend and have influence.[9]

This fact, though, has several unsettling effects. For one, it increases the pressure to be active online. While this certainly has its benefits, it also potentially devalues our online production. If our online presence is measured by our production, then "publish or perish" becomes a reality. To the extent that we exist online, we must contribute online. And the more time we spend online, the more difficult it becomes to separate this persona from our "real lives." Such an externalized, activity-oriented understanding of our identity, however, is deeply problematic, if nothing else because it contributes to the dilution of power and reflectiveness identified in the section above.

---

[9] I am indebted to Jonathan Olson for providing the language and examples for this paragraph.

There is a deeper problem, however, with communicating online. It is crucial in communication—whether in person or online—to be as authentic as possible. As new media are communally oriented, authenticity and honesty take on added importance. But online communication places us in charge of our own self-presentation. Even when we act "authentically" online, we act at our own discretion. In interpersonal communication, however, controlling our self-presentation is much more difficult, if not impossible. The astute and familiar observer can hear the subtle differences in tone that indicate contentment or anxiety, peace or frustration, just as the astute observer can see subtle differences in the face that betray the truth about a person's real state of mind (even if that truth is unknown to the person speaking).[10] In other words, in interpersonal communication, we communicate more than we consciously intend. There is a de facto self-revelation that comes from our body, giving away our internal states, as very few of us have the ability to hide ourselves as well as we think. Lack of ability, however, doesn't prevent most of us from *trying* to control when and how we disclose ourselves to the world, when and how we are "authentic."

This idea, though, that we can selectively self-disclose and control our own "authenticity" is the sort of problematic value that the new media reinforce. "Authenticity," on this understanding, becomes easy, as we get to tell others our sins and secrets in a way that feels safe to us. There is an inevitable sanitization that occurs when we decide what to tell others. This level of control over our revelations can even give us a sense of self-gratification for our "realness." The end result is a narcissistic hyper-self-awareness as we decide when we want to "be authentic" and disclose ourselves and when we don't.

When people are gathered together, authenticity happens whether we like it or not. Our very attempts to act in accordance with others' expectations reveals more about our own internal state than we might care to admit. The adage that 90 percent of communication is nonverbal is true, and in reducing human communication to that last 10 percent, new media run the risk of improperly shaping how we view communication in the rest of our lives.

---

[10]For instance, consider Paul Ekman's "Facial Action Coding System." For details, see his *Emotions Revealed, Second Edition: Recognizing Faces and Feelings to Improve Communication and Emotional Life* (New York: Owl Books, 2007).

LOSING REALITY—NEW MEDIA AND OUR RELATION TO THE WORLD

G. K. Chesterton did not offer his social criticism in essay form only. His novels are full of commentary, such that at their worst, they read like his essays. In his fanciful novel *Manalive*, Chesterton depicts a society that is trapped in a moribund melancholy, only to be rescued by the (autobiographical?) hero Innocent Smith. The novel is a frolicking portrayal of the fundamental goodness of reality over and against the dreary cynicism of German pessimism (which was in vogue at the time), scientism, and other social evils.

Chesterton puts the cause of the society's problem in the mouth of Arthur Inglewood, a young man who is an amateur photographer:

> "And yet I fancy all hobbies, like my camera and bicycle, are drugs too. . . . Drugging myself with speed, and sunshine, and fatigue, and fresh air. Pedaling the machine so fast that I turn into a machine myself. That's the matter with all of us. We're too busy to wake up."[11]

It is not hard to hear Chesterton's thought that people are "mentally paralysed by a flood of vulgar and tasteless externals" as a commentary on Inglewood's language about being "too busy to wake up." But it is Inglewood's interlocutor, Diana Duke, who asks the pertinent question: "What is there to wake up to?"

Not surprisingly, Innocent Smith provides the answer. Smith is a large but nimble man who announces his arrival by jumping over the wall of a garden and finds an extraordinary amount of joy in facts as simple as his having two legs. After all, had God decided otherwise, he could have had four. Writes Chesterton:

> [Smith] talked dominantly and rushed the social situation; but he was not asserting himself, like a superman in a modern play. He was simply forgetting himself, like a little boy at a party. He had somehow made a giant stride from babyhood to manhood, and missed that crisis in youth when most of us grow old.[12]

What do we wake up to? Smith has awakened and discovered the world,

---

[11]G. K. Chesterton, *Manalive* (Mineola, NY: Dover Publications, 2005), 28.
[12]Ibid., 14.

which is so fascinating, so complex, and so good that it is a source of perpetual wonder, joy, and enchantment. It is the external world—reality, or that which is outside of our minds—that we have been made for, and only in the apprehension of that can we find true and abiding joy. Smith's "forgetting himself" isn't a work of effort—it is a natural result of being engrossed by other things and people. Inglewood's point that we are "too busy to wake up" is a wise caution to us all, especially to those who wish to consume and create new media.

I have already mentioned the potential stultifying effect of consuming lots of information and the danger of reinforcing our inauthentic self-presentation. To those dangers, then, I would add a third: new media have the power to divorce us from the reality for which we have been created, effectively putting us to sleep.

As a novice blogger, I advocated adopting the medium on the grounds that it made me more attentive to things happening around me. "I am always looking for my next blog post," I claimed. Such an approach, however, crippled my ability to understand reality and experience it *as reality*. Just as the easy photography of digital cameras has caused people to interrupt their interactions to pose for a picture, so blogging disrupted my enjoyment of the world by making me conscious of it in a very different way than I would have been otherwise. I would tentatively suggest that the change made me more conscious of *myself* in that my own thought processes and preparation to write took precedence over the simple and direct experience of the reality itself.

Secondly, if we routinely place a form between ourselves and the manifold and diverse reality around us, we potentially stultify ourselves by *preemptively* managing our experience of the world. Reality is more than a potential blog post, and to experience it only as such undercuts our grappling with and apprehension of those aspects of reality that do not necessarily fit the medium. Only when such aspects thrust themselves before us are we confronted by the limitations of the medium, as happened with the Virginia Tech massacre. A blog post is an ill-suited commemoration for such a terrible tragedy. The hurried, transitory nature of blogging—think of how seldom people read the archives—is incommensurate with the profound and permanent pain.

Thirdly, seeing the world as a potential blog post threatens to reduce *reality to a tool for our own production rather than being an end in itself.* While this critique may be true of all artistic production, what makes new media different is the short turnaround time from *event* to *experience* (using Sayersian language) and the public nature of the media. The production of our interpretations of reality becomes a more important end than our own understanding of reality itself. The diminished lag time between writing and publication—from weeks or months to seconds—has changed the dictum examined above to "publish *frequently* or perish," increasing the danger of viewing reality as a means to our own end.[13]

The typical argument that new media are fundamentally narcissistic, then, does not go deep enough. The danger of new media is not only that they provide new means for our bloated desires for self-promotion. Rather, media—new and old—entice us to subordinate reality for our own ends and means, to bring reality into ourselves and shape it in our own image. If we give in, we will find ourselves unceasingly busy and stimulated, yet unrelentingly bored. Reality is a mystery rich enough, good enough, and powerful enough to hold our fascination, but only as long as it remains outside of us as a good to be sought for its own sake.

CONCLUSION

The world around us is hardly static, as the high schoolers I talked with seemed to think. New technologies continue to open new possibilities, extending individuals' and communities' means of transmitting information around the globe. The world is, in this regard, a very different world than during Jesus' time.

The modern world contains many new tools to preach the gospel, but with those new tools come new and hidden dangers, not all of which we currently understand. In this brief exploration I have attempted to articulate three such dangers: (1) that our souls will become shallow due to the imbalance between consumption of information and our reflection upon that information; (2) that the manifestly intentional nature of online communication will reinforce the notion that we can and should control our own self-presentations to the world; and (3) that seeing the world through new media can distort our relationship

---

[13]There is an underlying unity, then, with the danger of overstimulation, which we often (though not always) employ to avoid undesirable aspects of reality. This also makes the external world a tool for our own ends (constant pleasure) rather than an end in itself.

to reality by causing us to subordinate reality to our own ends and purposes (artistic creation) rather than seeing reality as an end in itself.

These dangers are not the final word on new media. Rather, that final word will ultimately be given by Jesus Christ, in whom dangers are overcome and threats abolished. Christians leery of engagement with these new tools should remember the comforting words of the answer to the first question of the Heidelberg Catechism—namely, that "our only comfort in life and death" is "that [we] with body and soul, both in life and death, [are] not [our] own." It is given to us to do the best with what we have: deliberating, deciding, and reflecting on our course of action, all the while taking a posture of prayerful trust that even if we err, the hand of God will yet prevail, both in our own lives, where all is "subservient to [our] salvation," and in the world around us.

4

BEGINNER'S TOOLBOX: BLOGGING

Joe Carter

www.EvangelicalOutpost.com

IMAGINE YOU ARE GIVEN THE opportunity every weekday to host a public conference. Five days a week an audience, ranging from a few dozen to several thousand, gather in one location for the sole purpose of hearing what you have to say. Many come because they want to learn or be entertained, while others come merely because they are given to disputation and contrariness. Yet each day they stop by to hear you give an opinion about current events, expound upon an obscure topic of personal interest, or hear you share an amusing anecdote. A few stay through your entire oration, while others leave after only a few words. But every day someone shows up for your briefing.

While this may sound rather far-fetched, the fact is that the tools of the new media have made this possible for the millions of people who have a blog. A blog that is read by more than a few dozen readers can have a bigger impact than most people realize. An educational blog with an audience of fifty has more people in its "classroom" than most professors at Harvard. A pastoral blog with ninety readers has more people in its "pews" than most pastors have in their churches every Sunday. And a literary blog with more than a thousand readers a month has a larger "circulation" than most poetry and short story magazines.

Starting a blog, therefore, can create an astounding opportunity to leverage your impact and influence. Yet it also raises some daunting questions for the Christian blogger: How will you handle the pressure of speaking to such an audience? How much time and effort should you put into your remarks? How will you use this incredible medium to bring glory to God and further the Kingdom of Christ?

One of the purposes of this book is to help those of you who are entering this new frontier to answer these types of questions. Part Two of this book focuses on content and provides models for engaging new media using a blog. This chapter, however, will cover the narrower topic of the tools you will need—both technological and conceptual—to become a successful blogger.

BEFORE YOU BEGIN

The seeds of blogging success are sown before you ever start a blog. Mistakes can often be overcome after the launch of your new site, but the correction always comes at a price, whether in time, money, or readership. The longer you wait to correct your initial errors, the more they will limit your success in this venture. Adhering to the following tips and principles, however, will keep you from falling into the traps that often snare new blogs:

Read First—Blog Later

How many different blogs have you read? If the number is below one hundred, then you have some catching up to do. You should be familiar with a wide range of blogs before you launch one of your own. Search around and visit various sites, both those that cover topics you plan to write about and those that are markedly different from your own intended subject areas. For example, if you plan to write about religion, include in your survey blogs that specialize in politics, fashion, or pop culture. Visit the TTLB Ecosystem (http://truthlaidbear.com/ecosystem. php), and randomly visit blogs in each tier level. Read the über bloggers who have a larger readership than most small newspapers. Read the up-and-coming stars (often the ones the well-known bloggers are linking to) who are gaining attention. And most importantly, read dozens of blogs that are on the "micro" level of readership, those with fewer than a hundred daily visitors.

You will learn a great deal from the exquisitely designed and well-written blogs; you'll learn even more from the slapdash, poorly edited, and boring sites. Once you understand what makes some blogs better than others you will be well on your way to creating a successful blog.

Know Your Role

Why do you want to start a blog? Before you begin, you need to be able to answer that simple question. Blogs can be used as a marketing tool for your company, as a means of staying in touch with friends and family, as a way to showcase your writing talents, or as a place to share your opinion with the world. You can even use your blog for all of these purposes simultaneously. As a general rule, though, gaining a readership will require you to focus your efforts on a fairly narrow range of topics.

The blogosphere is a market in which everyone is competing for "mindspace"—the attention, respect, and trust of blog readers. Fortunately, blogging is not a zero-sum game, and while the market is finite, it is also extremely large, constantly expanding, and with few barriers to entry. Attracting readers isn't difficult if you know what audience you are aiming for. However, if *you* don't know why anyone should read your blog, then you shouldn't be surprised to find that no one else does either.

You Get What You Pay For

You can start and maintain a blog without ever spending a dime. The low cost of entry is one of the primary reasons that so many blogs are started; it is also one of the reasons more than half of new blogs are abandoned within the first week. If you plan to take blogging seriously, you should spend a few dollars on this new venture.

Fortunately, blogging is a relatively inexpensive hobby. Using a cut-rate domain name registration and hosting service, you can start a blog for around twenty dollars. The cost of hosting the blog can also be as low as ten to thirty dollars a month. If you can afford it, pay a bit more for a hosting service that will allow you to upgrade your bandwidth. A single link to your blog from a news agency or established high traffic blogger can move your blog traffic from twelve visits a day to ten thousand visits an hour. What once seemed unlikely is now surprisingly common.

Be prepared by choosing a hosting service that will automatically charge you for surges in bandwidth. You don't want your site to crash under the weight of instant success. If the sudden increase in web traffic is temporary, it will only cost you a few dollars. If it becomes permanent, you can always sell advertising on your site to pay for the increase in bandwidth. If you aren't ready when success comes knocking, though, it likely won't be back for a return visit.

Choose Your Blog Name Carefully

Spend any time in the blogosphere, and you will soon notice an inordinate number of blogs with names that are confusing, inappropriate, or just plain silly. Many people give little thought to naming their blog and so choose a name they think is clever or funny. Big mistake. Your blog name not only represents your blog, it represents you. Companies dedicate a considerable amount of time and energy to choosing names for their products. You should do the same when choosing the name for your site. The name of your blog is one of the key components of branding, and getting it right is essential in marketing your site.

Whenever possible, try to choose a URL that is based on your own name. If the name is good enough to represent you, it should be good enough to represent your blog. It also has the added advantage of being defining and memorable. If you can remember the name of radio host Hugh Hewitt (http://www.hughhewitt.com) or pastor Mark D. Roberts (http://www.markdroberts.com), you will always remember how to locate their blogs.

Unfortunately, this isn't always a viable or even preferable option. Your name may be unavailable, too common to be distinctive, or a difficult to spell Slavic name (readers would have a difficult time remembering how to spell Dušan-Džamonja.com). If using your own name isn't an option, select a domain name that is short and memorable. It doesn't have to be obvious or boring—more people use Google and Yahoo in an hour than will use SearchEngine.com in a lifetime—but it should be something that you wouldn't be embarrassed to have on a business card. If you are an exceptional blogger, you may be able to compensate for a poorly chosen blog name. But there is no need to take that unnecessary risk.

Several years ago domain name registration cost upwards of thirty-five dollars a year for available URLs. Today the cost is less than a third of that, and it's getting cheaper every year. The differences between the services of major registration companies are negligible, so shop around for the lowest cost and pay for several years in advance.

STARTING YOUR BLOG

Blogging isn't about web design or the underlying technology but rather about content. What you write is far more important than the means by which you send it out into the blogosphere. Still, getting your content onto the Web requires a familiarity with a few essential tools. As you become more comfortable with the medium, you'll discover dozens of applications that you'll want to add to your toolbox in order to make the process of blogging more effective. Starting a blog, however, only requires a few basic items. Here are four invaluable ones you'll need to get started on the path to success:

Publishing Platforms

The interface between you and the blogosphere is the publishing platform (or Content Management System [CMS]) that translates your brilliant prose into a readable format and posts it onto your blog. A few of the more popular platforms are Movable Type (http://www.movabletype.org), Blogger (http://www.blogger.com), and Word Press (http://wordpress.org). Your comfort level with HTML and other web applications will play a role in which is right for you. Familiarize yourself with each one, and talk to other bloggers and ask their advice before settling on a specific platform.

You might also find it useful to read the user forums dedicated to each platform in order to get an idea of the problems that arise and the technical support available. Also keep in mind that your choice of hosting service will affect how simple or difficult it will be to install the platform. If at all possible, select a service that is blog-friendly and offers free installation.

Templates

Rather than creating the web design from scratch, most bloggers rely on a web template, a pre-built layout that places the design elements on your blog pages. The easiest way to determine what type of template you should use is simply to borrow someone else's idea. Originality—especially when it comes to blog design—is highly overrated. No matter how impressive your site's design may be, your success will be based on your content. Even a site that wins awards for its design will attract few visitors if the blogger has nothing to say.

Once you have a basic idea about layout and design for your blog, find someone who has something similar, and copy his or her style, tweaking it enough to make it your own. Ask him or her if he or she found his or her template online (there are literally thousands of blog templates offered for free on the Web) or if it is a custom design. Most bloggers are more than willing to help someone who admires their taste. (Keep in mind that your choice of templates might be limited by the type of publishing platform that you choose.)

Although the layout and design of your template will vary, a few key elements should be prominently displayed:

• *Blog name.* The first information that should be provided is your blog name. While this might appear obvious, many bloggers—particularly those whose URL is different from the blog name—fail to make this clear. Make it prominent enough that new readers will catch it quickly but not so intrusive that it gets in the way.

• *Contact info.* When the reporter for *The New York Times* or the producer for the local radio program stumbles across your blog and wants to discuss a brilliant post you've written (and it can happen), they will need to be able to find your contact information. Include an e-mail address somewhere on your site. Use a free service (Gmail, Yahoo, Hotmail) if you do not want to publicly display your primary e-mail address. A web-based form is also an option, though it is less useful than an e-mail address. Whichever you choose, ensure that you provide a way for readers to contact you directly. Most people will look for contact information either near the top of your blog or on the sidebar; so display it in an obvious and intuitive location.

• *Blogrolls.* A blogroll is a collection of links to other blogs, usually displayed on the front page sidebar. Every blog needs a blogroll. In fact, many bloggers find it useful to maintain several blogrolls. The reason is that blogrolls are the foundation of your blogging network. You cannot become a successful blogger without a blogroll any more than you could become a CEO without a Rolodex. The first blogroll you should have is a list of blogs you read often. Although the advent of the RSS reader has reduced the usefulness of blogrolls for this purpose, they still serve a function as artifacts that signal to others that you are a frequent reader and part of their "social network." While the primary blogroll should be a tool for your own use, it can also be valuable for your readers. If they appreciate your blog, they are likely to find other blogs with similar taste and interest on your blogroll. Choose carefully whom you add to such lists. Although no one should hold you responsible for the content on other blogs, including a site on your blogroll becomes a form of de facto endorsement. Along with your primary blogroll, you may want to add one of the hundreds of specialized blogrolls that are arranged around politics, religion, common interests, and other topics. If you choose to add them to your blog, limit them to two, or at most three. More than three and the blogrolls just become useless wastes of space.

Hit Counters

If it doesn't matter to you if anyone reads what you write, then you don't have a blog, you have an online diary. Most bloggers do care (perhaps more than we should) about readership and use a variety of tools to keep track of their site's visitors. Unfortunately, the process of measuring web traffic (the amount of data sent and received by visitors to a web site) remains an inexact science. Several metrics can be used—page views, unique visitors, site hits—that provide a rough approximation of how many people visit your blog.

Web traffic is a key barometer of your blog's impact; so you will want to keep track of how many people visit your blog on a daily basis. For this you'll need some form of hit counter. Currently two of the best and most used hit counters are Sitemeter (http://www.sitemeter.com) and Google Analytics (http://www.googleanalytics.com). Both tools are available for free and can be installed on your blog even by a technical novice. In addition to the numerical data, these tools can inform you about other blogs that are linking to your site. Knowing where your web traffic is coming from will help you engage with the blogging community and help you better connect with your own readers.

Although you should use these tools often, don't get too wrapped up in the numbers. Every page view your site receives represents a blog reader. Cherish every visitor, and make sure your readers realize that you appreciate their taking time out of their day to engage with you and your blog.

Link Tracking

While page views may be the reigning currency of most web sites, the true coin of the realm in the blogosphere is links (a link to your blog from another blog or web site). Page views are a measure of overall readership, while link count is a measure of your influence within the blogosphere itself. As a general rule, the more bloggers who link to your blog or to your individual posts, the more influential you are as a blogger. To find out who has added you to their blogroll or who was impressed enough by something you wrote to point it out to their own readers, use a link tracking site.

Link tracking sites are like search engines for blogs. Four of the most commonly used are Technorati (http://www.technorati.com), Blogpulse (http://www.blogpulse.com), Daypop (http://www.daypop.com), and Google Blog Search (http://blogsearch.google.com). Type your blog's URL into these online tools, and they will show you a complete list of sites that are linking to your blog. Pay close attention to the bloggers who link to you. It shows that they were impressed (or outraged) enough by what you've written to both visit your site and to include a mention of it on their own.

IMPROVING YOUR BLOG POSTS

The blog post is the most important information presented on your blog. Make sure it is readable and unobstructed by following these steps:

• *Correct your spelling.* Brilliant thought is rarely conveyed by sloppy writing. Proofread and spellcheck before you post any blog entry. Inevitably, typos and broken links will slip through your editing process. But make a habit of correcting such errors quickly after they are recognized by either you or your readers.

• *Correct our spelling too.* There are few things more embarrassing than finding a typo in your own blog post by reading an excerpt on another person's blog. Do unto other bloggers as you would have them do unto you: correct the obvious typos when you quote your fellow blogger.

• *Use headlines.* Always have a title for your post, preferably one that hints at the content within. Do not just drop a block of text onto the page and expect people to read it. Readers don't want to have to read two hundred words into a post before they find out you're writing about your cat. Better to give them a warning, even if it's nothing more than "Another Post About My Cat."

• *Consider using subheads.* Borrow a trick from newspaper layout. Instead of just writing a title, think about using a subhead as well: "Tabby Tales: Further Adventures of a Super Siamese."

• *Break up text.* Reading large blocks of text on a computer screen causes eyestrain. Break text up into readable chunks, typically no more than four or five sentences. Also use block quotations to set apart items that you are quoting and itemized lists when you have a sequence of items.

• *Use graphics and images sparingly.* Before you put a graphic on your blog, ask yourself if it conveys information that cannot be adequately expressed by using text. If that is the case, then by all means use the graphic. Otherwise think twice before adding it. Graphics increase the download time of your pages, so the use of images should always be a conscious choice.

• *Compress your images.* When you do use images, resize them for a proper fit, and compress them to the smallest size possible without losing their clarity. Image compression is a method of reducing the download time for JPEGs (the most common format for pictorial images). Squeezing a few bits out of every picture will allow your page to download faster. (If you don't have a program that allows JPEG compression, you can download one for free at IrfanView (http://www.irfanview.com/).)

KERR'S FOLLY AND THE CHRISTIAN BLOGGER

While familiarity with the previously discussed technical tools is essential for starting a blog, for Christian bloggers, certain conceptual tools are equally important. Christians must think differently about this task, which is why I recommend that before launching their site, every Christian blogger read Steve Kerr's *On the folly of rewarding A, while hoping for B* (available online at http://pages.stern. nyu.edu/%7Ewstarbuc/mob/kerrab.html). In 1975 the *Academy of Management Journal* published this article, which has since become a business classic. The premise of Kerr's paper is that most reward systems reward the type of behavior that is trying to be discouraged, while the behavior desired is not being rewarded at all.

Kerr provides numerous examples from activities and fields such as war, business, medicine, government, and the academy. While all are applicable to blogging, one of the most relevant for Christian bloggers is the reward system in sports:

> Most coaches disdain to discuss individual accomplishments, preferring to speak of teamwork, proper attitude, and one-for-all spirit. Usually, however, rewards are distributed according to individual performance. The college basketball player who passes the ball to teammates instead of shooting will not compile impressive scoring statistics and is less likely to be drafted by the pros. The ballplayer who hits to right field to advance the runners will win neither the batting nor home run titles, and will be offered smaller raises. It therefore is rational for players to think of themselves first, and the team second.

The two primary means of "rewarding" the work of bloggers are site traffic (the number of readers) and links (the number of links from other blogs). What type of behavior do we hope for, and what are we currently rewarding by using this system? Over the years the Christian blogosphere has wrestled with several particular difficulties inherent in this reward system. As you start your blog, consider how you might be able to help our community resolve these situations.

We hope for community, *but we often reward* individuality.

The tasks associated with blogging—sitting at a computer, typing an opinion, posting it on the Web—are by nature individualistic. It is no surprise, then, that the rewards of blogging also tend to be conveyed on the individual. Yet as Christians this emphasis can be destructive to genuine community. We become both envious of other people's achievements and filled with pride (or false piety) about our own. We become jealous of bloggers who have more links or readers. We become frustrated when our efforts are not gaining enough attention or when we are not duly rewarded for our brilliant insights.

The question we wrestle with as bloggers is, how do we imbue our individual efforts with godly ambition, helping others as we form a genuine community? How can we change this focus on the individual over the communal?

> We hope for faith, hope, and love, *but we often reward* doubt, pessimism, and a lack of charity.

Bloggers, and the audiences who read them, have access to one of the most powerful and transformative technologies in the history of mankind. We not only have access to information that was unavailable to Augustine, John Calvin, John Wesley, Jonathan Edwards, and Francis Schaeffer, but we possess the ability to communicate instantly with people across the globe. Are we going to squander this profound tool? When our Creator asks how we used this gift, how are we going to explain that we hoped for B but rewarded A?

> We hope for eternal perspective, *but we often reward* focus on the trivial and ephemeral.

Almost every blog has an archive listed by date and category. Yet the average blog reader will never take advantage of this resource. Why? Because we assume that anything that was written in the past (i.e., last month) will be of little relevance today. We accept the absurd notion that the latest news is more necessary for understanding our times than the past. But, to paraphrase the historian Arnold Toynbee, the blogger trying to understand the present is like the man with his nose pressed against the mirror trying to see his whole body.

This is not to suggest that blogging should never be timely or focused on the latest news. But how can we provide an eternal perspective while keeping our noses pressed against the mirror of current events? Why do we not reward bloggers who attempt to address eternally important issues?

This last item is of profound importance. Your audience is giving you two of their most precious possessions—their time and attention. What are you doing with this gift? Are you using it to improve their life, influence their worldview, feed their mind, and strengthen their faith? Or are you wasting it by giving them junk food, blather, and trivia that provide a momentary amusement but have only a fleeting impact? What interest will be paid to your readers in return for loaning you their treasure of time and attention?

As you join the community of Christian bloggers, consider this question and how you will respond. Consistently striving to maintain an eternal perspective is far more important than chasing after the ephemeral attention span of a large blog-reading audience. It will also be more rewarding. You'll get to know your readers as people rather than as statistics. You'll engage with them and sharpen your own thinking in the process. You'll find that your readers shift from being a passive audience to being part of a thoughtful community. Mostly, though, your blogging will gain a Kingdom-centered purpose, and you'll begin to understand what it truly means to be a successful blogger.

5

BEGINNER'S TOOLBOX: NEW MEDIA—PODCASTING, VIDEO PODCASTING, AND MORE

Terence Armentano and Matthew Eppinette

http://terenceonline.blogspot.com; http://blog.aul.org

INTRODUCTION

Digital media players have become nearly ubiquitous. Sometimes it seems that almost everywhere we look, we see people listening to them and watching them—at the gym, on the bus, while walking down the street, while working, or while just relaxing. What, one might wonder, are all of these people listening to and watching? Well, no doubt many are listening to their favorite songs or watching their favorite TV series, which they've purchased online or copied/ripped from their own collections. But some may be listening to free content—called podcasts (audio blogs) and video podcasts (also referred to as videocasts, video blogs, or vlogs)—that has been automatically downloaded to their computer and synced to their digital media players.

Think of a podcast as an Internet-based radio show that will automatically download to your computer. Content creators (people creating blogs and podcasts) can now "push" the written or audio content using RSS feeds. Content consumers (people wanting to read blogs, listen to podcasts, or watch video podcasts) can "pull" the content into their computers with RSS feed readers (e.g., Google Reader, Netvibes) or podcatchers—also known as podcast aggregators, podcast finders, or podcast catchers (e.g., iTunes, Juice). Many people use RSS feed readers to automatically download the content of blogs to their computers. Similarly, one can use a podcatcher to automatically download the content of podcasts to the computer.

PODCASTING

Let's get one thing out of the way right off the bat: you do not need iTunes (Apple's digital music management software) or an iPod (Apple's digital audio and video player) to create or listen to podcasts. However, it can be noted that Apple has invested substantial time and effort into making the process easier for the consumer with their products. For example, iTunes is a good option to search for and listen to podcasts, iPods are a good option to listen to your podcast on a mobile device, and Apple's GarageBand enables the recording of podcasts.

According to the *New Oxford American Dictionary*, a podcast is "a digital recording of a radio broadcast or similar program, made available on the Internet for downloading to a personal audio player." The generally accepted definition has expanded to include video as well as audio content. Technically speaking, podcasts are digital media files, audio files (e.g., MP3), or video files (e.g., M4V) that are uploaded, along with an RSS feed (a specially formatted text file) containing the Internet addresses and descriptions of the media files and their content, to a server connected to the Internet. Special software programs or web sites called podcatchers, such as iTunes, can read these RSS feeds and automatically download the audio or video files to the computer, which can then be synced to a portable device such as an iPod or other MP3 player. One of the great things about a podcast as opposed to a live radio broadcast is that you can download and listen to podcasts at your convenience.

The term *podcast* comes from the fact that the technical coding that allowed RSS feeds to encapsulate or "broadcast" audio files was first developed to work with the Apple iPod. IPod + broadcast = podcast. Because of the "pod" in podcasting, many associate podcasting with Apple. However, the Apple, Windows, and Linux Operating systems all support podcasting, as do digital media players from a number of manufacturers.

- To learn about podcasting tools for Microsoft Windows, see http://www.microsoft.com/windowsmobile/articles/podcasts.mspx.
- To learn about podcasting tools for Apple, see http://www.apple.com/itunes/store/podcasts.html.
- To learn about podcasting tools for Linux, see http://www.linux.com/articles/43055.

One key aspect of podcasts is that instead of having to visit web sites to look for new audio files, podcasts can be automatically downloaded via podcatcher software such as iTunes, Netvibes, or Juice whenever they are made available. Anyone can subscribe to a podcast with the right software or can create a podcast with the right tools.

Many people use podcasting technology to publish Internet-based radio or television shows. In fact, some of the most popular podcast offerings are actually professionally produced offerings from Public Radio, ESPN, HBO, and Comedy Central. In addition, many churches are using the technology to podcast weekly sermons, teachings, music, events, etc. In fact, some of the most innovative podcasts are done by churches.

A WORD ABOUT VIDEO PODCASTING

Video podcasting, also known as vlogging or vodcasting, is a bit newer than but is closely related to podcasting. The term *vlogging* is a portmanteau of a portmanteau—video and blogging (web + log). Even as we've been at work on this chapter, the line between podcasting and vlogging has become less and less clear. In fact, iTunes and other services generally list both as podcasts, noting parenthetically that some are video. Further, many podcasts are available in either video or audio form, where the audio version is simply the soundtrack stripped away from the video and uploaded as a separate file.

Video, of course, offers a wider range of options for entertaining, informing, and persuading. Given the proliferation of video-capable digital media players, such as the video iPod, it's not surprising that "video" has become just another form of podcast. In this chapter, then, when we speak of podcasting, we are speaking generically of either audio or video podcasts. When what we are saying applies to only one or the other, we will attempt to point that out.

PODCAST EXAMPLES

Examples of podcasts range from a guy in a room with something to say to universities podcasting class lectures, guest speakers, and events. For example, Terence is currently spearheading a project at Bowling Green State University in Bowling Green, Ohio to enable both blogging and podcasting for the entire university community (faculty, staff, students, alumni). The goal is to empower an education-focused community with the ability to easily publish text, audio, and video online. UC Berkeley, Stanford, and Harvard are just a few other universities using podcasting and blogging technologies to make available some or all coursework. One reason educational institutions are placing the once proprietary course content online is that they understand that while there is no shortage of information in the world today, information does not equal education. Education involves engaging in active learning, academic discourse, problem-based learning, and rigorous assessment. However, by making available specialized information to the global community, universities are contributing to the potential betterment of the world, which, one must admit, is great PR as well.

Perhaps one of the best ways to learn about podcasting is to begin by listening to a variety of them. Our first example is in many ways what many podcasts aspire to imitate. *This American Life* (http://thislife.org/) is a Public Radio International/Chicago Public Radio program where each episode generally consists of three or four mini-"documentaries" on a theme. It is all very well done—entertaining, informative, thought-provoking—and consistently ranked as a top podcast.

Some of Matthew's favorite *This American Life* episodes include "Pray" (episode 77, September 26, 1997; http://thislife.org/Radio_Episode.aspx?sched=682); "Somewhere in the Arabian Sea" (episode 206, March 1, 2002; http://thislife.org/Radio_Episode.aspx?sched=913); and "Superpowers" (episode 178, February23, 2001; http://thislife.org/Radio_Episode.aspx?sched=860). The staff of the show has put together a list of their favorite episodes on the show web site (http://thislife.org/Radio_Favorites.aspx).

Another podcast that is very well done, although with a much smaller staff—actually it's a one-man operation—is *Fly with Me* (http://flywithjoe.com). The host, Joe d'Eon, is an airline pilot who records interviews, stories, and other sounds as he works and travels. Episodes don't seem to come out on any kind of regular schedule, but they are always interesting peeks into airline life. One or two episodes contain harsh language, but this podcast is still worth checking out. The *Fly with Me* podcast was featured on the Slate.com podcast (http://www.slate.com/id/2119317), which is simply a professional voice reading a column that was written by a professional writer/columnist.

43 Folders (http://www.43folders.com/) is another amateur offering, but it makes for interesting listening. In the older episodes, the podcaster, Merlin Mann, simply records himself talking about a particular topic for two to ten minutes. In later episodes he conducts interviews, which is a change of pace. Taken as a whole, the episodes are a good study in someone finding his style and growing in his podcasting skill.

Matthew started *The Bioethics Podcast* (http://www.cbhd.org/podcast) in February 2006 in order to make the bioethics articles that The Center for Bioethics & Human Dignity was posting to its web site even more accessible. Interest was immediate and enthusiastic. Each week's episode is downloaded an average of 650+ times in the weeks and months after posting. Episodes on particularly interesting topics, such as the Terri Schiavo case, have been downloaded more than 1,600 times. The primary audiences for *The Bioethics Podcast* are physicians, academics, and students—very busy people who appreciate being able to listen on the go.

Many churches now make their sermon audio and/or video available as podcasts. And it's not just enormous mega-churches. Blackhawk Community Church in Madison, Wisconsin, a medium-sized church, makes available both audio and video podcasts. Blackhawk's podcasts are the work of a single volunteer, Terrell Smith, who caught a vision for "broadcasting" the services over the Web after hearing international students talk (in February 2001) about the lack of access to biblical teaching in their home countries. By May 2001 Terrell was posting sermon audio (transferred from cassette tape) to Blackhawk's web site. Each sermon is now listened to or watched more than 820 times in the weeks and months after it's posted, pretty evenly split between the video and audio versions. Blackhawk has received positive feedback from regular attendees who appreciate the ability to review sermons during the week, from pastors of other churches who otherwise might not be able to take in sermons, and from people from as far away as France, China, and New Zealand, some of whom have no access to local biblical teaching.

HOW TO SUBSCRIBE TO A PODCAST

Subscribing to a podcast means that whenever a new episode is created and uploaded to the Internet by the author, your computer will automatically download it and have it ready for you to listen to or transfer to, or synchronize with, your digital media player. Subscribing to a podcast—audio or video—requires two things, a directory and a podcatcher. Podcast directories are typically web sites but occasionally are part of a software program such as iTunes. A podcatcher may also be a web site or a software program. One can find and subscribe to individual podcasts by locating them via the search engine of one's choice or by simply coming across them on web sites one is visiting. Most often, though, it is helpful to have a single place to browse many offerings, and it can be helpful to see what others are subscribing to and rating.

While there are dozens of podcast directories, the clear leader is iTunes, which is both an online podcast directory and an offline podcast aggregator. Other online sites include Podcast.net (http://www.podcast.net), Podcast Alley (http://podcastalley.com), and Odeo (http://odeo.com).

Many digital media players come with software for aggregating podcasts. Such is the case with iTunes, which is shipped with the iPod or alternatively can be downloaded free of charge from Apple's web site (http://www.apple.com/itunes/download). Another popular player is Juice, which was formerly known as iPodder (http://juicereceiver.sourceforge.net). It is also possible to subscribe to podcasts through Windows Media Player, and even a properly connected and set up TiVo.

Because there are so many different ways to subscribe to a podcast, let's go through a real-life example. We both enjoy *RELEVANT Magazine*, and their web site (http://www.relevantmagazine.com) is a place for readers to access additional articles and other Internet-only features such as the weekly *RELEVANT Podcast*. Having found this podcast, we would like to regularly listen to the podcast, and we have several options to make that happen.

• Option 1: Go to the *RELEVANT Magazine* web site each week, click on the "listen to podcast" button, and listen to the new podcast right from the web site.

• Option 2: Go to the podcast section of their web site and, since we have iTunes installed on our computer, click on the iTunes button icon. This launches iTunes and subscribes us to the podcast feed, which enables iTunes to automatically download new episodes whenever they are uploaded by the magazine staff.

• Option 3: Go to the podcast section and, if iTunes is not installed on our computer, click on the XML button icon, which brings up an XML webpage in our browser. We can then copy the URL of the page and paste it into the appropriate place in our podcatcher (note: this works with iTunes as well, but the iTunes button icon as described in option 3 makes the process automatic).

• Option 4: Go to a podcast directory such as the one in the iTunes music store or at Yahoo! (http://podcasts.yahoo.com) and search for the *RELEVANT Podcast*. Once the podcast is located, we can click on the subscribe button, and it will automatically queue up the latest episodes as they become available. The process for other podcatchers is similar.

Note: Since we use iTunes, Option 2 is usually the best option, though Option 4 makes sense when we want to search the iTunes podcast library/directory to find and subscribe to podcasts.

WHY PEOPLE CREATE AND SUBSCRIBE TO PODCASTS

The reasons people create podcasts are probably as varied as each of us are individually. For many, it clearly is a creative outlet. While *This American Life* (http://www.thislife.org) is a great example—and probably the gold standard—of a professionally produced creative outlet, *Fly with Me* (http://www.flywithjoe.com) is an outstanding example of an amateur or armchair creative outlet. For others, it's about informing or persuading. *Captain's Quarters Radio with Ed Morrissey* (http://www.captainsquartersblog.com/mt) is a prime example of this. Many churches already record the sermons and distribute them via CD. It's a logical technological progression to turn the sermons into podcasts.

Likewise, people subscribe to podcasts in order to be entertained, informed, and to hone their persuasive skills. Other podcasts have cropped up to help people learn a foreign language (http://www.radio lingua.com), for audio city tours (http://iaudioguide.com/), and for a variety of other purposes. Some museums (and museum enthusiasts) have created podcasts as virtual tours so people can download the audio tour to their digital media players and listen to the tour as they walk through the museum.

One of the main benefits of podcasting, which we've already mentioned, is the fact that listeners automatically receive the latest updates without having to constantly check for new content. In addition, listeners can enjoy content when and where they choose—no tuning in at a set time and place. Finally, the cost of both production and consumption is so low that niche content becomes not only possible but in fact a reality. So, while train spotting and quilting are both relatively obscure topics of personal interest, podcasts exist for both: Centralized Traffic Control (http://ctcpodcast.libsyn.com) and Quilting Stash (http://www.simplearts.com/blogs/index.php).

YOUTUBE: A VIDEO SOCIAL NETWORK

YouTube is the most popular video-sharing web site on the Internet. YouTube doesn't require any special software to watch or subscribe to video since it is entirely web site driven. Though there are many other video-sharing web sites such as Google Video, Bebo, and JumpCut, we will focus on YouTube as it is not only the most popular site, but much of what we will say applies generally to these web sites. The idea behind YouTube is simple: create a video, upload it to the YouTube web site, and share it with the world. The users are both the producers and consumers of content on YouTube.

One of the most powerful aspects of YouTube is the social networking and tagging aspects of the system. By registering and creating a profile, a person can create their own YouTube "channel" and upload any kind of video content they choose. YouTube users can then "subscribe" to that channel within the web site. The entire platform is Internet-based; so, unlike a podcast, you do not download software to your computer.

Being able to find the content you are looking for is crucial, and therefore accurately tagging items is critical to the success of a video-sharing site. For example, if we were to upload a video we created about how to create a podcast, it would make sense to title it appropriately, "How To Create a Podcast" and to use keywords/tags such as "how-to," "podcast," "audacity," "MP3," and "podcatcher" in order to make it easy to find. By tagging a video appropriately, one can easily use search engines much more effectively to find the most relevant videos.

CREATING A PODCAST

First, an important note: copyright is an important consideration for both individual and ministry podcasts. Generally churches do not include the music portion of their services in podcasts because they do not have a broadcast copyright clearance. In addition, care must be exercised with photos and other visuals that may appear on a PowerPoint that might be included in a video podcast.

That said, there are several sources for free and freely usable music and images. The Wikimedia Commons (http://commons.wikimedia.org/wiki/Main_Page) is a good source for images, sound, and video. Sites devoted to music that can be used in podcasts include The Podsafe Music Network (http://music.podshow.com) and Podsafe Audio (http://www.podsafeaudio.com). A number of sites offer free images, including Stock Exchange (http://www.sxc.hu) and the Creative Commons section of Flickr (http://flickr.com/creativecommons).

Second, before starting your own podcast, spend some time listening to and watching different podcasts to see what others are doing, and try and find a style that fits you. The more podcasts you listen to, the easier it will be to craft or find your own style, and the less likely it is that you'll simply copy someone else's style, which may or may not really be you. So set aside some time to listen to multiple episodes of several of the podcasts we listed above, as well as others that you come across on the Internet.

When you're ready to create your podcast, you will need something to record it with, something for editing (unless you're very good on the first take), a place to upload and host the podcast, and a place or places to distribute your podcast.

HARDWARE

You can record directly onto your computer using any of the editing software we'll talk about later. But if you want to do anything "in the field," you'll want a portable recorder. You will probably want to use a digital and/or solid-state recorder rather than something that uses tape, in order to ease the transition from recording device to computer to Internet, etc.

The Bioethics Podcast uses a Marantz PMD660 (http://tinyurl. com/cxpzj). This device records in MP3 onto a compact flash drive that can be inserted into a laptop using a PC card adapter (http://www.buy. com/retail/product.asp?sku=10391451).

Also very popular is the M-Audio MicroTrack (http://www.m-audio. com/products/en_us/MicroTrack2496-main.html). It too is solid-state, using compact flash and recording in MP3 or WAV format. The latest generations of iPods can also act as recorders, although they require an external microphone. Several manufacturers offer such mics.

The quality of the microphone that you use can make a great difference to how your podcast sounds. There is a huge difference between a twenty-dollar mic and a two-hundred-dollar mic, and a small difference between a two-hundred-dollar mic and a two-thousand-dollar mic. More than price, one of the most important things is that it is a digital rather than an analog connection. For example, at Bowling Green State University instructors can use a fifty-dollar USB mic and get crystal-clear sound.

Originally developed for network television use at the 2000 Olympic Games in Sydney, Australia, the Sennheiser SEMD46 (http://www.bhphotovideo.com/bnh/controller/home?O=Search&A= details&Q=&sku=223940&is=REG) has a great sound and has internal shock mounts that reduce handling noise for "in the field" interview situations. You might also want to consider purchasing a desktop stand for the mic for your "in the studio" recording sessions, so your hands will be free and you won't have to worry about handling noise. A Porta Brace case will help protect the investment you've made in the recorder and mic (http://www.bhphotovideo.com/c/

product/398726-REG/Porta_Brace_AR_PMD660_Audio_Recorder_ Case.html). If you're planning to do "in the field" interviews, a pro- fessional-looking setup goes a long way in terms of first impressions of your credibility.

Many podcasters use a small mixing board, like the Behringer UB802 (http://www.behringer.com/UB802/index.cfm?lang=ENG) for in-studio interviews. A number of hardware- and software-based audio processing options are also available, but these are beyond the scope of this introductory chapter. Besides, they aren't really necessary for producing a podcast.

To create a video podcast, obviously you'll need something that captures video. Like most technologies, video cameras are ever chang- ing, with newer and newer models being introduced all of the time. For quick snippets of video, many point-and-shoot digital cameras like the Sony Cybershot or Canon Elph PowerShot will capture video perfectly suitable for vlogging.

For higher-end video production, you might want to consider investing in a camera that shoots High-Definition (HD) video. Most of the video editing software we'll talk about below will allow you to edit HD and output it in either HD or standard format. You'll want to be mindful of whether you intend to post the video as HD or standard when shooting, to ensure that you frame your shots properly.

When buying a video camera you'll want to look for something that is easy to connect to your computer and that has the features and functions you want and need. A number of Internet sites offer reviews and comparisons of video cameras and camcorders, but as you shop you'll want to go to a bricks-and-mortar store and try several models to get a feel for how they operate, how they fit in your hands, and how easy they are to use.

SOFTWARE

Software varies by operating system. The good news is that no matter what operating system you're using, good tools are readily available. In fact, one of the most popular audio-only tools, Audacity (http:// audacity.sourceforge.net), is available free of charge for Windows, Mac, and Linux/Unix.

Windows Movie Maker is a free tool, included with Windows,

for editing and saving movies in a variety of formats. Adobe makes high-end software for audio (Audition) and video (Premier) production (both Windows only), but these are probably considerably more in terms of function, complication, and cost than most podcasts will want or need.

Apple, though, has some of the most powerful and yet easy to use tools for both audio and video production. Apple's iLife program includes GarageBand for audio production and iMovie for video production. GarageBand offers a host of music samples, sound effects, and post-production fine-tuning for all but the most demanding podcasts. When editing a podcast in GarageBand, you can insert digital pictures alongside the audio track, so that the pictures will display on the screen of an iPod or on your computer screen if listening to the podcast in iTunes. This is a kind of Apple-specific halfway step between a podcast and video podcast that would allow you, for example, to have PowerPoint slides or photos to accompany the dialogue in your podcast.

GarageBand can also be used to produce the soundtrack to accompany video edited in iMovie. Perhaps the one drawback to GarageBand is that it can only export audio to a .Mac account or to iTunes. Once you have the audio in iTunes, though, you can easily convert it to MP3 and upload it to the host of your choice. The version of iMovie shipping with early versions of iLife '08 has received such negative reviews that Apple has continued to make available the very highly rated version from iLife '07. In addition, Apple also offers a slightly stripped down version of its studio-quality video editing package, Final Cut Express HD. While it's not as easy to use as iMovie, Final Cut Express HD offers virtually the full array of features used in editing Hollywood blockbusters like *King Kong*. It has plenty of power for your video podcast.

One challenge brought by writing deadlines and publication schedules, particularly when it comes to writing about hardware and software, is that things can change drastically with the release of a new software version or a new piece of hardware. Fortunately, a number of bloggers write specifically about podcasting hardware and software. Matthew particularly recommends Scott Bourne, the PodcastGearGuy (http://www.podcastgearguy.com and http://www.onlinemediatips.com

com). In addition, Apple has a section of iTunes devoted to podcasts on podcasting (http://phobos.apple.com/WebObjects/MZStore.woa/wa/viewRoom?fcId=154803340&id=1).

In the end, though, we both have found that the simplest solution for audio is the free product Audacity, and the simplest solution for video is Apple's iMovie.

MAKING YOUR PODCAST AVAILABLE

Once you've created your podcast, you will need to upload it to a web site. Most web site hosting plans include enough storage space to hold several to many episodes of your podcast. Over the long term, you will want to pay attention not only to your storage limits but also to your bandwidth transfer limitations. I (Matthew) have used 1and1 (http://www.1and1.com) for years to host my personal web sites, church web sites, and organizational web sites, and I highly recommend their combination of price and performance. Alternatively, a number of podcast hosting-specific sites include large storage space and high transfer volume for little or no fee. Examples include Liberated Syndication (http://www.libsyn.com) and PodcastPeople (http://www.podcastpeople.com). *Podcasting News* has a list of hosting services (http://www.podcastingnews.com/topics/Podcast_Hosts.html).

It would be quite surprising to find someone who did not want to make their podcast available through iTunes. To that end, Apple has on their web site (and available through the podcast section in iTunes) detailed instructions—http://www.apple.com/itunes/store/podcaststechspecs.html. In short, you have to create an RSS feed, which is simply a text file in XML format. According to Apple's web site, "There are a number of applications and online services that will assist you in the creation of your podcast's XML feed; you can even create one by hand using nothing but a text editor." Indeed you can, but you may not want to. One of the most popular online services to assist you with feed creation is FeedBurner (http://www.feedburner.com).

Some web sites enable people to create and publish podcasts for free without downloading any software. ODEO (www.odeo.com) is one such web site. ODEO Studio (http://studio.odeo.com/create/home) enables a person to create an account and use online tools to record a podcast. ODEO automatically generates a podcast web page where all of your ODEO podcasts will go. Users can submit the feed to the ODEO podcast directory as well as the iTunes directory and others. People can then use their podcatchers to subscribe to your podcast or they can listen right there on the Web. The upside to this method is that it enables anyone to create a podcast with limited knowledge of the technology involved. The downside is that hosting a podcast on ODEO is less customizable than a personal web page and therefore may not give you the professional look you would want.

CONCLUSION

We are living in an age of information and communication unlike anything ever seen before—a world in which everyone is given a voice. *Time* Magazine named "You" "Person of the Year" because of the new media revolution in content creation, distribution, and consumption. Blogging, podcasting, and vlogging are staples of this new media revolution. It is vitally important for Christians to give serious consideration to ways that this affects life as we know it, to what doors this might open for the gospel, and to how we can use these new media to effectively transform the world. In this chapter we've attempted to address a number of technical questions in order to help expand your understanding of podcasting and video podcasting so that you can dive into the new media age headfirst. So jump into the waters of innovation and change, and let the world hear your voice.

PART TWO

ENGAGING
NEW MEDIA

6

THEOLOGICAL BLOGGING

David Wayne

http://JollyBlogger.typepad.com

ON JANUARY 3, 2006 PAUL GILLIN admitted that he had made a mistake. In a column for CIO News he said:

> One of my worst predictions ever was from 2003: "Blogging's wave has already crested now that millions of online diarists are realizing that not that many people actually read this stuff." I missed the point, which is that small but passionate audiences are the core of "long tail." The technology world is already being reshaped by blogging. Sites like Technorati and Tech.Memeorandum are the kingmakers who choose who gets heard. Podcasting is an explosive new phenomenon that takes blogging to another level. The mainstream media is already taking cues from the blogosphere. Get to know it because it counts.[1]

It turns out that many people do read "this stuff," even when "this" is theological stuff. And it is fair to speculate that blogging may be helping reshape the theological landscape just as it has the technological and mainstream media landscapes.

Traditionally, theology has been the domain of the theologians, academics, and professional ministers who have had specialized "theological" training. In that setting, the specialists have done the study and delivered the product to the "people in the pew," whose duties were to receive and obey.

---

[1]Paul Gillin, "2006 Outlook: Open Source, Offshoring, Web 2.0," January 3, 2006; http://searchcio.techtarget.com/originalContent/0,289142,sid183_gci1155797,00.html (accessed March 20, 2006).

With the growth of the Internet, blogging, and other new media, the people in and out of the pew have gained a voice in the theological conversation, whether the specialists like it or not. The Internet in general and blogging in particular democratizes knowledge, and each voice carries as much weight as any other voice.

Blogging is becoming a new means of delivering the product of theological study, but it is also shaping the study itself. This chapter will focus on how blogging is changing the way theology is studied and delivered.

Before looking at how blogging influences the theology task, it will be useful to understand what theology is in the first place.

WHAT IS THEOLOGY?

Theologians have often defined theology in an academic fashion—theology as study.

While study is central to it, an overemphasis on academics and studies can keep theology locked up in the classroom, never letting it out into the highways and fields where it belongs. John Frame defines theology this way: "I would suggest that we define theology as 'the application of the Word of God by persons to all areas of life.'"[2]

Frame's definition takes theology from the exclusive domain of the theologian and pastor and extends it into the lives of mechanics and managers, housewives and teenagers, athletes and artists, bloggers and Luddites, ballerinas and surfer dudes.

Defining theology as the application of Scripture to life reminds us that the task of theologizing is always incomplete. The last word has yet to be written in theology. We can never exhaust the knowledge that the Scriptures reveal to us about God. Since theology is an ongoing task, a discussion of theology and blogging is warranted as the blogosphere has become a new arena for doing theology.

HOW DO WE DO THEOLOGY?

If the last word on theology is yet to be written, it is fair to ask the question, how do we do theology? For many the answer is simple—we just read the Bible and say what it says about any particular topic. And there is a good deal of truth in this simple expression. The goal of theol-

---

[2]John Frame, *The Doctrine of the Knowledge of God* (Phillipsburg, NJ: P&R, 1987), 81.

ogy is to say what the Bible says about any given topic. Yet it is more complicated than that. To do theology well there are many matters we ought to consider, but I will highlight three—exegesis, experience, and community.

Exegesis

Exegesis is the process of studying the text of Scripture to understand its meaning. This involves the study of the grammar, syntax, genres, and the historical and canonical contexts of individual passages and books. Exegetes must also practice the principle of interpreting Scripture with Scripture, and they must pay attention to redemptive-historical concerns, interpreting individual passages in light of their place in the grand story of redemption. The fruits of exegesis become the basis of theological statements, which are simply summary statements of what the Bible teaches on a given topic.

Experience

The role of experience in theology is a controversial topic in itself. But even those who are most insistent that experience not determine our theology will admit that it informs our study of theology. The Bible was not given to us as a textbook on theology. Our theological statements answer questions we bring to the text of Scripture, questions that derive from our experience of life in this world.

There is a reciprocal relationship between theology and experience. Our experiences give us the questions we ask of Scripture, and through our study our theology informs, explains, critiques, and corrects our experience.

Yet there is a real sense in which experience helps correct errant theology. For instance, it is possible to read the Bible in a way that suggests that the earth is a flat plane, the edge of which an unwary traveler may fall off. After all, the Bible suggests the earth has "four corners" (Isaiah 11:12; Revelation 7:1; 20:8) and that there is an end, or ends, to the earth (Psalm 22:27; Daniel 4:11; Mark 13:27). But if you were to get into a boat and sail west, or east for that matter, and someday arrive back at your starting point, your experience would tell you that you may have misunderstood those Scriptures and that you may need to adjust your theology.

Of course, there is the danger of giving too much weight to experience or of misinterpreting experience. This can (and often does!) lead to
aberrant theology. These dangers are real and must be guarded against.
Yet, the existence of these dangers ought not to prevent us from giving
experience its proper place.

Community

Recognizing community as a resource in the theology task affirms the
biblical picture that each individual is a member of a larger body. God
is building his church, a connected body, not a group of disconnected
individuals. And this group includes Christians of all times and ages.
As the Westminster Confession of Faith states:

> The catholic or universal Church, which is invisible, consists of the
> whole number of the elect, that have been, are, or shall be gathered
> into one, under Christ the Head thereof; and is the spouse, the body,
> the fullness of Him that filleth all in all.[3]

Theology is done in conversation, in community, and that community includes those who have been and are members of the church.
We can think of this community in terms of present representatives
and heritage.

As the name implies, present representatives are members of our
present church community. This includes everyone from the lady who
sits next to you in church to the person you were discussing theology
with on the Internet or over lunch to pastors, teachers, popular speakers, authors, and contemporary scholars.

Yet we are all part of a much larger community of all the believers who have gone before us, a group that G. K. Chesterton refers to
as "the democracy of the dead." At every moment of the day we are
surrounded by a great "cloud of witnesses" (Hebrews 12:1), many of
whom have left records of their study of theology in commentaries,
creeds and confessions, systematic theologies, and devotional and
other writings. C. S. Lewis reminds us of the importance of knowing
our heritage:

---

[3]*The Westminster Confession of Faith* (Bellingham, WA: Logos Research Systems, 1996), Chapter
XXV, 1.

We need intimate knowledge of the past. Not that the past has any magic about it, but because we cannot study the future, and yet need something to set against the present, to remind us that the basic assumptions have been quite different in different periods and that much which seems certain to the uneducated is merely temporary fashion. A man who has lived in many places is not likely to be deceived by the local errors of his native village: the scholar has lived in many times and is therefore in some degree immune from the great cataract of nonsense that pours from the press and the microphone of his own age.[4]

Keeping in mind that we are part of a much larger heritage reminds us that the Holy Spirit has been speaking to the church for thousands of years. "There is nothing new under the sun" (Ecclesiastes 1:9), and we need to remember that the temptations of our present age are not unique (1 Corinthians 10:13), and the theological issues we address today often, nearly always, were addressed in some fashion in the past.

So, doing theology in community corrects our faulty exegesis at the same time that our exegesis is correcting our faulty ideas about community. Doing theology in community broadens our perspective— it helps us see that we don't know it all. In fact, it reminds us that we haven't come up with all of the questions that could be asked of Scripture. The community supplies us with questions and insights that can deepen our understanding of Scripture and correct our misunderstandings of Scripture.

As we move to discuss the relationship of blogging and theology, my fundamental assumption is that blogging doesn't change the way we do theology. For bloggers, theology is still the application of the Scriptures to life. Theology is still a necessity for bloggers, and all bloggers who in any way attempt to apply the Scriptures to life are theologians.

Furthermore, blogging does not provide a new resource for theology, but it does supply a new means of delivery for the three resources mentioned above.

But most importantly it is changing the way we use all of the

---

[4]C. S. Lewis, "Learning in War-Time," *The Weight of Glory* (San Francisco: Harper San Francisco, 2001), 58–59.

aforementioned resources as it alters the way we deliver and receive information, and it alters the way we engage in community.

Some of these alterations are helpful, and some are challenging at best and potentially harmful at worst.

BLOGGING AND THEOLOGICAL RESOURCES

Resources for Exegesis

Before there was an Internet, many preachers, Sunday school teachers, and zealous laymen were exegeting Scripture as they prepared sermons and lessons or just boned up on a topic of interest. Back then they used these things called *books*. Now much of the content of books is available online.

Those of us who have become comfortable on the Internet may forget just what a revolutionary thing it is to have access to the resources that are available on the Net. Any Christian with an Internet connection now has access to a library of materials that most pastors, through most of history, could only have dreamed of. Here are a few examples.

At the date of writing, Bible Gateway (http://www.biblegateway.com) allows you to read and search twenty different English translations of the Bible. The search capabilities go far beyond what you could do with a concordance before the Internet was available. With Bible Gateway you can look up individual words, passages, and phrases. Advanced search options enable you to do even more precise searches.

The Christian Classics Ethereal Library (http://ccel.org) provides access to hundreds of high-quality theological books that few people could have afforded a generation ago. With the Worldwide Study Bible (http://ccel.org/wwsb) anyone can click on the title of a biblical book or look up a particular passage, and it will provide anywhere from a few to dozens of links on that passage in commentaries, dictionaries, and the like.

And this only scratches the surface—there is an explosion of some of the finest exegetical and theological resources the church has produced throughout its history.

In addition, many bloggers are sharing the fruit of their exegesis online, including many well-known biblical scholars who now have blogs of their own. This makes exegetical material that was formerly available mostly to specialists now available to the masses. Material that has traditionally been contained in technical commentaries and scholarly journals and was housed in libraries is now available to anyone with an Internet connection.

Christian Experience

In 1998 George Barna predicted the rise of the cyberchurch, an alternative way of doing church. His prediction is coming true in many ways. The blogosphere has become a new "sphere" where the Christian life is being lived out, where Christian experience is being lived out. Andrew Careaga summarized Barna's position this way:

> In 1998, Christian pollster and sociologist George Barna predicted the emergence of a "cyberchurch" in the early years of the new century. This cyberchurch will not be anything like the bricks-and-mortar gathering places that pass for churches in our culture today. Rather, Barna's cyberchurch will be an online church—one that is entirely on the Internet. Its congregation of millions "will never travel physically to a church, but will instead roam the Internet in search of meaningful spiritual experiences." As the Internet becomes more integrated in our culture, and as traditional church become less relevant in a globalized, consumerist culture, Barna concludes that we'll see "a majority of Americans . . . completely isolated from the traditional church format." Not only will they be surfing the Net for spiritual guidance, but many will also meet in cell groups and home churches, while others will simply have forsaken church altogether.[5]

This is deeply troubling in many ways, but there is no doubt that it is happening. But no one can (or no one should) doubt that the Internet and blogosphere are providing an alternative "sphere" for Christian living. This is reshaping Christian experience, including the experience of doing theology.

Community

As Careaga and Barna intimated, the greatest way the Internet/blogosphere is influencing Christian experience is in reshaping Christian

---

[5]Andrew Careaga, "Embracing the Cyberchurch," http://www.next-wave.org/dec99/embracing_the_cyberchurch.htm.

community. As Andrew Careaga says, "the Internet is radically reshaping lives, perceptions of reality, communication, community, relationships and culture."[6]

There is a good deal of debate about whether or not real community can take place via the Internet. I am one of those who have reservations about this. But whether I, or anyone else, have reservations about this, there are many who perceive and are looking to the Internet/blogosphere for true community.

Jordon Cooper shares an example of how the blogging community ministered to him in a time of need.

> When my wife Wendy had her miscarriage a little over a month ago, I went downstairs and posted it when we got home in the middle of the night. By the next morning, many people who only know me through my weblog had e-mailed, commented on the site and later on made several phone calls to see if we needed anything. At the time, I was on staff of a church of 1500 people who went on and on about being an authentic community. Outside of my son's godparents, not a single phone call from any of the staff and leadership.
>
> There is a reason we flock online. There are people, interaction, and community here that in many ways is more real than in the offline world.[7]

Of course, we may argue that the real moral of this story is the failure of a church to care for its members, and I am sure there are those who might quibble about whether or not the cyber well-wishes that Jordon and Wendy received constitute real community. Wherever you stand on those things, it is undeniable that Jordon and Wendy received true expressions of Christian love and that this was facilitated through the blogosphere. And there are many other stories like this around the blogosphere.

There is a real sense in which the Internet/blogosphere has created a parallel Christian universe for us. But the real significance is not in its creation of a parallel Christian universe and a parallel delivery system for the three main theological resources. The real significance is in the way it is reshaping the way we use the very resources themselves. In

[6]Andrew Careaga, "The Church-Internet (dis)connection," http://www.next-wave.org/jun02/disconnection.htm.
[7]Quoted in Tim Bednar, "We Know More Than Our Pastors," http://djchuang.googlepages.com/WeKnowMoreThanOurPastors.pdf, pp. 15-16. Jordon Cooper blogs at http://www.jordoncooper.com.

this respect blogging has the potential to help and harm us in the task of doing theology.

HOW BLOGGING MAY HELP THEOLOGY

It remains to be seen if and how the blogging phenomenon will make a long-term positive contribution to the theological task. If it does so, it will be because of the expanded community resources it provides. Specifically, the blogosphere may provide better access to our present resources and to our heritage.

Blogging and Present Representatives

The particular benefit that blogging brings to us is the increased interaction with the present representatives of our Christian community. I'll introduce that thought with a story from my own experience.

During seminary I benefited immensely from the lectures of excellent professors and the great books we read. But for me and many of my fellow students the after-class informal conversations with fellow students and professors were as valuable as the in-class time. Obviously the classroom lectures were of primary importance in the education, but it was in those informal, off-the-cuff discussions and debates outside of class where many things sunk in. It was in these discussions that students who "got it" could explain things to those who didn't get it. Students could offer other illustrations and insights, they could say "yeah, but," and talk about things the professor didn't mention or bring up other books they had read that might add to the learning. And it was outside class where we could often talk to the professors to get clarifications on many points. In short, much of our learning took place outside the formal class time. A good deal of theologizing took place outside the theology class.

With its conversational style, blogging is the closest I have come to duplicating this after-class aspect of the seminary experience. The feedback allowed in comments on blogs and in the cross-posting that takes place as blogger A interacts with blogger B has a terrific sharpening effect on our theologizing.

Here are some particular benefits that come from interacting with the present representatives of our community through blogging:

Quick feedback: Theology is perfected as it is discussed and debated. In the past a scholar might offer his theological insights through a book or an article in a theological journal. Hopefully this scholar would have interacted with critics before publishing the book or article, but the real feedback came after publishing. Professor A might write a journal article that was responded to by Professor B in another article, and others may jump into the fray. Something similar might take place through the writing of books.

Whether it is professional theologians or the theologians in the pew who are interacting, blogging dramatically shortens the feedback loop. This can have many beneficial effects.

First of all, errors and misunderstandings can be corrected quickly.

Second, with blogging it becomes increasingly harder to misrepresent your theological opponents and create straw men. To be sure, a good deal of misrepresentation and straw-man-making goes on in blogs, but at least these things don't go unchallenged for long.

Third, the quickening of the feedback loop can lead to greater clarity and precision as errors, misunderstandings, misrepresentations, and straw men are dealt with in a timely fashion.

Expanded horizons: Most of us spend most of our time talking to like-minded people. This is appropriate and understandable, but when doing theology, it is helpful to have a broader perspective.

Blogging expands our communities. It does help us deepen the conversation within our own denominations and theological traditions, but it goes deeper than that. Blogging exposes us to many people from many different communities. This not only opens up new resources, but it helps clear up some of the misunderstandings and misinterpretations we often have regarding people of other traditions.

It is one thing for a Reformed or arminian or dispensationalist or _____ (insert your tradition here) Christian to criticize the errors of his theological opponents when he is among members of his own tradition. But in the blogosphere there is a good chance that when you criticize your opponents, those opponents are going to be reading and responding, and this can only be helpful.

Blogging and Heritage

Along with the above, blogging can enable us to know more of our heritage. Many bloggers write from within a theological tradition, and many blogs are devoted to bringing the fruits of their tradition to the forefront today.

Blogging helps us with the theological task of making our Christian heritage available to us today, thereby strengthening and challenging our theological convictions, helping us avoid being deceived by the local errors of our native village, as C. S. Lewis said.

HOW BLOGGING MAY HARM THEOLOGY

It is often the case that our greatest strengths are also our greatest weaknesses, and blogging is no different. There is a flip side to the freedom and access that blogging provides for us to interact in community. That freedom can be a blessing, and it can also be a curse.

Along those lines I offer some thoughts on ways that blogging may harm, hinder, or confuse the task of theologizing. None of these things have to happen, but blogging is a medium, and Marshall McLuhan's famous quote ("the medium is the message") applies to blogging just as it does to other forms of media. The medium of blogging not only transmits a message, it has potential to shape the message.

With that in mind, part of the task of doing theology in the blogosphere will be to recognize and critique the blogging phenomenon itself. I'll offer a few thoughts on potential dangers to theology in the blogosphere, all the while acknowledging that these aren't necessary consequences of blogging, just potential consequences.

I'll also point out that it seems to me that the potential dangers I address would fall loosely into the category of habits of the mind. If the medium of the blogosphere shapes the message, it does so by shaping the mind, by creating certain potentially harmful habits of mind.

The Cult of the Amateur

In choosing the title for this section I am purposely borrowing the title of Andrew Keen's book of the same title. This captures the nervousness many feel toward theological bloggers. Andrew Keen has made this moniker popular with his book *The Cult of the Amateur*.[8] The subtitle of the paperback edition of Keen's book gives a good idea of its argument—"How blogs, MySpace, YouTube, and the rest of today's

---

[8]Andrew Keen, *The Cult of the Amateur: How Today's Internet is Killing Our Culture* (New York: Doubleday/Currency, 2007).

user-generated media are assaulting our economy, our culture, and our values." Keen's sentiments are shared by some who evaluate the evangelical/theological blogosphere. *The Texas Observer* questioned Richard Land, head of the Southern Baptist Ethics and Religious Liberty Commission, and Land offered the following observation:

> "[Blogs] increase the level of communication among Southern Baptists without a commensurate level of responsibility." As a result, he says, "a lot of stuff gets out there that's irresponsible and inaccurate and misleads people." Does he read the blogs? "I never read the blogs," he says. "I have staff people who monitor them, and if they think there's something I really need to read, I read it, but I'm too busy. I have a job to do, and I'm way too busy. I can't read as fast as they blog. I have a full-time job."[9]

Land's comments reflect a potential hazard of theological blogging. All who have a computer and a network connection can speak authoritatively about any matter they are interested in, regardless of their theological training or lack thereof.

The "cult of the amateur" criticism is a dangerous one to make as it smacks of a kind of elitism that seems to take theology out of the hands of the common man and make it the sole prerogative of professionals.[10] Protestants in particular may want to watch the vigor with which they proffer this criticism. With its emphasis on vernacular translations and the priesthood of the believer, Protestantism has sought to put the treasures of the faith into the hands of the common man. Thus they will want to be careful to avoid making theology the prerogative of professionals.

Giving proper weight to those caveats, it still remains that God has given a gift of teaching to the church, and this is a gift that is given to some and not to others. There are leaders in the church who watch over the souls of their charges and who must give an account to God for their work. The church is called to submit to their authority and obey them (Hebrews 13:17). Elders, or overseers, are distinguished in

---

[9]Michael Erard, "Don't Stop Believing," *The Texas Observer*; http://www.texasobserver.org/article.php?aid=2547(accessed September 21, 2007).
[10]A stimulating online debate on these matters between Kevin Kelly (pro-Internet) and Andrew Keen (anti-) can be found at Jewcy online magazine. The debate begins with an article called "Can We Save the Internet?" by Andrew Keen at http://www.jewcy.com/dialogue/2007-05-29/can_the_internet_be_saved. On that page there are links to the rest of the dialogue.

the church by their ability to teach (1 Timothy 3:2). James warns the church that not many of them ought to become teachers (James 3:1).

All of this suggests that the democratizing process in blogging (and the new media in general) is not an unmitigated good. On the plus side there are many gifted teachers who have gained a greater audience through blogging. The downside is that blogging also can grant a platform and sense of authority to some whom the apostle James says ought not to teach.

Individualism

America is famous for being a nation of "rugged individualists." This is a good thing in that it resists an unbiblical elitism and honors the dignity of the individual. It can be a bad thing when it resists the communitarian impulse. In her book *Total Truth* Nancy Pearcey speaks of the revivalistic tradition of the seventeenth century and how it focused on the individual to the detriment of the community. Seventeenth-century society was "highly communal and organic," and people did not think of themselves in distinction from their community. This changed for the revivalists as an "individual was addressed *as an individual*, apart from membership in a church."

> Thus it was a radical departure when the revivalists directed their message to individuals, exhorting them to make independent decisions in regard to religion—and to act on those decisions regardless of their effect on the larger society. "Piety was no longer something inextricably bound up with local community and corporate spirituality," explains Stout. "The emphasis shifted to a more individualistic and subjective sense of piety that found its quintessential expression in the internal, highly personal experience of the 'New Birth.'"[11]

The individualism that Pearcey identified in seventeenth-century revivalism has become a given in evangelicalism; yet few of us recognize the damage this has done to community. Blogging may (again, not necessarily "will") further this individualism and further degrade community.

Though there is a sense in which blogging can build community,

---

[11]Nancy Pearcey, *Total Truth: Liberating Christianity from Its Cultural Captivity* (Wheaton, IL: Crossway Books, 2005), 270.

it is equally true that blogging offers a substitute for face-to-face community. It creates a kind of community where no one is truly accountable to anyone else. Any individual can excommunicate himself from a blogging community at any time or excommunicate the rest of the community simply by turning off the computer, de-linking, or removing someone from an RSS reader or leaving the blogosphere. The blogosphere is a "sphere" where the individual reigns supreme.

Egalitarianism Run Amok

I realize that the word *egalitarian* is a controversial one, given modern debates about the roles of men and women. I am not using it in reference to that debate but rather in its more general sense of equality. In that regard, Andrew Sullivan says of blogging:

> And it harnesses the web's real genius—its ability to empower anyone to do what only a few in the past could genuinely pull off. In that sense, blogging is the first journalistic model that actually harnesses rather than merely exploits the true democratic nature of the web.[12]

That is good news indeed for bloggers and all who read them. With its democratic nature the blogosphere promotes equality and diversity.

But this is not an unmitigated good. At its heart, the Christian faith is not a purely democratic movement. Everyone's opinion is not as good as everyone else's.

Tolerance is a hot topic in our day, but we have lost the true meaning of tolerance. There is a true, biblical tolerance that teaches us to accept all men as equals, as fellow image-bearers. But to accept every person is not the same as accepting every idea and behavior. If we are not careful, the very democratic nature of the Web that is being exploited in blogging can lead us down the road of an extreme and unbiblical individualism/egalitarianism.

This doesn't mean the blogosphere needs some kind of priesthood or hierarchy to vet bloggers and their posts. It does mean that bloggers and their readers need to be aware of how the medium may be shaping their theology, and it calls them to use their theology to critique the medium.

---

[12]Quoted by Josh Claybourn in his blog archives—http://www.joshclaybourn.com/blogger.html.

A Loss of Authority

Finally, the blogging phenomenon can create a habit of mind that weakens our ability to submit to legitimate biblical authority. This potential danger comes from two sources—the conversational nature of the blogosphere and the development of sovereign individualism.

The blogosphere is uniquely able to foster conversation, and this is one of its greatest strengths. In one sense this is all to the good. Because the blogosphere is open to anyone with an Internet connection, anyone can join the theological conversation. But when conversation becomes the default mode of communication, we may train ourselves to reject anything that smacks of authoritative proclamation. Taken too far, this mind-set will lead us to question and debate everything, and we may develop an allergy to anything like authoritative proclamation. Further, if we develop a habit of mind that can't receive authoritative proclamation, we will be hard-pressed to give any weight to any theological statement.

In regard to sovereign individualism, I borrow the term from the book *The Sovereign Individual: Mastering the Transition to the Information Age* [13] by James Dale Davidson and Lord William Rees-Mogg. Those who are familiar with these authors know that they are quite controversial, both for their political views and for their claims to prescience. In fact, in this book they seem to have bought into a good deal of the failed Y2K hype. Yet, I do believe they accurately capture a mind-set that is developing here in the information age. They write:

> The coming transformation is both good news and bad. The good news is that the Information Revolution will liberate individuals as never before. For the first time, those who can educate and motivate themselves will be almost entirely free to invent their own work and realize the full benefits of their own productivity. Genius will be unleashed, freed from both the oppression of government and the drags of racial and ethnic prejudice. In the Information Society, no one who is truly able will be detained by the ill-formed opinions of others. It will not matter what most of the people on earth might think of your race, your looks, your age, your sexual proclivities, or the way you wear your hair. In the cybereconomy, they will never see you. The ugly, the fat, the old, the disabled will vie with the

---

[13]James Dale Davidson and Lord William Rees-Mogg, *The Sovereign Individual: Mastering the Transition to the Information Age* (New York: Touchstone, 1993).

young and beautiful on equal terms in utterly color-blind anonymity on the new frontiers of cyber-space.[14]

They go on to say that this is creating the "Sovereign Individual," one whom nation-states and traditional institutions will lose their power to control. In gaining more control over their lives, people will have less and less accountability to traditional institutions.

My concern is that the more and more "sovereign" people perceive themselves to be, the less and less willing they will become to bow the knee to another sovereign. The task of theologizing assumes a posture of submission to the Word of God and recognition of the sovereignty of God. How will the increasing self-perception of sovereign individualism change the ways that people view the sovereignty of God?

How will such sovereign individuals relate to the Word of God? How will they relate to the broader Christian community? Will there be any hope of reaching theological consensus in the church?

CONCLUSION

The theological task is more nuanced than most of us think, and maybe a bit more complicated, drawing on a few more resources than we ordinarily think. If the theological task is more complex, though, it is a complexity that leads to beauty as more of the richness of Scripture is found and made useful for living.

Blogging may provide some unique benefits for us and could enable us to move the theological task forward. In particular, blogging may expand our communities and in so doing bring greater resources to bear on the theological task. Blogging can expose us to more exegetical tools and then enable us to have wider and deeper interaction with present and past representatives of our Christian community.

And blogging may create situations that will diminish our ability to do good theology. But even where it may harm, it need not. The potential danger blogging poses to theology is mainly that it may create habits of the mind that militate against habits of the mind that are necessary for good theologizing. But these are things that may be effectively resisted as we live in submission to the Word of God.

---

[14]Ibid., 17-18.

7

BLOG AS MICROWAVE COMMUNITY

Tod Bolsinger

http://Bolsinger.Blogs.com

HAILED AS THE "GREATEST DISCOVERY SINCE FIRE" forty years ago, the Amana Radarange promised to change the way America cooked. Twenty years earlier a World War II-era engineer had walked by a microwave radar tube one day and noticed that the candy bar in his pocket had melted. Before long they were sitting around the office trying to use "radar" to pop popcorn and explode eggs. It took twenty years of engineering and tinkering for the microwave oven to be made compatible for Mom's kitchen, and it would be another twenty before the price would come down to make it affordable enough to be considered a household item. But all along, the real question was whether this new "microwave oven" was going to rid the world of the need for fire to prepare food or whether it would just be a passing fad that could endanger the "fine art of cooking."

Today microwave ovens are in 90 percent of American households (there are more microwaves than dishwashers), and without a doubt the device that you probably used to reheat a piece of pizza last week is here to stay. But take a look around your kitchen and you'll notice something else. You probably also have a conventional oven. In fact, unless you live in a dorm room, you very likely use your conventional oven as much (in elapsed time anyway) as your microwave. The microwave didn't replace your conventional oven—

it simply took its place alongside it. And the key to really enjoying your microwave—and even more important, cooking well—is to know how and when to use your microwave and at the same time what it is *not* good for.

A generation after the microwave oven entered mainstream America, we are amidst another revolution, this time one of "new media." And like the microwave oven, some are convinced that these new media will make newspapers and books and magazines go the way of the eight-track tape player, the dial telephone, and the mangle. *Huh? What's a mangle?* My point exactly.

There are also those who believe that the new media will change the way we do a lot of "old" things, like go to church and build community. And in a "flat" world where you can communicate with Christians in Singapore as easily as you can with those who live on your same street, it is tempting to believe that Christian community will soon become a mostly "virtual" reality.

Anyone who ever tried to bake a cake in a microwave understands that the key to using technology well is being really clear on what technology does and doesn't do best. Similarly, it will take time to understand what the new media do and do not do best in furthering Christian community. But in this chapter I would like to suggest some insights that we can use to guide our use of the new media, especially blogs (my main area of experience). So, after a brief definition of what Christian community should be and how any "virtual community" can never be a replacement for genuine life together, I will pose two questions to consider:

> 1. What can new media *do* to encourage Christian community? That is, to what end can blogs, instant messaging, Facebook, and other new media contribute to growing healthy, faithful, Christian community?
>
> 2. What can new media *undo* that may actually hinder or lead to the decline of healthy Christian community? What warnings or pitfalls should make us pause and consider carefully the proper role of new media?

Then finally, I want to offer a few suggestions for how best to consider new media, especially blogging, as tools that can and will stand alongside but cannot and should not replace more traditional forms of communication and community building.

To be sure, the variety and relevance of the answers to many of the questions I will pose are based largely on age and temperament. My teenage son's primary mode of connection with his friends is text messaging and cell phone calls. But my wife has never sent a text in her life. (If she received something on her phone that read "IMHO, U shld go 2. BRB. LOL," she would likely think that a list of car license plates had been sent to her in error.) My son started a Bible study on his junior high school campus and at the same time started a blog to further discussion and post meeting times for the group (which had made an agreement with the school administration not to pass out fliers or other publicity for the Bible study on the school campus.) While Beth will e-mail a friend, use a cell phone to tell me she is running late to pick up our daughter, and shop on the Internet, she still reads the daily newspaper that plops on our driveway each morning to keep up with the world, barely reads my blog, and very likely doesn't know how to post a comment to a blog if she wanted to. Without question, the new media affect my son's world and the way he develops, cultivates, and stays connected to his friends and sense of community more than they do my wife.

At the church I pastor, our two directors of high school and junior high ministry have Facebook and MySpace pages, communicate events and activities through e-mail and text messaging almost daily, and freely give out their cell phone numbers to the teenagers. Our director of senior ministries just started a new paper-and-ink, "snail-mail" newsletter that is published and sent out monthly. In a multi-generational church like ours, multiple forms of communication are necessary. But, and this is perhaps the most important point, if you ask my teenager why he is texting and calling his friends, the most common reason is to arrange plans to get together—face-to-face. And that, to me, points to both the beauty and built-in limitation of the new media as community builders, especially if our focus is building *Christian* community.[1]

---

[1]Since I am a blogger, I will limit most of my reflections on the use of blogs, but I believe that most of the points apply more broadly to other new media.

CHRISTIAN COMMUNITY: THE EMBODIMENT OF THE LIFE OF GOD ON EARTH

In another book, I have written extensively about Christian community as the embodiment of the triune life of God for the expressed purpose of becoming transformed into the likeness and participating in the ministry of God in the world.[2] Christian community is not a strategy for church growth or a means for getting our personal spiritual needs met. *Christian community is the very life of God* that we enter by faith and express in faithfulness (1 Peter 2:9–10). While a life of witness to the life-transforming, world-transforming presence of Jesus Christ is the flower, community is the bulb, and they are of the same seed and belong to each other. Separating community from witness or witness from community leads to the death of witness and the barrenness of the community. Indeed, the essence of the Christian life is the love of God expressed through the community of believers as fellowship. As Emil Brunner wrote a half century ago in *The Misunderstanding of the Church*, "togetherness of Christians is . . . not secondary or contingent: it is integral to their life *just as is* their abiding in Christ."[3]

With this definition as a backdrop, it becomes more clear that blogs in and of themselves are not a true Christian community *and can never be*. No virtual "group" of "members" can express the inherent realities of the Christian life that is expressed in the incarnation of God in Jesus Christ. The language of *embodiment* and *abiding*, of *fellowship* and even *church* speaks of a tangible, connected life together that includes praying, spending time together, learning, and eating (Acts 2:42), as well as a host of other ordinary activities that make up life together. These everyday disciplines and experiences cannot be replaced with "virtual" connection, any more than a married couple can bring a new life into the world through love letters or intimate e-mails.

While the language of "community" permeates cyberspace and the blog world (we even have the "Godblogging community" running events like GodBlogCon),[4] it is probably better to consider these

---

[2]Tod E. Bolsinger, *It Takes a Church to Raise a Christian: How the Community of God Transforms Lives* (Grand Rapids, MI: Brazos Press, 2004).
[3]Emil Brunner, *The Misunderstanding of the Church* (Philadelphia: Westminster Press, 1953), 12 (emphasis mine).
[4]The promotional web site for GodblogCon 07 included this line: "Today, GodBlogCon continues its growth by joining with the BlogWorld and New Media Expo as the sole representation of the GodBlogging Community at what is the premier New Media trade-show in the nation"; http://www.godblogcon.com/schedule#history (accessed September 5, 2007).

"groups," "blogrolls," and cyber-groups as "lifestyle enclaves"[5] rather than genuine community, let alone Christian community. "Lifestyle enclaves," a term coined by sociologist Robert Bellah, refers to a group of people who share and enjoy similar things, mostly related to one segment of one's private life. While certainly a sense of shared interest (even shared mission!) leads people who have never "met" (in the traditional sense) to call themselves "friends" through their blogs and MySpace pages, to call these virtual conversations and points of connection "community" is to devalue the depth of connection, shared life, and mutual commitment that the gospel calls us to embody as a "covenant people" as well as asking the new media to do what they cannot do well. And further, this can actually hinder the very community that we hope to create. So, what do blogs and other sources of new media do to encourage genuine Christian community?

First, *blogs and new media offer fuel for the journey, not a feast for community*. Blogs and other new media allow us to "eat on the run" and to get fed spiritually with insights, encouragement, and conversation with a wide variety of readily accessible spiritual "food." At its best, this can be like a giant gourmet salad bar, with many different, fresh resources for learning and growing. At its worst, it can resemble a fast-food drive-through where people gobble down spiritual morsels to sustain them until the next quick bite, with ease of access and simplicity of understanding winning the day. In similar fashion, blogs allow input and even some quick discussion by way of comments, but it is a far cry from the combination of "semiotic and non-semiotic" experiences that make up truly nourishing human interaction. In the same way that a Thanksgiving feast is more an experience of family, ritual, and celebration than it is a mealtime for getting healthy nutrients, Miroslav Volf points out that all human communication is both the message and the means of communication, including always the personal and experiential way in which that content is communicated.

> Think of the stories at bedside and the radiance of a face reflecting the love of Christ, words of admonition and the silent holding of the hand of a person in pain, eating and drinking the bread and wine, worship of the one true God, holiness and failure, manipula-

---

[5]Robert Bellah, et. al., in *Habits of the Heart: Individualism and Commitment in American Life* (Berkeley, CA: University of California Press, 1996, orig. pub. 1985), 72ff.

tion and sword, the blood of the martyrs, the lives of the saints, hypocrisy and lust for power among church dignitaries and the rest of us, and economic interests and political machinations.[6]

This means that *who communicates Christian teaching and how it is communicated* is as important as the fact that is being passed on. Christian education is always a combination of the content and the communicator. While blogs at their best can give Christian content and some degree of interaction, they can't replace the genuine slow, "crock-pot" discipleship of a community learning and living out faith together.

Second, *blogs offer spiritual nourishment to those who can't get to the feast*. Perhaps the most touching comments on my blog have come from those who are, for whatever reason, outside of genuine Christian community. I have received e-mails from missionaries, military service personnel, and even friends who have recently moved to a new area and are without fellowship. The content, interaction, and ability to stay in touch across the miles are mercies to those who aren't able to be in a Christian community setting. One of my friends is a Marine Corps Chief Warrant Officer who spent a year away from his family deployed in Iraq. He and his wife both set up separate blogs so friends and family had a convenient and quick way to keep updated on their needs and struggles as a family separated by war and could offer prayers and support. Even more, that Marine's blog became a way that many of us "back home" could better understand the challenges being faced by a Christian leader serving in the military. While a blog is not the same as a meaningful face-to-face conversation, it did allow deeper understanding, greater care, and the opportunity for one Christian who was very far away from his community of faith to keep a sense of connection.

Third, *blogs offer community-like connection for those who are nourished by similar "tastes."* Related to the last point but some-

---

[6]Miroslav Volf, "Theology, Meaning and Power: A Conversation with George Lindbeck on Theology & the Nature of Christian Difference," in Timothy R. Phillips and Dennis L. Okholm, eds., *The Nature of Confession: Evangelicals and Postliberals in Conversation* (Downers Grove, IL: InterVarsity Press, 1996), 57. It seems beyond doubt that a person becomes a human being not only by learning her mother's language but also by feeling her mother's touch and hearing the sound of her voice. Similarly we become Christians not only by learning the language of faith but also by being "touched" by other Christians and ultimately by God on a non-semiotic level. The Christian semiotic system lives in the lives of the people of God through the interplay of non-semiotic dimensions of church life (which are meaningless without the semiotic) and semiotic dimensions of church life (which are powerless without the non-semiotic).

what different, blogs offer encouragement or fellowship with other Christians who share passions and callings but are not within convenient relational distance or who are having trouble finding others who share those passions in their immediate community of faith.

When I took a team of leaders from our church to Malawi, Africa to begin a project with World Vision and some other Christian ministries to do outreach and AIDS and poverty relief, I posted our team devotional on my blog and offered blog post updates whenever possible. Our families back at home were able to keep up with us and even post notes back to us that we could read. But even more, when I returned and blogged on my experiences in Africa and the impact that I was experiencing in my own faith and life, I was soon contacted by others who had similar experiences or shared a common conviction about the church's need to be part of the AIDS pandemic in Africa. But as a pastor of a church I have to lead our church in more than just awareness and mission for Africa. Indeed, long after my Sunday sermon topics had to move on to other areas of life and faith, the blog allowed for an ongoing conversation with others who wanted to keep concern for Africa in the forefront of their own minds, while others who were called to other issues could easily move to another topic.

As a pastor, my blog has allowed me to have a place to write about and discuss a number of different topics or areas of interest that are not directly related (at least at this time!) to my church's mission and calling, without my having to impose my passions and interests (for example, adventure travel as worldview education, Christian stewardship of the environment, leadership development issues, and the joys of cheering on the Los Angeles Angels of Anaheim baseball team) on them at every turn. On many occasions I have encouraged those members of our faith community who are particularly called to an issue or cause to form a blog to aid them in finding others who share that calling in a convenient way. Again, this isn't exactly Christian community, but when a "lifestyle enclave" includes a joint sense of passion and calling, new media tools can help foster and mature that connection in a mutually edifying way.

Fourth, *blogs are the perfect place to reheat spiritual "leftovers."* Anybody who has ever cooked a big Thanksgiving dinner knows that the bonus is the three days of leftover turkey, stuffing, and cranberries that will satisfy empty stomachs at lunchtime. And while the meal itself was most likely cooked over several hours using conventional means, the microwave oven is perfect for a quick hot turkey sandwich the next day and the next. Similarly, the inexhaustible storage capability of the World Wide Web enables Christian communities to keep, store, access, and serve up teaching, resources, and even discussions for later consumption. As a repository of ideas or discussions, blogs offer timeless storage that is easily accessed anytime (including, as it is often pointed out, negative comments, false teachings, or unwise off-the-cuff posts) and in any place. While the concerns about intellectual property and copyright issues surrounding the new media will certainly need to be worked out in the years to come, our "flat world"[7] allows those pastors, churches, and leaders who may not have educational opportunities or do not have proximity to seminaries and libraries (especially in the global south or rural areas) almost limitless access to resources that will enable them to "feed" themselves and the "flock" to which they are called.

Thinking of new media as a "microwave community" does indeed allow us to understand both the limits and advantages of applying this technology to Christian community building. And within the inherent limits, the advantages are indeed numerous. However, blogs and the new media, if utilized indiscriminately, ruin the very community they should be serving.

Most blogs, like a microwave, instantly "heat" up whatever it is focused upon, the result being that without constant attention and wise use, it is easy to get burned. The stories of bloggers who jumped on a political story and created a "storm" of interest are legend. And for even the most humble pew-sitter, the power to quickly communicate one's views, concerns, and opinions all over the world is intoxicating. The Bible is filled with exhortations and warnings about the correct kinds of speech, one-to-one private confrontation, and the prohibition of gossiping. In a "public" forum like a blog, frequent reviews of the "rules of engagement" are even more necessary. I have been stunned as a pastor to read vitriolic blog comments by people who would never make such remarks in a face-to-face setting. Especially for those who are of a gen-

---

[7]Thomas Friedman, *The World Is Flat: A Brief History of the Twenty-first Century* (New York: Farrar, Straus and Giroux, 2006, revised edition).

eration that did not use e-mail as standard business practices and therefore were never trained in e-mail etiquette, I have often had to remind the members of my church that public blog posts, discussion boards, and e-mails are not license for gossip (cf. Romans 1:29; 2 Corinthians 12:20), slander (Psalm 101:5), indirect confrontation (Matthew 18:15), or unedifying conversation (James 3).

So, with that warning, what can we do to insure that the new media serve healthy fuel for the spiritual journey? Let me suggest a few quick principles.

The new media require us to revisit "old" moral teaching. Everything that your mother told you that applies to speaking in civil society ("Gossip kills two reputations," "Sticks and stones will break my bones, but names will *put me in therapy"*—or something like that!) is doubly applied to new media, because every comment, post, or podcast has the potential to be both "broadcasted" and "archived" for posterity. While a careless or thoughtless slip of the tongue may harm a friendship, a comment posted to a web site in anger can take on a life of its own and last far longer than anyone expected, tarnishing both reputations and legacies.

We in the church need to make sure that our new media communications are built on the ethics of biblical relationships ("speaking the truth in love," Ephesians 4:15) and not "media." We need to insure that the *quality* of our conversation is more important than the *quantity*; that thoughtfulness, discernment, and consideration are valued as much as some of the highly prized values of the new media like "giving voice," "flattening the world," and "swarming" and "long tail marketing." Perhaps one of the most challenging issues of discernment in the future will be the degree to which virtual relationships are becoming, for many, primary (or at least quite significant) relationships and how confusing lines become when that is so.

Second Life (http://secondlife.com) is an "online community" that boasts nearly ten million registered users. People make up complete identities (often more than one) that may have little or nothing to do with their real identities. Cyberchurches exist in this virtual world that invite (virtual?) people to come to faith in Jesus Christ, become members, and even donate (certainly non-virtual) dollars to support the ministry.

I must admit that I am all too quick to dismiss these kinds of phe-nomena. I see them as nothing but video games, like my kids' Wii on steroids. But if the growth of this online community is any indicator, and if the seriousness by which these Christian ministries take their charge to minister in the midst of the novelty of a "virtual world" is any indicator, there needs to be more discernment here, not less. One church (http://almcyberchurch.org) asserts that Jesus' command to "go into all the world" and make disciples (Mark 16:15) necessarily includes the *virtual* world, too. While the leaders are sincere and sim-ply hope to use the new media to bring genuine change in the lives of people who come to "experiment," there are very likely people who now worship solely within a "virtual community." The most interest-ing question is whether these are "real Christians" who are finding community in a virtual world or whether people are becoming "virtual Christians" as one of the many different identities that they "try on," so that ultimately (ala Marshall McLuhan) the *medium* of "virtual" inevitably becomes the *message* of "community."

Building community through new media requires more commit-ment to community than to new media. In his book on building com-munity, M. Scott Peck writes that community "happens" when those who usually speak up shut up, and those who usually shut up speak up. In a similar way, the blogosphere will never be the tool it could be for fostering community and fueling the spiritual journey if only the same few post comments, engage in discussions, and have blogs to begin with. At the same time, "microwave connections" can never replace the long, slow process of building deeply rooted, enduring relation-ships. To that end, when it comes to building community, blogs are best when they better and more consistently connect people who are already connected to each other *within* a community or who are trying to build deeper connections with those *within* a lifestyle enclave who draw support from each other to fulfill their callings.

The new media offer us a powerful tool for building, maintaining, and supporting Christian connection in an increasingly disconnected world. We can be grateful to live in a time when the ability to get "fuel for the journey" or a connection with fellow travelers that we would otherwise never have is available to us as we walk the way of Christ. But let's also be clear that we need more than just "fast-food" faith, no matter how "healthy" and "nutritious" the offering. A microwave oven can never fill a house with the aroma of good home cooking like Grandma's old conventional oven. And in the same way, the ethos, environment, and traditions of community will need to be cultivated through the "slow cooking" of face-to-face friendships, conversations over coffee, arguments and making up, and many, many good family meals.

8

PASTORS AND THE NEW MEDIA

Mark D. Roberts

www.MarkDRoberts.com

IN THIS CHAPTER I WANT TO CONSIDER a simple question: How can the new media help pastors be better pastors? Of course, pastors can have blogs, put up YouTube videos, and make friends through Facebook, just like anybody else. But can any of these activities help pastors excel in their primary calling?

Let me show my cards right at the beginning. I believe the new media *can* help pastors be better pastors. But this will happen only when pastors carefully consider the needs and context of their particular ministry, as well as their own unique combination of gifts, talents, and calling. Like other ministry tools, the new media don't necessarily help one to be a better pastor, but they can if we use them wisely.

Before I elaborate, let me say a bit about my background as a pastor and how I discovered the pastoral value of the new media. I should also suggest some of what is essential to pastoral work, so that I might show why the new media can be truly useful to pastors.

MY PASTORAL BACKGROUND

I spent several years as an associate pastor at the First Presbyterian Church of Hollywood before becoming senior pastor of Irvine Presbyterian Church, where I served for sixteen years. I have just begun a new role as senior director and scholar in residence at Laity Lodge, a multifaceted ministry in the Hill Country of Texas. My new work continues to be pastoral in many ways, though I don't serve in a parish. Plus, a substantial chunk of my current ministry includes supporting and encouraging pastors.

The center of my ministry at Irvine Pres was preaching and teaching God's Word. At the end of my tenure there, we had four services each weekend in which I was the primary preacher. I also taught a midweek Bible study. Additionally, I provided leadership for leaders (staff and elders), offered pastoral care, prayed for individuals and the whole church, performed weddings and memorial services, and you name it. In all I did, I sought to help Irvine Presbyterian Church become the faithful, active, loving, praying, serving body God had called us to be, so that he might be glorified in our fellowship, worship, and ministry in the world.

Shortly after I arrived at Irvine Presbyterian Church in 1991, I had a conversation with a woman named Mary. She was working in the Computer Science Department at the University of California, Irvine. Her project was something unfamiliar to me—the World Wide Web. Mary told me that the Web would revolutionize communication and that one day everybody would have web sites, even churches and pastors. *Sure,* I thought to myself, *just like we all have 8-track tape decks, rowing machines, and pet rocks.* I didn't take Mary's prediction too seriously.

A decade later, as we entered the new millennium, I had to admit that Mary had been right. The Web had revolutionized communication, though I still had no intention of having my own web site. It was enough, I figured, for our church to have one. I was quite familiar with online bulletin boards and blogs, in addition to static web sites. I could even imagine how these forms of new media could be useful to pastors. But I was happy to ignore them. I couldn't see how I could add anything else to my overly crowded calendar.

Then, in early December of 2003, I had dinner with my friend Hugh Hewitt. He talked enthusiastically about blogging and how it was transforming the world. "It's changing everything," he exclaimed, reminding me of Mary's twelve-year-old prediction. Then, zeroing in on me, Hugh said, "Mark, you have to get into the blogosphere. Voices like yours are desperately needed. And the opportunity is vast. You just have to start a blog."

I tried to dodge Hugh's attack, but he's not an easy person to fend off. When I protested that I didn't have time for blogging, Hugh almost relented. "Yes, a blog is a harsh mistress," he conceded, "but you have to do it." So, pummeled into submission by Hugh's visionary zeal, I agreed to start a blog. Three weeks later, on December 22, 2003, I put up my first blog post. Ironically enough, it was a short piece called "*The Da Vinci Code* Is Truly Fictional." (Later on, I posted more than a hundred thousand words on *The Da Vinci Code* and related subjects.)

Though Hugh envisioned my blog as impacting the larger virtual world, I couldn't imagine that anyone "out there" would care what I had to say, except for my mother. So I began to think of my blog as primarily for my own church members. I wrote as their pastor, addressing topics I knew would be of interest to them. If a couple dozen folks from my congregation were to read my blog each day, I reasoned, it just might be worth my time.

As it turned out, many more than two dozen in my flock became regular blog readers. Other members tuned in when looking for my views on particular subjects. But the impact of my blog grew beyond my own congregation and way beyond my expectations. Soon I started getting e-mails from blog readers throughout the country, even across the world. Today I'm averaging about four thousand visitors a day to my principal blog, markdroberts.com. But during my tenure at Irvine Pres I continued to think of my blog primarily as a pastoral tool, a way to speak with my own congregation. If others chose to eavesdrop, so much the better. But I have been, at core, a pastor-blogger. And I continue to fill this role even though I no longer have a local parish.

PASTORING AS COMMUNICATION

I discovered, quite accidentally as you have seen, that the new media can help pastors in the core of our work. Pastoring entails preaching, teaching, praying, counseling, studying, writing, leading, community-building, leading worship, and so forth. All of these discrete actions have something in common. They all involve communication. Some flows from pastor to flock (preaching, teaching, writing newsletter columns, leading worship). Sometimes it includes lots of listening (counseling, moderating meetings). At other times pastors facilitate communication among members (forming small groups, prayer chains). Praying is itself an essential kind of pastoral communication.

The new media are basically new modes of communication, many of which can enhance pastoral work. That which was once incredible, like letting the world see your home movies, is now commonplace. And that which once took hours and dollars now takes minutes and cents. For example, when I began at Irvine Pres, if I wanted to communicate with my board of elders, I would dictate a memo, which would be typed by my secretary, then copied and mailed. In a day or two, my elders would receive the memo. This process required about an hour of staff time, not to mention postage and stationery costs. Thus I would send a memo to my elders only when something merited the time and cost. Once my elders had e-mail, I could send a group e-mail that involved no cost other than my time and that reached my elders almost immediately. In this way the Internet helped me be a more effective leader. (Sometimes it also led to a time-consuming and confusing mess of communication as my elders enjoyed the power of the "Reply All" button. Technological advancement always brings new challenges, new frustrations, and new dangers and requires new disciplines.)

From here on in this chapter I want to examine in detail many specific ways that the new media can assist pastors in their core work as they enhance and expand communication. This discussion will be more practical than theological. I'd love to address the theological issues associated with pastor-blogging but must reserve that for another day.

PREACHING AND TEACHING

At first glance, the new media have little impact on preaching. (In this chapter I'm not wading into the controversial bog of digital projection.) Preachers stand up in front of a congregation and speak God's Word in the power of the Spirit. Can the new media make a positive difference in preaching?

Yes, indeed they can. Let's begin with sermon preparation. The Internet makes available a wide array of tools for Bible study. Classic commentaries and translations can be consulted in a flash. Illustrations can also be found at preaching illustration web sites and through clever use of search engines. I used to keep extensive files of magazine and newspaper articles for possible sermon use. Now I no longer need to do this because I can find what I need more quickly online than by searching through my files, and I can do this while sitting at Starbucks a thousand miles away from my study.

Preachers who use the Internet for sermon preparation face several dangers. One is plagiarism. Too many preachers find it easy to borrow liberally from their online pastoral colleagues without appropriate attribution. If you quote another pastor in a sermon, admit it. If you are tempted to borrow whole sermons, you're probably in the midst of burnout and should quickly find a wise Christian in whom to confide.

Another danger is passing along urban legends as if they were true when in fact they are fictional. Hundreds of preachers, including a guest preacher in my own pulpit, have told the touching "true" story of Teddy Stoddard, the struggling student whose life was transformed by his kind teacher, Mrs. Thompson. Unfortunately, this story is a work of fiction that was once published as such in *Home Life* magazine. Before you tell any story as if it really happened, be sure to verify its truthfulness. (Snopes.com is a great help here.) Laziness in verification can quickly undermine your trustworthiness as a preacher.

Perhaps the greatest power of the new media to enhance preaching comes after the sermon has been delivered. Not too long ago, a sermon lived only as long as the words echoed in the sanctuary or in the hearts of the congregation. Tapes and CDs expanded the life of the sermon but in a limited way. Now online streaming, podcasting, and posted manuscripts make sermons readily and indefinitely available to church members and others. If your digital recordings and/or manuscripts are indexed on a web site, then people can use them as a reference library. I had many church members tell me that they went back months later to listen again to a sermon I had once preached.

The Internet can also facilitate communication among church members in response to preaching. If I had continued on at Irvine Pres, I would have implemented an interactive web site I had been developing. This site, an adapted blog, would have enabled people to put up their responses to my preaching. I envisioned a virtual place where folks could make comments, ask questions, and, most importantly, share what God had done in their life through his Word.

Some pastors put up on their blogs not their finished sermons but

their study notes as they prepare. Tod Bolsinger, blogger at It Takes a
Church (http://bolsinger.blogs.com/weblog), has done this. His readers
get to see in advance what Tod is working on, and Tod gets to read their
comments. With their help he can clarify his points, sharpen his focus,
and enhance his effectiveness as a preacher.

What I've said about preaching pertains equally to teaching. Pastors
can put up their notes from their midweek studies or can even post special teaching series on their blogs, as I'll illustrate in a moment.

CONGREGATIONAL COMMUNICATION BEYOND PREACHING

For years, one of my greatest frustrations as a pastor was the limited
input I had into my parishioners' lives. I delivered a weekly sermon
(heard by about two-thirds of my flock), a midweek Bible study
(attended by fewer still), and an occasional newsletter column. Yet
there were so many topics I felt the need to address but had no forum
in which to do it. How could I help my flock think rightly about *The
Passion of the Christ* or exercise their earthly citizenship in a biblical
manner or respond to a friend who had just read the latest Bart Ehrman
book attempting to debunk the Bible?

Blogging answered this question in marvelous ways. No longer
was I severely limited in time and topic. Through my blog I could
address a wide variety of pressing issues and still make sure my sermons
focused on the expository preaching of Scripture. When church members asked me questions like, "What should I do with *The Da Vinci
Code*?" I could answer their questions online. Not only did this allow
me to formulate thoughtful responses, but also these essays became
available to others. Soon the others included not only members of my
congregation but also their colleagues at work, family members, and
friends in the neighborhood. My pastoral ministry was having a wider
impact through my blogging, and I'm not even thinking of blog readers
who had no connection with my flock.

Once again, I need to add a word of warning. Pastors must think
carefully about what topics are appropriate for their blogs. For example, I chose not to blog on political topics in a partisan way. I have
written extensively on biblical perspectives on politics in general, but
I have not expressed my personal preferences with respect to specific
candidates or issues. I chose this course because my congregation was

diverse politically. In fact, in a recent election both the Democratic and the Republican candidate for Congress were church members. If I waxed eloquent about my political views, not only would my congregation have seen just how little I know about politics, but also I would have run the risk of erecting unnecessary barriers between me and those who disagreed with me.

I am not saying that all pastors should follow my lead here. I am saying that we all must think carefully and prayerfully about the topics we address and their impact on our primary ministries. We can generate lots of blog traffic by taking controversial stands on political issues, yet thereby damage tender pastoral relationships. Moreover, I'm not sure the blogosphere needs more ignorance writ large. We pastors would do better to blog on that in which we have some measure of genuine competence.

TALK WITH YOUR LEADERSHIP BOARD

I would strongly suggest that you talk in depth with your church leadership board before beginning to blog. Or if you already have a blog and have not had this conversation, by all means initiate it. (If you're an associate pastor, a conversation with your supervisor may suffice. If you're part of a larger staff, you should talk with your colleagues as well.)

I did not talk with my board of elders before I started blogging. This was one of the biggest mistakes I made as a pastor-blogger. In my defense, let me say that I greatly underestimated the impact of my blog, and that's why it didn't occur to me to talk with my elders about it in advance. But my failure to have this conversation led to unfortunate misunderstandings. Many of my elders affirmed my choice of topics, and some became regular readers. But others saw my blog more as a mistress stealing away my affections from the church than as an integral element of my pastoral devotion to my own congregation. If I had taken time to talk with my board about the potential of blogging before I began, I would have avoided unnecessary conflict, and the impact of my blog within my own church would have been more positive from the beginning.

If it turns out that your board is not enthusiastic about your desire to use new media in your pastoring, it is better to learn about this before you start than afterward. You may find that you need to take more time to bring your leaders up to speed or that you need to refine your own vision for your ministry. The discussion with your leaders could well become a clarifying conversation about pastoral priorities, one that may be long overdue. I would encourage you not to rush this process with your fellow leaders.

PASTORAL CARE THROUGH THE INTERNET

This section title might raise a few eyebrows. How can pastoral care happen through the Internet? Doesn't the impersonality of digital communication virtually contradict the essence of pastoral care?

Let me say at the outset that I do not believe the Internet can replace personal pastoral relationships. Pastors need to look people in the eye, listen to their voices, shake their hands, or offer a supportive hug. Nothing can take the place of genuine, one-on-one conversation.

But the Internet can enhance and extend that which is centered in immediate fellowship. To cite an obvious example, Marc, a member of Irvine Pres, chose to put aside his military retirement in order to serve a year's term in Iraq. While he was overseas, he listened to my sermons online. He read my Pastor's Letter (see below). And we kept in touch through e-mail. Our personal relationship continued electronically, so that when I saw Marc again face-to-face, it felt as if we had hardly been apart.

Speaking of my Pastor's Letter, this was another of my surprises from the new media. My Pastor's Letter was an e-blast (an e-mail that was sent simultaneously to all church members who had signed up for it). I began the letter partly because I realized that many in my flock, especially older adults, didn't visit blogs, though they did read e-mail. Also, I was looking for a more personal and intimate way to address issues of concern within my church family, the sort of thing I wouldn't post on my public web site. See, for example, the letter I sent to my congregation when I announced my new calling to Laity Lodge (http://www.markdroberts.com/htmfiles/pastorsletter/07.08.10-letter.htm).

When I began sending the Pastor's Letter, I was astounded by people's response. Though they knew this was an e-blast, they received what I had sent as if it were written personally to them. They talked about reading and rereading my letters. I received many e-mails in response. In some cases my Pastor's Letter opened up new opportunities for teaching or pastoral care. It extended and enriched my relationship with my flock in blessed new ways. I would say that in most cases this mode of Internet communication is more immediately useful to pastors than blogging.

Although I greatly prefer face-to-face conversation for pastoral counseling, I found that some people prefer the safe distance of e-mail. I had some members who would never in a million years make an appointment with me open up about deep struggles in an e-mail. Sometimes this led to personal meetings; sometimes an e-mail relationship sufficed. By the end of my tenure at Irvine Pres, though, my number of weekly counseling meetings remained the same as at the beginning of my ministry there. To put it differently, the Internet enabled me to do four times more pastoral care than I'd have been able to do in person.

NEW MEDIA DEVOTIONS

The Internet also allowed me to offer devotional input to my congregation on a daily basis. I began with a web site called Pray the Psalms (www.praythepsalms.com). This web site focused on a psalm each day, offering a short excerpt for reflection, a link to the whole chapter, my prayer based on the excerpt, and a brief postscript or question for further reflection. In actuality, I was putting online a portion of my own daily devotions, inviting my flock to join me as I spent time each day with the Lord. Now my daily devotional appears on a web site associated with Laity Lodge, The High Calling of Our Daily Work (thehighcalling.org). It is also e-mailed to several thousand subscribers each day.

You could use the Internet in other ways to help members of your flock grow deeper in their relationship with God. A regular devotional e-blast is one obvious option. Another would involve sending or posting devotional links rather than original devotional thoughts.

GO WITH YOUR STRENGTHS

I realize that what I've described about my own online pastoral ministry, with a blog, the Pastor's Letter, e-mails, and my devotional web sites, might feel overwhelming to you. In particular, if you're not an especially quick writer, you can't imagine imitating my efforts. So let me say it clearly: Don't! Don't try to do all that I have done. Rather, let me serve as one example of an effort to use the new media to strengthen pastoral ministry. What I've done fits my particular mix of talents and gifts and makes sense in my particular community. You should do what fits you and your pastoral context.

As you consider how you might make use of new media options, be sure to pay attention to your personal strengths. Do you write fairly quickly and easily? Then a daily blog might work for you. If not, then blogging may not be best. Or you might choose to blog on a weekly rather than a daily basis. A successful blog needs to have regular input, but *regular* could mean once a week or twice a week. A pastor friend of mine blogs each Wednesday. His congregation knows this and looks forward to his weekly posts.

If you're not especially good with the written word but are better in person, you may wish to investigate the world of online video posting (on YouTube and similar sites). Or you may have talent in making videos in which you're behind the camera rather than in front of it. Or you may be inept in this technology but an expert at motivating others to do it. However you move forward with the new media, go with your strengths.

BUILDING COMMUNITY

Pastors are called not merely to care for the souls of individuals but also to build healthy Christian community. Our responsibility is to equip our people for the work of ministry, so that they might build up each other in love and live out their faith in the world. We build community in a variety of ways, often by training leaders or by forming relational networks (small groups, classes).

The new media offer plenty of help in this endeavor. Blogs can become centers of congregational communication. Church bulletin boards and discussion groups can broaden and enrich fellowship. A particularly striking example of this happened in the fall of 2005. As Hurricane Katrina pounded New Orleans, Canal Street Presbyterian Church took a major hit. Their building, though not destroyed, was badly damaged. Their members were scattered, and most lost telephone service. But this church had recently begun a bulletin board. In the aftermath of the hurricane, this became the primary context for church contact. Through the bulletin board (which "lived" on a server far away from New Orleans), the Canal Street Church was able to stay connected, checking on lost members, reaching out to the hurting, finding housing for the homeless, and praying for each other. Pastor Mike Hogg, who had to move his family to Arizona, remained in close contact with his flock through the bulletin board and e-mail. (Now Canal St. Pres uses Facebook to facilitate its online fellowship.)

In this connection, I should mention an experience we had in our church. One of the surprising aspects of MySpace is the extent to which its users openly share some of their deepest secrets. This enabled the high school leaders from my church to minister to kids at a deep level. In one case, a young man shared his unhappiness in a way that sounded suicidal. One of our youth leaders saw this and quickly contacted the parents, who were able to intervene in their son's life, getting him the help he needed right away.

Now I realize that some pastors discourage their congregants from entering such forums altogether, and for good reason. In my setting, however, it seemed better for our leaders to enter their students' MySpace world than to try to get them to leave it. So I began my own "Pastor Mark" MySpace. I filled it with pictures of my wife and kids to avoid looking like a predator. Before too long, I found myself interacting with many of the youth from my church. Several told our high school director that it was "sweet" that their pastor had a MySpace. Again, I'm not suggesting that this strategy would be right for all pastors. But I expect that many will find through MySpace or Facebook an opportunity to connect with church members in new ways, as well as to encourage community among members. With a variety of age groups signing on to the social networks, the possibility for ministry in them is extending beyond just the youth.

PASTORING BEYOND THE FLOCK

So far I have focused on how the new media can assist pastors in leading their own flocks. I should add that several forms of the new media (blogging, YouTube, MySpace, Facebook) facilitate outreach beyond the local church. This can open up doors for new ministry, even for building your own church. I'd estimate that in my last couple of years at Irvine Pres, at least a quarter of church visitors had read my blog and were attracted to the church through this means. Of course, blogging can also allow a pastor to have a wider influence in the world.

But there are dangers lurking here as well. We blogging-pastors can get so wrapped up in getting more hits that we forget our first calling. Or we can spend hours responding to comments on our web sites that should have been invested in pastoral care of our flock. It's great that the new media can get pastors out of our Christian ghetto. But we must also beware of the temptation to neglect our first priorities as pastors.

CONCLUSIONS

A few years ago when blogging was relatively new, some folks got a bit carried away. "All pastors should have blogs," they insisted. Leaping onto the bandwagon, thousands of pastors began blogging. Many, perhaps even the majority of these, stopped before too long. Blogging turned out to be, like most pastoral efforts, hard work with limited rewards (at least this side of heaven). Many pastors realized, rightly so I believe, that they weren't cut out for blogging and that they might better invest their time elsewhere.

The new media offer tools to pastors—blogging, e-mail, e-blasts, podcasting, streaming, online video, online community, and so on. By the time this book is published, I'm sure there will be more tools to add to this list. Once we get through the hype, we realize that these tools are just like other pastoral tools, in that they may or may not be useful depending on a wide variety of personal, theological, cultural, and ecclesiastical factors. Our challenge, as pastors, is to look carefully and clearly at what these tools offer and to consider prayerfully which ones are best suited to us and our ministries. We might find it helpful to discuss the possibilities with our colleagues or covenant group. Or we might simply want to experiment and see what God chooses to bless.

From my own experience and that of many other pastors, I'm convinced that wise, thoughtful, disciplined use of the new media can in many cases help us be better pastors. With greater effectiveness we can care for people's souls, communicate God's truth, build up the church, and reach out to the world.

9

NAVIGATING THE EVOLVING WORLD OF YOUTH MINISTRY IN THE FACEBOOK-MYSPACE GENERATION

Rhett Smith

www.RhettSmith.com

ONLINE JOURNEY

It seemed to me as if everyone was doing it, but that type of reasoning was just what I was careful to avoid, especially after hearing it from college students in our ministry over the years. Most of the time that phrase was used when it came to issues such as underage drinking, drug use, and sexual behavior, but now I was finding it being used in an entirely different context, and I was beginning to feel like everyone was doing it and I was missing out. What was everyone doing that I was not? They were social networking on the Internet, primarily on sites such as MySpace and Facebook.

Now let me first say that I am not naive to the Internet or the phenomenon of social networking. I decided to jump into blogging in the summer of 2004 by launching a blog first at our college web site (www.thequestbelair.org) and then launching my own site in 2005 (www.rhettsmith.com). Although blogging could be considered another form of social networking, I was finding myself very hesitant to join MySpace, which was sweeping through our college ministry, our church, and my own personal social circle. There were many good reasons why I didn't jump onto the MySpace bandwagon at that point, but my primary concern was that social networking sites lacked any type of control. For example, I could launch a MySpace profile for our college group, but ultimately I had little control of what took place on that profile. People could post comments, photos, videos, as well as other forms of content onto our profile without my approval or prior knowledge. Sure, there are many layers of security and control that a group could choose to enable on their profile, but in the end that inhibits the purpose of the site, which is to empower users and encourage social networking.

My college students would come to group each week and tell me to start a MySpace profile, but I resisted. I was aware that they spent much of their time on that site, but why should we as a ministry create our own profile? Instead, feeling overly righteous as I remember, I put my foot down, drew a proverbial line in the sand, and was determined to make a statement by not joining MySpace. Whatever my reasoning, in the end I felt like an ostrich with his head in the sand when I realized that regardless of my own convictions and beliefs, my students were going to carry about their business on MySpace whether I approved of it or not. In fact, I began to notice that the forums we had created on our own web site to encourage social networking were empty and lifeless with few or no visitors, while I would hear stories from the students about some of the interesting forums they were involved in on MySpace. And eventually I realized that a great majority of ministry was taking place on its own between students on MySpace, while I was left wondering about my decision to be so dogmatic and resistant to the social networking revolution sweeping the college scene.

So in the summer of 2005 I did the inevitable and created a MySpace group for our college ministry. Along with a profile photo of some students in our ministry attending a beach bonfire, I listed some details about who we were and what kind of things we would be doing that summer and into the school year. It wasn't long before one student after another, some of whom I knew and others I didn't, began to join the online group. I showed up to the college group the following Wednesday, and as the new people introduced themselves, I asked them how they heard about us, expecting to hear the typical, "a friend told me" or "I heard about your group on campus." Instead I heard a couple of new people tell me how they had found our MySpace page and decided to check us out. Any doubts I had about its effectiveness in networking and reaching out to college students in the local area were forever put to rest.

IDENTITY FORMING

Though I was late to the MySpace phenomenon, it was not long before I began to realize its addictive nature and the incessant desire to log on and check and update my profile while I read through others. If you have never been a part of a social networking site or actively engaged students on their profiles, it is quite possible for you to fail to realize just how alluring and addictive this process can be. Every day millions of students log on to their profile, often through a pseudonym, or with their real name, and find out what type of activity has been taking place in their network since they have been away. When students do this, they get a window view into the lives of their friends from updated photos of the party or retreat that took place over the weekend to finding out what musical tastes their friend has listed. And on Facebook it is possible to update your online status as often as you would like, so that you can see that "John is studying" or "Chris is watching *Lost*" or "Jamie is pondering the meaning of life." Pretty soon your status and profile become an image of who you are, at least in the virtual world. After a while, one begins to wonder just how powerful these sites are in shaping one's personal identity. When it comes to online profiles and the shaping of identity, I can't help but think of the words of Thomas Merton: "It is a spiritual disaster for a man to rest content with his exterior identity, with his passport picture of himself. Is his life merely in his fingertips?"[1] And for students on social networking sites, their identity and life are often at their fingertips on a daily basis.

When I was growing up, the concern for many parents was the amount of TV their children watched. The issue at hand was the correlation between the amount of TV children were watching, coupled with what type of material they were being exposed to, which in turn would have certain effects upon their development and behavior. But somewhere along the way that discussion has tapered off, and the question being posed today is, how many hours are kids spending in front

[1]Thomas Merton, *The New Man* (New York: Bantam Books, 1981), 70.

of the computer? One of my biggest concerns is, how is a student's identity being shaped by the Internet? I see that students are spending several hours a day online, and I have to wonder what kind of impact that makes on their identity, who they perceive themselves to be, and who they are becoming. Unlike TV, users of the Internet interact and live in a virtual world, with a profile that they have shaped for themselves. Every day students are interacting online with individuals from a wide range of backgrounds, beliefs, and values. As they process these interactions, I can't help but wonder how their own profile or identity is being shaped by what they see, hear, or experience during the hours they spend online.

Throughout these interactions, students continue to create and define who they are online. It is not uncommon to come across a profile and find that there is incongruent behavior between the student you know in person and the student you interact with online. In the virtual world that students inhabit, there seems to be a place of "disconnect"[2] where the lines are often blurred. This type of incongruent behavior often manifests itself in a couple of different ways, from the more benign inconsistencies of facts and information that students portray about themselves on their profile to the more malignant discrepancies in behavior that exist and are displayed through photos, videos, and posted comments. In these cases I often begin to wonder if it's even the same person online as the individual I know personally.

One of the concerns in youth ministry is what to make of students who present themselves as Christian and talk about the virtues of their faith, yet also display a life that appears completely inconsistent with those virtues. All it takes is a click of the mouse to peruse their profile and see that their professed beliefs and actions are often in complete contradiction to one another. This is nothing new to Christianity as we ourselves are often accused of being hypocrites when our beliefs and actions don't align. Before the Internet, we typically only had knowledge of our students' lives when we directly interacted with them, not knowing what they did away from church. But now we are being exposed to both in ways and degrees that have never existed before. Something else has shifted over the years as more and more of our

---

[2]Chap Clark and Dee Clark, *Disconnected: Parenting Teens in a MySpace World* (Grand Rapids, MI: Baker, 2007). This is an excellent book for an in-depth look into the world of adolescence and the challenges teens face in an Internet culture.

students are living less anonymous lives and are actually quite proud to display them for the world to see.

With the rise of these online social networks and our ability to create an online identity that is either similar, close to, or completely different than our real identity, one begins to wonder who the real person actually is. Pastor and author Shane Hipps states, "When we fail to perceive media as extensions of ourselves, they take on godlike characteristics, and we become their servants."[3] Is there a real identity that is being formed, or are we and our students living completely duplicitous lives that aren't cohesive or bridged in one way or another? Do we end up using these online social networking sites to our benefit, or do we become slaves to them? Rather than being a black or white issue, I think what we are witnessing is much more gray, and that can tend to bring about confusion in the lives of many of our youth over their identity, and sometimes social networking sites can fuel this confusion. When we have limited time with our children and students each day versus the few hours a day they spend with MySpace and Facebook, we are at risk of being of little or no consequence in shaping their identity. The influence of these social networking sites with millions of voices is often no match for the person trying to influence them through one or two short interactions each week. When a student is in these communities for hours a day, how do we help shape and transform their identity, whether it be online or in the personal time we get with them?

LEADING WITHIN

This is when I realized that I had a couple of choices before me. I could continue to see my college students once, maybe twice a week during our programs and meetings, or I could enter into their social networking sites, hoping to have more influence than the one to two hours I was interacting with them personally. Henri Nouwen expounds upon the idea of leaders leading within when he says, "I am deeply convinced that the Christian leader of the future is called to be completely irrelevant and to stand in the world with nothing to offer but his or her vulnerable self. This is the way Jesus came to reveal God's love."[4] Rather than being out front or above, a leader places himself in the

---

[3]Shane Hipps, *The Hidden Power of Electronic Culture* (Grand Rapids, MI: Zondervan, 2005), 36.
[4]Henri Nouwen, *In The Name of Jesus: Reflections on Christian Leadership* (New York: Crossroad, 2001), 17.

midst of his or her people and leads from a position of vulnerability within. This style of leadership is different than the type of leadership to which most of our students are exposed. Many of our students are in ministries where the pastor, director, or youth worker leads from a place of hierarchy rather than alongside and with the students. Leading within is a style of leadership that joins with the students as the leader stands in the midst of them. We have the choice to stand with our students and offer our vulnerable selves in the way that Nouwen is speaking of, or we can choose to distance ourselves from them and become completely irrelevant. This is an empowering process and one that I think is very evident on social networking sites, and one of the reasons that many students are drawn to it.

Students may not think of their experience in these terms, but by entering into social networking sites, students are encouraged to be a part of a group where they are empowered to lead and create content that benefits the whole. This is attractive to students who in their daily experiences may not feel the type of empowerment they are craving. Whether it's in the context of a parent, teacher, or youth worker, sometimes our relationships with students are not empowering enough to help them find their voice and to help them use it for the benefit of those relationships. Is it any surprise that they are drawn to a site that welcomes them, encourages them to create content, and places them in the midst of groups where they have a voice and can lead?

This world of social networking is a world of little to no hierarchy, and the leadership that exists is one that is centered within the groups in the online communities and encourages a leadership style that is horizontally structured, striving to give equal voice to everyone involved. In terms of its impact to the world outside of them, these online social networking sites encourage a bottom-up style of leadership, where change comes from grass-roots movements within the sites and moves out into the world. If a student does not feel empowered in any of the relationships that exist in his or her day-to-day life, he or she is going to find it online where there are little to no rules and no parental control or authority to tell him or her what, when, or how to do something. Students are masters of their own universe, and they shape their profile and identity around the idea that they are valuable to the group and can offer meaningful opinions.

This is crucial for youth workers to understand. Most churches operate using a hierarchical approach, where structure and authority are organized in a top-down manner. In most cases this means that the voices that are given the most importance and are usually the most heard are those of the senior pastor, the ordained staff, or those in positions of employed leadership. This is not the case for MySpace or Facebook. Everyone has a voice and place along the continuum of leadership in these communities. When Nouwen states, "The way of the Christian leader is not the way of upward mobility in which our world has invested so much, but the way of downward mobility ending on the cross,"[5] I would argue that online social networking sites offer in terms of leadership a trajectory more aligned with downward mobility than do most church structures. This is what happened in our ministry in 2006 when one of my students decided to create for us a Facebook profile without my knowledge. This is often what scares most youth workers away from these sites, knowing that they can't control what happens online and that the power and position they hold in the real world sometimes means nothing in the virtual world. But looking back over the last year I am thankful that he took the initiative and didn't feel like he had to get approval through me.

So we come back to the two choices. Avoid these sites and continue to exert our power, influence, and leadership on the students only a couple of hours a week or enter into their midst and lead within and among them, encouraging them to find their voice, create content, and impact those around them. That choice eventually became clear to me after realizing that I could completely avoid the site and have no influence on what was happening online, or I could enter the site and hope to set a better tone by influencing those around me.

This lack of hierarchy encourages multiple users to create content, and that is what is so appealing to our youth. It is what draws them in when they feel they don't have that same sense of importance in the larger church structure. A student can have a great idea but often comes upon roadblocks as he tries to push it through the leadership and hierarchy of the church. Alternatively, the student can bypass any red tape by going online, creating a group, and then getting others to join, all before it's time for bed that night. "This shift toward information

---

[5]Ibid., 62.

diffusion and the subsequent diffusion of power are providing us with a helpful corrective to the long history of centralized, top-down authority in the church. Electronic media allow us to retrieve the more participatory and egalitarian forms of leadership where authority is dynamic and based on relationships rather than on fixed job descriptions."[6] This is an exciting and scary time, and I believe that youth workers must be a part of this journey; otherwise we are left with no voice at all. So we must enter into the lives of our students, on their turf, and hope that by leading within and among them, our voice as well can contribute to the creation of content and the shaping of their identity.

INTERMINGLING LIVES

When we decide to enter into the lives of our children and students by going online and joining with them on social networking sites, we automatically place ourselves at risk of being exposed to the good, bad, beautiful, and ugly in the lives to which we minister. I think the most appropriate term for this is *intermingle*. In my experience youth workers are often afraid of coming into too much contact with the messy lives of students. We fear that we may be associating with things that we don't agree with or with which we know our students are struggling. But when we intermingle with our students on their turf, we are suddenly faced with the intermingling of all the things that their life entails, both good and bad, light and dark, clean and messy, and it comes pouring out when we interact with them in person and many times online.

For many people in the real world, this conjures up the image of the pastor elevated up on the pulpit, looking down from a distance at those to whom he is preaching and ministering. This type of distance has no place or opportunity to exist in the virtual world of online social networking. If we as youth workers choose to enter these sites, we must be prepared to put our guard down, come humbly, and enter into the messy lives of our students, up close and personal. We must be willing to be surrounded in online community by people who choose to live differently and do things with which we don't agree. This is a scary prospect for those of us in ministry who have spent so much time polishing our "glittering image."[7] Why would we put our reputation at risk like that?

---

[6]Hipps, *The Hidden Power of Electronic Culture*, 130.
[7]Susan Howatch, *Glittering Images* (New York: Fawcett Crest, 1987).

Because Jesus did (see Luke 5:27–31; John 4:1–26; 8:1–11; etc.). The person whom we worship and teach others about did not try to keep himself away from those to whom he was ministering. Rather, he put himself in close, intimate proximity with the messy lives around him, with no regard for his own reputation or how it would look to the religious leaders who were constantly trying to throw judgment on his character and leadership. Our reputations are important to us, and they should be. But I think it's important to be online where our students are, and by doing so, we say something about our willingness to walk through the heights and depths of their lives. "Jesus is not repelled by us, no matter how messy we are, regardless of how incomplete we are."[8] By being online with our students, we show that we too are not repelled and that we truly do care for them.

Being online allows you to intermingle with both saints and sinners in your student community. Where else are you going to see the gritty world of junior high, high school, and college life so up close? If your students let their guard down around you online, then you have the privilege of seeing the struggles and temptations they face on a daily basis. Your heart will ache at some of the decisions they make, but it will also present to you the reality of how important it is for us to be in their midst and to help guide them through the murky waters of adolescence and emerging adulthood. And it is not all messy either. You will be inspired, encouraged, and hopeful as you see the amazing things your students do online in their communities. You will see them join online groups that actually lead to their involvement and action in their local communities in areas such as social justice, racism, and poverty. You will witness them standing for truth by resisting the temptation that comes their way as they choose to live out God's truth in small groups at their church or on campus. You will see them launch groups that invite them and their friends over to a person's house in need of prayer. And you will have the privilege to see the joy and fun that come with being an adolescent and young adult.

By being present online, students have a sense that you are more readily accessible to them than you might otherwise be. It is not uncommon for students to contact me via social networking sites and feel vulnerable enough to pour their heart out about the difficult issues in

---

[8]Michael Yaconelli, *Messy Spirituality* (Grand Rapids, MI: Zondervan, 2002), 17.

their lives. Often the issues are related to some of the personal struggles
they are facing such as alcoholism, a sexual addiction, or issues in their
family. One of the more poignant interactions was with a student about
a death in her family. Her presence on my network every day kept her
struggles and difficult situation front and center for me. It was a daily
reminder of the difficulties that many of my students face in their lives,
and through this communication I was able to help walk her through
some of the processes of grieving. In talking about the death in her
family and her grieving, I was able to minister to her in ways online
that she was not ready for in person. This online interaction eventually
moved to more pastoral care in person, but I credit social networking
with opening up the lines of communication when the student felt like
I might not have been accessible before. Stories like this have been
common since I have been online, and it is not unusual for someone
completely unknown to me to send me a message seeking help because
he or she feels alone and doesn't know where to turn.

    We are not presented with many opportunities to do "life
together"[9] in this day and age. Most of the students to whom we
minister live very disconnected lives, and the only opportunities we
have to live life together are a couple of hours a week at church or
during some extended mission trip. So when that student leaves our
midst, we are not privy to the actions, struggles, and ups and downs
that others get to witness in their lives. But in online community your
senses will be inundated with photos, books, quotes, movies, music,
and more from the students to whom you minister. Here their lives are
exposed, sometimes to great degrees. Though it is not the real world of
flesh and blood in front of us, we can take what we learn online, and
from the interactions we have with our students we can better position ourselves to help transform their lives through our presence and
through the message of Jesus Christ that we bear.

TRANSFORMING COMMUNICATION

I came to the realization that at times my students inhabited parts of
these online communities and that as a minister to them I was missing
out on a huge opportunity to use the importance of communication to
transform their lives where they are. Whenever an invention related to

---

[9]Dietrich Bonhoeffer, *Life Together* (New York: Harper & Row, 1954).

communication in the past was available, there have been those who have made advantageous use of new technologies. Martin Luther took the momentum of the Reformation and capitalized on the ability of the printing press to communicate his message to as many people as possible.[10] Today I believe the most effective technological medium for communicating to our youth online is social networking.

Whether we realize it or not, we are always communicating. If we are always communicating, then by not being online with them, I was communicating to them the message that I didn't want to be a part of their whole life. I was sending out the message that I was too righteous to engage them in the messy parts of their lives. They wanted to see a youth director who could embrace them for who they were and would love both the good and the bad as they continued to seek Christ and be transformed. At some point the risks no longer outweighed the benefits, and I decided that bigger things were at stake and that I could use this medium to help transform their lives by engaging them where they were assembling.

I am fond of the maxim attributed to St. Francis of Assisi: "Preach the gospel at all times. Use words if necessary."[11] For me, I had the opportunity not only to use words to help transform students' lives online, but it was possible to use video, photos, art, music, and other forms of media to communicate the gospel to them. We not only have the opportunity to communicate words to students through messages, announcements, and advertising, but we also have the means to engage them and communicate the Word to them. Along with the positives and negatives, our words ultimately convey our beliefs, views, and thoughts about the Word that transforms lives.

On one level I am communicating information to them, such as who we are as a ministry, what types of events we will be doing this year, and what our preaching topics will cover. I can communicate information by sending out messages regarding outreach projects or announcements regarding a local concert, and I can post my blogs for them to read, when most likely they never would have read my thoughts by going to my web site. This is the most basic level of com-

---

[10]Hugh Hewitt, *Blog: Understanding the Information Reformation That's Changing Your World* (Nashville: Thomas Nelson, 2005), 51–59.
[11]Father Pat McCloskey, O.F.M., "Ask A Franciscan," *St. Anthony Messenger*; http://www.americancatholic.org/Messenger/Oct2001/Wiseman.asp.

munication online, the transfer of information. But there is another level of communication that we must keep in mind that is much more subversive. I communicate what type of person I am and who I long to be by what I post on my profile. What kinds of photos are appropriate? What kinds of comments on my wall are appropriate? What do they see me reading, watching, and listening to? By living out my beliefs online I am trying to communicate to them the process of having Jesus Christ continually transform my life. So on the one level I am communicating bits of information to them, but on the other level that information communicates something much deeper about what I stand for as a Christian. If we choose not to inhabit their worlds and act as "salt" and "light" (Matthew 5:13–15) in their world, who will?

It is a slow and sometimes frustrating process to live out our faith online, especially when it seems like everyone else is doing something with which we disagree. But over time I believe that by being online with our students we can make a great impact, and probably in ways that we will never realize. As a college director, I am now choosing to stand in solidarity with and in the midst of my students. I am choosing to minister to them completely by being exposed to everything in their lives and by living out faithfully in the community what it means to follow Christ, so that by my example they may be witnesses to the transforming work of Jesus Christ in me (Galatians 2:20).

10

EVANGELISM AND APOLOGETICS IN THE NEW MEDIA

Roger Overton

www.AteamBlog.com

A. B. SIMPSON ONCE WROTE, "The Christian is not obedient unless he is doing all in his power to send the gospel to the heathen world."[1] With the dawning of new media, what is in the Christian's "power" is potentially expanding. There appears to be almost no limit to the opportunities for those who take seriously the charge of spreading the good news to every tongue, tribe, and nation. We must do everything we can toward this great cause, but we must also be wise about how we go about it.

It is important for us to remember that though it is the Holy Spirit who regenerates unbelievers so they can believe the good news, God has decided to include us in the process of revealing his truth to the lost. The Bible is clear that God does want us to go, teach, disciple, and baptize, as was commanded by Jesus before he ascended into heaven.

In Acts 10 we are told of a centurion named Cornelius who had a vision of an angel who told him to send for Peter. The narrative tells how Peter arrived and preached the gospel to Cornelius and to his household and how they were all saved and baptized as a result. God didn't have to use Peter. If he can give a man a vision of an angel, then he could have simply had the angel tell the man the good news.

---

[1] A. B. Simpson, "Mission Work," *The World, Work and World*, 9 (1887), 104.

Similar stories are reported even today, and I've heard several from Muslim countries. Typically there is some sort of vision or dream, followed by the preaching of the gospel by faithful Christians. In every testimony I've heard, including the one I recited from Acts, at least two principles are clear:

> 1. God is sovereignly deciding whom he will save. Only those whom God has chosen receive these visions and dreams.
> 2. For whatever reason, God is still using Christians to proclaim and defend the good news of the gospel.

This should be quite humbling. Though God could save every person in the world without us through direct revelation, we find in the Bible and in the world today that God uses his people to advance and enlarge his Kingdom. Why is this? The only answer I can give is that he does so for his own glory and good pleasure.

This should also be inspiring. If we are faithful to proclaim and defend the good news, God will use our work for his glory. We get to be part of the process of expanding God's family! And these principles are just as true today in new media evangelism as they have been throughout history.

In this chapter I will first explain why we ought to consider doing evangelism and apologetics in new media. Then I will offer some principles for faithfulness and provide examples for how some Christians are currently being faithful through their use of various media for the proclamation and defense of the gospel. The chapter will close with some considerations for the future of evangelism in new media.

ARE NEW MEDIA WORTHY OF THE GOSPEL?

Are new media, such as blogging and social networking, really adequate or effective avenues for Christian evangelism and apologetics in our postmodern age? One problem is the necessary limits of written communication as it pertains to blogging and social networks. Writing lacks inflection, body language, and tone. Inevitably confusion over criticism, jokes, and sarcasm can lead to vicious retorts and hurt feelings. Perhaps the strongest objection to evangelism through new media is the inhibited nature of the relationships it produces. With any type of relationship, the more obstacles there are between two people, the more limited the relationship will be. Not being able to hear the reader's voice, see him or her face-to-face, or share meals together means the relationship formed will be somewhat impersonal. Personal approaches to evangelism are typically preferred; therefore, some might argue, new media are inadequate means for evangelism.

There is some legitimacy to this argument. No book, blog, or YouTube video should take the place of face-to-face evangelism. The apostle Paul taught that the primary means for communicating the gospel ought to be people. In Romans 10:14–15 he asked, "How are they to believe in him of whom they have never heard? And how are they to hear without someone preaching? And how are they to preach unless they are sent? As it is written, 'How beautiful are the feet of those who preach the good news!'" Paul didn't even suggest passing out Bibles as the way to get the good news to people. The gospel was intended to be communicated through spoken words between individuals. The Bible is the foundation for training in the gospel, and everything else, including new media, are tools toward the goal of evangelizing face-to-face.

New media should not be viewed as replacements of face-to-face evangelism but as extensions of it. Throughout church history, Christians have used various tools to extend the reach of their influence and always with the goal of bringing people from every tongue, tribe, and nation into the live fellowship of Christ's body, the church. Popular among these tools have been books and tracts. These have limitations in regard to communication, and they are actually far less relational than blogs. There are very few opportunities for book and tract readers to interact with authors in any forum, depending on how the literature is distributed. And yet many Christians have found writing to be a great tool for evangelism.

Beyond the opportunities for discussion with the author and other readers, new media take advantage of wider audiences. Books and tracts are limited by the publisher's ability to market the book within a given country and by the time and cost of publishing. Blogs can be read worldwide within minutes of publication, cost far less, and can instantly be translated into over a hundred languages. When writing printed literature, authors can only point to or briefly quote an article available somewhere else. Blogs can link directly to articles and other resources available online, making them far richer in content.

In a nutshell, the versatility of the new media supplies a wider, more diverse audience and more accessibility to resources than do books and tracts. These strengths do not make new media better instruments for evangelism than any other. We must humbly remember that God chooses to use a variety of means to call the lost to him, even those means we may dislike or in which we are less gifted. As with any other method, Christians must keep in mind the inherent limits of their chosen medium, but we should also take advantage of the unique opportunities the medium provides.

FAITHFUL EVANGELISM IN THE NEW MEDIA

Every time we communicate something important, we run the risk of distorting, oversimplifying, or perverting our message. This is true of the gospel and especially true when we attempt to use new media to communicate it. Along with the new opportunities we have been given with which to spread the good news are new opportunities to make mistakes. Since I've made many of these mistakes, I hope I can help you avoid them.

We must be faithful to the message of Christ. Jude 3 says that we are to "contend for the faith that was once for all delivered to the saints." Regardless of our time, culture, language, location, or philosophical persuasion, the central message we must preach as Christians is the same as the one passed down from the earliest followers of Christ. How we communicate it may change, but what we communicate is not good news if it is not the simple gospel found in the pages of the Bible. For all that we might do in attempting to share the gospel, salvation ultimately comes down to what God does. As Paul said in Romans 1:16, "[The gospel] is the power of God for salvation to everyone who believes."

Being faithful to the message requires that we have some knowledge of it, and when it comes to the theology of the gospel and apologetics, there's a lot of knowledge to be had. Most of us have not had time to learn that much. However, one of the benefits of conversing in new media is that the Internet is at our fingertips. It is like having lunch with a friend with a library in our backpacks. Instead of just mentioning a book or trying to quote an argument or piece of an article from memory, we can link directly to the material, quote it accurately, and engage it bit by bit. In live conversation it is easy to unintentionally misremember something or misrepresent a position. In the new media we have fewer excuses. With such a wealth of resources available to us for research through the Internet, it is our responsibility to take the time to get things right.

This means we must find reputable sources to link to for our information and claims. Too many people have fallen for the idea that "if it's on the Internet, it must be true." We must evaluate each resource in light of what God has revealed as well as general truth and rationality. Below are a few web sites I've found to be reliable and helpful:

• www.TheGospelCoalition.org. The Gospel Coalition exists to serve the church by drawing Christians together in renewed passion for the gospel of Christ and teaching them to clearly communicate the gospel through speech and lifestyles that are submitted to the lordship of Christ over all things. The ministry's web site provides valuable videos, audio lectures, articles, and other aids toward this cause.

• www.STR.org. Stand to Reason is an organization dedicated to training Christians to make a thoughtful defense of traditional Christianity in the public square. On their web site readers will find information that helps clarify the teachings of Christianity and Christian living and offers discernment on issues of contemporary culture; most of the material is written by Greg Koukl. The material serves not only as a great starting point for conversations (and blogs) but also helps Christians further cultivate knowledge, character, and especially wisdom. Stand to Reason also utilizes the new media through their popular and insightful blogs and podcasts.

• www.CARM.org. The Christian Apologetics and Research Ministry, run by founder Matthew Slick, is an informative site dealing with topics from the defense of mere Christianity to the exposing of problems in cults and other religions. Go to the CARM site for straight facts such as a list of the prophecies Jesus fulfilled or archived incriminating statements by The Church of Jesus Christ of Latter-day Saints (Mormons) and The Watchtower (Jehovah's Witnesses).

We must be faithful to the virtues of Christ. In 1 Peter 3:15 we are told, "But in your hearts honor Christ the Lord as holy, always being prepared to make a defense to anyone who asks you for a reason for the hope that is in you; yet do it with gentleness and respect." In other words, the words that we say in defense of the gospel or in proclaiming it must be matched by how we act. Josh McDowell, a popular author in evidential apologetics, notes, "Our motivation in using [apologetics] is to glorify and magnify Jesus Christ—not to win an argument. . . . One should have a gentle and reverent spirit when using apologetics or evidences."[2]

The overarching virtue upon which all of the other virtues depend is love. We must be able to say to non-Christians, "I am going to love you more than you love your sin because in this same way I was loved until I came to know the Lord Jesus Christ."[3] But even more important than our love of non-Christians is our love of fellow Christians. "After we have done our best to communicate to a lost world, still we must never forget that the final apologetic which Jesus gives is the observable love of true Christians for true Christians."[4] If we dismiss the prayer of Jesus in John 17:21 by lacking love for fellow Christians, we would do better to shut our mouths and silence our keyboards than profane the name of Christ whom we claim to follow. In our lives we must seek opportunities to live out this love in a manner apparent to the world around us.

Very rarely will our lifestyles be explicitly visible through new media. However, the individual choices we make on a day-to-day basis will impact the character with which we write. One of the most important virtues for us to cultivate is the ability to be charitable. Charitability can be unpacked in a number of different ways. Unless we have good reason to believe otherwise, we ought to assume people are being honest about what they believe. Accusing someone of believing something other than what they have said can be a quick way to end the conversation. We also ought to assume people have the best of intentions. This means that if a comment could possibly be taken positively or negatively, we ought to take it positively. To put it simply, we must be charitable by giving people the benefit of the doubt by assuming that those we converse with are acting as honest individuals. They might not be, but worthwhile conversations and relationships are not often begun by displaying distrust.

Part of the Christian apologetic enterprise is to criticize contrary

[2]Josh McDowell, *The New Evidence That Demands a Verdict* (Nashville: Thomas Nelson, 1999), xiv.
[3]R. Albert Mohler Jr., "Homosexual Marriage as a Challenge to the Church: Biblical and Cultural Reflections," in *Sex and the Supremacy of Christ*, ed. John Piper and Justin Taylor (Wheaton, IL: Crossway Books, 2005), 126–127.
[4]Francis A. Schaeffer, *The Mark of the Christian* (Downers Grove, IL: InterVarsity Press, 1970), 17.

beliefs. A serious danger comes when we fail to draw a line between beliefs and the people who hold them. We are to *disrespect ideas* foreign to Christianity, but we are to *respect people* who hold those ideas as fellow creatures made in the image of God. Especially when conversations get heated, we should make it a point to mention our reverence for our challengers. Remember that though our message is necessarily offensive (we're telling people they need to be saved from their sin), our character should not make it more offensive. We are not blogging to win arguments but to win people. Our concern must be more for the people than about their ideas, even though we express our concern through addressing their ideas and sinfulness. Also, while we ought to be careful when attacking beliefs to affirm the people who hold them, we should be prepared for those who do not give us the same courtesy. We will be insulted and ridiculed, but that is never an excuse for responding in like manner. It will help if we refrain from taking attacks personally and overreacting, but ultimately we must remember that it is not really about us anyway. Our proper reaction to offense is to encourage better dialogue.

I must admit that I learned this lesson the hard way. The leader of a Christian organization had been making comments on his blog that I found offensive. When he eventually made a comment about me, I decided it was time to rant on how poorly his comments reflected on his organization. Regardless of whether my points were valid, my attitude and approach were not. My response generated more damage than good. After I posted my response several friends e-mailed me to weigh in on where *I* went wrong. Had I sought their wisdom prior to posting I would have either severely edited my response or silenced it altogether. I learned that when it comes to controversial posts such as that one, out of humility I should seek the counsel of wise friends before going public with my criticisms. Out of humility we must be ready to admit when we are wrong, even when we are initially convinced we are right.

We must be faithful to the wisdom of Christ. Christians are regarded as sheep among wolves; so we must "be wise as serpents and innocent as doves" (Matthew 10:16). In extreme cases, being wise means we "do not give dogs what is holy, and do not throw [our] pearls before pigs" (Matthew 7:6). We must be aware of whether what we are doing is even worth our time—whether it is the time to pursue a relationship or simply give someone something to think about. Wisdom involves making the right choices in complex situations and knowing how and when to say the right words in challenging conversations.

How can we be wise with our words and time when blogging? First, we must be selective about what topics we post about and how we approach those topics. To do this, it is a good idea to know something about our audience. The best way to find out what interests your readers is to try a number of different things. I have found that posts on Mormon theology generate a lot of conversation, so I make it a point to post on it periodically. In order for this to work, our readers must have the ability to comment on our blogs, perhaps on a message board or via e-mail. The ability to comment is fundamental to doing evangelism in new media. When readers and viewers have a voice, they are more likely to return, and they are more likely to engage the content, even if they do not actually leave a comment. Conversations are the first steps toward relationships, and relationships are a cornerstone of effective evangelism.

Being wise in the new media often requires the use of tactics. Tactics involve the ability to listen and to discern when to speak and when to ask probing questions. Greg Koukl has explained the importance of questions: "Asking simple, leading questions is an almost effortless way to accomplish balance. You can advance the dialogue and make capital of the conversation for spiritual ends without seeming abrupt, rude or pushy."[5] In a chapter entitled "Ask at Least a Half-Dozen Questions . . ." Hugh Hewitt says, "When you ask a question, you are displaying interest in the person asked—and in most settings this is a great boon to the pride and self-worth of the person being asked."[6] There are different types of questions, and the ones most useful for evangelism and apologetics are clarifying and exposing questions. *Clarifying questions* are used to gain information, such as "Why do you believe that?" or "Can you further explain your beliefs about . . . ?" The second useful type is *exposing questions*. These are questions used to expose a problem or weakness in someone's position or reasoning. For example, if

[5]Gregory Koukl, "Tactics," in *To Everyone an Answer*, ed. Francis J. Beckwith, William Lane Craig, and J. P. Moreland (Downers Grove, IL: InterVarsity Press, 2004), 55. I recommend his full-length book on the subject: *Tactics: A Game Plan for Discussing Your Christian Convictions* (Grand Rapids, MI: Zondervan, 2008).
[6]Hugh Hewitt, *In but Not of* (Nashville: Thomas Nelson, 2003), 172–173.

someone were to claim, "There are no true propositions," an exposing question would be, "Is that proposition true?"

It is not a rare occurrence for someone to leave a good question or two and then never return to the conversation. If we are going to make effective use of our time, fly-by comments and questions are rarely going to cut it. We need to stick around and engage people's ideas. Real conversations that lead to relationships require attentive interaction from both sides, and fly-by comments tend to detract from conversations rather than help move them forward.

NEW MEDIA EVANGELISM IN ACTION

Many Christians and organizations are already making use of new media for the proclamation and defense of the gospel. One organization in this field is the Mormonism Research Ministry (www.MRM. org). This ministry has been around since 1979, but they're discovering the importance new media can play in the future of their outreach. I asked their web developer, Aaron Shafovaloff, to explain how they've been using new media.

> At Mormonism Research Ministry we have used YouTube (http:// youtube.com/MRMdotORG) and other video sharing sites to promote our message. YouTube is like a modern town square. So many people are willing to watch a video that aren't willing to read an article. Where we don't fill in the gap others will. Spending the extra time to get videos up is a no-brainer, especially when you experience the popularity and effectiveness of the medium. Every day I get a dozen or so messages from people asking questions or making comments about the apologetic material. One thing that has definitely made an impact is the personal testimonies of ex-Mormon Christians. The little seed of effort it takes to videotape one person while they share their testimony at a Utah church and then upload it often turns into thousands of views and hundreds of comments.
>
> Bill McKeever, the president and founder of our ministry, is a walking encyclopedia of Mormonism. Like a lot of people, he understandably felt uncomfortable in front of a camera, but I convinced him to simply sit down and talk in front of my video recorder about a topic. Months later there were 5,000 views and a

lot of dialog. Needless to say, YouTube has become an important part of our outreach.

Between a few of us, we make it a point to post to our blog, humorously called "Mormon Coffee" (http://blog.mrm.org), three times a week. This has evolved into a hub of Mormon/evangelical interaction with hundreds of unique visitors everyday. We use this to address current events, contrast Mormonism and Christianity, and frequently share the gospel.[7]

The experiences of Mormonism Research Ministry are similar to those of Rob Sivulka, who also does evangelism to Mormons. Rob runs the web site MormonInfo.org, which operates under the umbrella ministry of CourageousChristiansUnited.org. He had already been doing street evangelism for many years but found that the new media expanded his ministry opportunities. Using social networks such as MySpace and Facebook, Rob has increased the awareness and flow of traffic to his web sites. "These networks all make an effort in one way or another to point people back to my two main sites. I also have a discussion board on MormonInfo.org and blogs on all the rest. I have also taken video testimonies and posted them on YouTube, Google, etc."[8]

When asked how new media have impacted his ministry, Rob said, "I'm an author who is read all over the world now. My main site—MormonInfo.org—averages around 100 visitors a day. It is quoted and linked to around the Internet. I have received many positive responses as well as many negative ones (which I also take as positive since I know the opposition is interacting with my ideas), many of which are documented in my monthly newsletters. Many people have changed their mind on various topics as a result of my sites. This is no different from people changing their minds when they read books. Often times, it's the site that attracts one to write me; a dialogue ensues, and repentance happens—both with them as well as me. . . . I expect to build more sites for Jehovah's Witnesses, the immorality of ethical issues such as abortion, generally speaking, etc."

YouTube, and other video broadcast platforms like it, can be a great place to discuss any topic. Jay Smith works with Answering-Islam.org and teaches weekly at the Speaker's Corner in London

---

[7]Private e-mail, September 13, 2007.
[8]Private e-mail, August 28, 2007.

(a public forum for dialogue). He uses YouTube videos (username PfanderFilms) to present challenges to Islam and rebuttals to Muslim challenges against Christianity, and thousands of comments in conversations have ensued.

Other ministries are finding the value of podcasting. Many people use iTunes to find and download podcasts that pique their interest. The folks at Apologetics.com broadcast a weekly radio show in Los Angeles. By podcasting their radio shows, they have exponentially increased their listening audience and regularly receive responses from around the world.

These are just a few examples of what's already being done in new media. Many more can be cited, but it should be clear at this point that when used wisely new media provide opportunities to reach wide audiences and to engage in conversations that lead to fruitful relationships.

THE FUTURE OF EVANGELISM IN NEW MEDIA

Thus far I've explained why I believe Christians should be involved in evangelism and apologetics through new media and what it looks like to be faithful when doing so, and I've offered some examples as to how this is currently being done. But there's one area of faithfulness I've left out since it is an area that is currently lacking.

The proclamation of the gospel to all nations is not simply the responsibility of individual Christians; it is more generally the responsibility of Christ's body, the church. While some churches have attempted to utilize new media as part of their ministry, for the most part churches are absent. Once someone becomes a Christian, being a part of a local church community plays a vital role in his or her spiritual development.

The church needs to establish its presence through more than just sermon podcasts. Being intentionally active in social networks, for example, will not only help the community be more connected but will also provide opportunities for nonmembers in the church's community to see how God is moving in the church and to provide new converts more avenues for becoming connected to a local church. Most churches today have static web sites that provide information about the church's ministries. The next step is to make the web sites dynamic and interactive through blogs and message boards that foster and encourage more relationships throughout the community. This step has begun to take shape through the MyChurch.org social network, but it needs to be integrated more directly with what local churches are already doing. Until local churches become intentionally involved in new media ministry, the opportunities for evangelism through new media will not be fully utilized.

When asked how Christians can "foster the encounter of people with Jesus Christ," C. S. Lewis responded, "You can't lay down any pattern for God. There are many different ways of bringing people into His Kingdom, even some ways that I specially dislike!"[9] While we cannot know for sure whether or not Lewis would have liked the idea of evangelism through new media, they certainly represent some of the many "different" methods available. Throughout history God has used many different means to advance his Kingdom, and today those means include new media. It is our responsibility to wisely and prayerfully make use of the opportunities that new media provide by continuing the proclamation and defense of the gospel to all nations for the glory of God.

---

[9]C. S. Lewis, "Cross-Examination," in *God in the Dock: Essays on Theology and Ethics*, ed. Walter Hooper (Grand Rapids, MI: Eerdmans, 1970), 262.

11

PROFESSORS WITH A NEW PUBLIC: ACADEMICS AND NEW MEDIA

Fred Sanders

www.ScriptoriumDaily.com

IF THERE IS ANY CATEGORY OF PEOPLE who stand in obvious need of the resources of new media, it is the category of people known as professors. Academics need new media. The main reason is that the old media of academia—that constellation of behaviors, networks, and institutions by which academics get their work done—make little sense and have little coherence.

In other spheres, advocates of the old media can plausibly argue that while their old systems might be growing obsolete now, they were at least appropriate for their time. They can also argue that the old media systems still manage to perform well within certain restraints. In journalism, for example, it may be the case that a network of daily newspapers, wire services, and broadcast news, all standardized by style books and driven by commercial ratings systems, may have once done the job of informing the public. No such case can be made for academia. The old media of modern academia have always been a baffling welter of incoherent behaviors: journals, academic presses, conferences, and visiting scholar positions, standardized by regional accreditation collectives and driven by tenure and promotion systems. Was there ever a workable system under that chaotic mess of inadequate programs and redundant planning loops? If there was, it must have been a system that served the needs of a quaint, one-campus, medieval college where a small faculty was in constant contact with each other around shared lives, tasks, and even meals. Today when professors in the diverse and sprawling colleges and universities try to study, teach, and publish using available systems, they constantly run into unnecessary limits imposed by the old media of academia. New media solutions are already ameliorating some of the problems. Indeed, academic users have been important early adopters of many of the electronic breakthroughs of the computer age, especially in information storage and retrieval. But a thorough rethinking of academic media is something from which professors stand to benefit greatly.

The necessary rethinking of academic media should take three basic elements into account: first, the nature of academic work and its tasks; second, the old media through which this work has been done up until now; and third, the possibilities offered by new media. To survey the new media possibilities, this chapter includes some observations by major academic bloggers in the author's field, theological studies.

ACADEMIC WORK

What is the work that professors need to do in order to be professors? We should narrow the focus as much as possible, excluding first of all the tasks that fit under the heading of institutional maintenance. A professor's work week may be filled with committee meetings and paperwork of all kinds, but none of these tasks are unique to academic work. They are the things that any responsible member of any institution will have to do to keep things moving, but they do not mark the specifically academic calling. At the other end of the spectrum is the important work of teaching and advising students, which is obviously a hallmark of professorial life. But education itself is too fundamental to be treated as one element of academic work, and another chapter in this book handles the subject of education and new media (Chapter 12). My point is that to be hired as a college teacher, a person has to be qualified as an academic, with some certification of scholarly expertise in hand and a research program ahead, along with an ability to interact meaningfully with other experts in the field. It is this properly scholarly work that I would like to focus on, discarding committee work on one hand and teaching on the other. I will describe scholarly work, as much as possible, in abstract and content-neutral terms that emphasize the general form of each activity. That will enable us to see how these forms of work can be carried out under the old media and the new media respectively.

Proper academic work involves three tasks: research, peer review, and dissemination of information. What is research? It is progress in a knowledge tradition. The place where you can see research happening most dramatically is in the hard sciences, especially in the applied sciences where successful research leads to nifty gadgets. But there is also such a thing as research in the humanities, where scholars identify a problem or an unexplained phenomenon and devise a way to understand it better. The key idea in research is progress, or the production and synthesis of new knowledge. Properly identified research problems tend to be fruitful, opening up new lines of inquiry and new areas for exploration. One good idea leads to many others, whereas bad ideas tend to shut down further investigations. A cluster of related lines of inquiry constitutes a research program, and a scholar with a research program is somebody who correctly identified a researchable problem and then investigated it so thoroughly that it transformed from one project into a whole career of things to examine. In most fields, progress in research requires the scholar to have a clear and up-to-date understanding of the current state of research. What has already been investigated? What areas need further exploration? How have advances in one area changed the field's understanding of other areas, and have those connections been examined yet? Research, in other words, tends to take place on the cutting edge of knowledge, and scholars need to know where that edge is.

The second major component of scholarly work is peer review. When a scholar moves forward with a research program, that work needs to be scrutinized by the other scholars in the field who have the relevant expertise to make independent judgments about the quality and adequacy of the work. Peer review covers a broad range of interactions, all the way from hard scientific verification on one hand (if cold fusion was produced in one lab under specifiable conditions, another lab should be able to duplicate it) to establishing and enforcing standards of good writing for academic prose. Professors have an enormous amount of freedom in how they conduct their scholarly work, which makes peer review an important time of reckoning. Probably the most exciting variety of peer review arises when scholars sharply disagree and review takes the form of extended debate. Competing scholars can disagree not just about results but about methods, interpretations, and even about the very definition of the field of inquiry. Debates of this nature are not things that can be resolved neatly or conclusively; instead they tend to generate competing teams of scholars that emerge as intellectual movements or schools of thought. At its worst this situation can degenerate into rival dogmas, but ideally it develops new forms of collaboration and competition that open up new lines of inquiry. Even extended conceptual conflicts, in other words, continue to be a form of peer review.

The third major component of academic work is disseminating information. We have already seen how fundamental this is for research itself, since scholars cannot make progress unless they know the current state of research. For this to be possible, there must be some way of making the results of scholarly inquiry available to other researchers in the field. Publishing is therefore necessary, even if the public is only the handful of other experts in a given subject. Beyond that tiny public, however, is the other public, people in general, who in a variety of ways may want or need to know what the scholar has learned. Some subjects are too difficult, detailed, or dull to be shared with the whole world. Even when the subject is interesting or accessible, not all researchers are capable of communicating with people outside their field of advanced research; they go so far into their subject that they can only talk meaningfully about it with other experts. In this gap there emerges a category of scholarly activity that is completely devoted to popularizing and simplifying the more difficult information to a less specialized audience of general readers. On campus, the first type of professor teaches narrowly focused advanced seminars, while the second type thrives on introductory courses covering an entire field.

These three tasks (research, peer review, and information dissemination) are the main tasks involved in academic work. Beyond the internal evaluations built into the system, academics are further assessed and held accountable in a couple of ways. First, individual professors are evaluated by a promotion and tenure system. These systems vary widely from school to school, but the basic idea is a kind of holistic peer review that looks at the overall career path a scholar is pursuing. Second, institutions are evaluated by accrediting agencies, which in America are large regional collectives that maintain uniform standards for higher education. In another way, educational institutions are evaluated by academic reputation, which is a less structured system of public relations, market demand, and perceived prestige. Where will you send your children to college? Academic reputation in part determines the answer.

THE OLD MEDIA OF ACADEMIA

These are the basic elements of academic work. How have they been carried out under the regime of the old media? By *old media*, I do not mean the truly ancient systems of pre-modern university life. How Socrates may have thought about his "research" in fourth-century B.C. Athens is a fascinating question, and not as anachronistic as it first sounds. He knew he was moving into fruitful lines of questioning beyond what had been achieved by the Ionian nature philosophers, and he knew that his rivals, the Sophists, were engaged in a kind of spurious education that didn't meet his peer review standards any more than his work counted by their standards. Disseminating information in that ancient world apparently took the form of making speeches at drinking parties, and committee meetings apparently were held on the highway to the harbor town, or in prison. It would also be interesting to study the forms of research, peer review, and information dissemination for Plato's Academy, the schools of the Carolingian Renaissance, or the first medieval universities. But for our purposes, asking about old media means asking how the scholarly task is accomplished in a world where multiple centers of scholarship need to be connected to each other across larger spans of geography and history. When Athens is the only hub of Western intellectual inquiry, *media* just means talking to Socrates, *research* is whatever he's thinking about, *peer review* is when he tells you you're wrong, and *information dissemination* is when Plato writes it down. When many schools need to communicate, however, the medium of their communication begins to emerge as a system worth considering in its own right.

The old media of academia include scholarly journals, academic book publishing, scholarly conferences, and guest lectureships. Business as usual in modern academia means carrying out the scholarly task through these old media, learning these systems, and working according to their standards of success. Taken together, the whole system forms a subculture with its own expectations and attitudes. Tenured academics can easily forget how odd the whole thing is, but newcomers who have to learn the system like a new language are keenly aware that they are being introduced to a new culture. Which journals are good? How do you write book reviews for them? Who do I know who knows somebody I need to know? Which conferences are mandatory?

This alternative culture created by the old media of academia is where things begin to get strange for the academic life. Professors play a strange game in this second culture. Consider one of the basic units of scholarly exchange, the academic article published in a scholarly journal. When they are functioning at the highest levels, professors are often writing scholarly works so specialized that only a few dozen people are capable of understanding them (never mind caring about them), but it is absolutely crucial that those few dozen people be able to find the right articles, for the sake of their own research. Established scholars usually know those few dozen people personally and could probably mail printed copies of their work to each of them for less expense than the whole journal-publishing system will end up costing. When you consider the printing, binding, mailing, cataloging, and shelving in libraries that it takes to get that article into the right hands, it is astonishing how much labor and expense is required for such a small result. The periodical budget at good academic libraries is astronomical, and the results are meager. This is obviously a system that cries out for new media solutions.

Peer review of academic journal articles is also peculiar because of the comical way in which the large scale of the enterprise collides with the small scale of the scholarly community. The writer submits his article to the journal editor, who sends it out for "blind review" to an anonymous qualified expert. Often the anonymous expert is somebody the author knows, whose work is cited (or ignored) in the article. The reviewer's identity is easily guessed from the nature of the comments he or she provides on the article. I have even heard of a case in which a professor's own office mate was selected as the blind reviewer for an article, which means that the article made the trip from its office of origin to the office of the editor and back twice.

The same system of peer review is in place for books from academic presses, where the situation is further complicated by the even smaller number of copies printed. For the average academic book, the potential readership is so small that only the smallest print runs are justified. The market is exclusively university libraries, so a few hundred copies will suffice. In order for this kind of micro-publishing to be profitable or even supportable, the price of the volumes has to be disproportionately high. It is now common for a scholarly hardcover of about three hundred pages to cost well over a hundred dollars. This high price, in turn, guarantees that individual professors will not consider purchasing it but will instead ask their university libraries to purchase it. This has the advantage of making the book available to the whole university community, but there is some unintentional comedy involved in the fact that the only person on campus qualified to read the book has the same access to it as everybody else ("Who checked out Volume 3 of Hypothetical Vocalizations of the Late Sanskrit Subjunctive Mood?").

Of course, the publication of the expensive books could be subsidized, and that is how the business has been conducted for a long time. The subsidizing is taking on new forms in recent years. When a university subsidizes its own academic press, it is a way for the school to keep its academic publishing on justifiable life support: these books are a basic form of scholarly communication, without which academic life would dry up. So it is in the university's own best interest to publish books at a loss. But like any system of institutionalized subsidizing, this system needs to be closely monitored, and while individual presses are held accountable, it is hard to imagine who could track the performance of the whole industry. Prestigious universities try to manage their subsidy and subvention systems in order to prevent the perception that plenty of money is available to bail out any book project, and one of the ways they manage that perception is by keeping the subvention system quiet. Another form of subsidy is when publishers ask for subvention payments to defray the cost of printing and distributing an individual academic book. These subventions increasingly are being required from authors themselves, which creates a situation of great ambiguity. Numerous academic presses will publish a scholar's book in exchange for a complete subvention of the cost of publishing, while some presses only ask for a partial payment, a few thousand dollars to offset potential financial losses. Others will publish the book if the author agrees to buy every copy of the book printed. In some of these cases, the press will only accept a manuscript that has been scrutinized and recommended by external reviewers. In other cases, no such external review is required, and any academic manuscript with money attached will be printed. In such cases, it is hard to distinguish between the widely accepted author subvention system and the unacceptable zone of the vanity press.

The main pressure point on this publication system is where it collides with promotion and tenure standards. In order to be promoted to a higher rank, a professor needs to publish a book somewhere along the way. Imagine a young professor in need of the next promotion with its accompanying pay raise, whose book on an advanced topic is not publishable because it is not profitable. He finds a publisher who is willing to put it into print in exchange for a subvention covering all costs. It may be crass to consider the transaction in purely financial terms, but he can easily calculate that a one-time three-thousand-dollar payment to the publisher will translate into an annual six-thousand-dollar salary raise plus the security of tenure. Grant money may even be available for the publication expense. The committee that makes decisions about promotion now has to decide whether this book is a "real publication" or the result of academic vanity press printing. To make this decision, they have to consider how much money was paid to the publisher, whether the work was externally reviewed by peers, and the general academic reputation of the press. Decisions of this nature are being made at universities all over the world now, and there is no obvious bright line of demarcation between acceptable subvention and unacceptable vanity publication. Generally speaking, a publisher has crossed the line into the zone of vanity press if certain conditions are all present: if there is no peer review, if the author is required to do all the editing and layout, if the author pays for the cost of publication, if there is a guarantee of publication. But since any of these conditions can be present in a reputable press, promotion decisions have to be made on a case-by-case basis, which sometimes means the desperate measure of ad hoc peer review after publication—a sure sign that the original system has malfunctioned. Though the coming crisis is most obvious in the world of academic books, the journal scene is beset by the same problems. It can be extremely difficult to identify the difference between a peer-reviewed and a non-peer-reviewed journal. Young professors trying to get early works into print are often advised to try placing their work with a journal that is "peer-reviewed . . . but not too peer-reviewed."

The real showpiece of professorial old media, however, has to be the academic conference. They are almost too easy to mock. Once a year most academics travel to a major city for a multi-day extravaganza of meeting others who work in their field. Armies of tweed-clad experts converge and confer with each other. The heart of these conferences is "giving a paper," an event in which one professor stands in front of a roomful of other professors reading aloud a drastically shortened version of a scholarly article. Meanwhile, dozens of other professors are doing the same in dozens of other rooms to thousands of other listeners who had to decide which paper to hear and which ones to skip. Considered simply as information exchange, it would be hard to invent a less efficient system. If ever a system needed to be re-imagined in light of new technology, it is the academic conference. Sitting in a conference room listening to somebody read a paper, all scholars must have had the question occur to them, *Why wasn't this paper just e-mailed to me? Why did I have to fly to this city and stay in a hotel for three days to hear this research presented orally?* Further, the more successful a scholarly society becomes, the more unwieldy its annual meetings become. The Modern Language Association draws about ten thousand attendees every year, taking over major hotels and convention centers with mobs of philologists and critics. The respective societies for history and religion also draw an attendance in the thousands, and along with the business of presenting papers, these scholars do job interviews, buy books, and network with each other.

And here is a paradox. Here at academic old media's weakest point, the bloated academic conference, we can see the thing that can never be replaced by new media: the human contact of scholars meeting each other. You can look around you in a paper presentation and see who else made the same decision you did, to attend this particular paper out of all the options being offered in this exact time slot. The third time you see the same person shuffling into a room you are shuffling into, it begins to dawn on you that here is a person who is interested in what you are interested in, and a scholarly friendship forms. The academic conference is a dreadfully inefficient way of exchanging information, but it is a place where you can take the name you've been reading books by for years and attach things to it like a face, a voice, and mannerisms. It is remarkable how much more intelligently you can read a dry scholarly book after hearing the author present some of the ideas in person.

This last benefit of academic conferences crosses the line from tangible exchange of information into the intangible realm of interpersonal contact. We described the work of academics as involving research, peer review, and information dissemination. But professors are human, and they live in a human subculture where friendships and rivalries are formed, colleagues become acquainted, and freedom of association is permitted. There is actually something quaint and cozy about academic work. Perhaps it should always have stayed at a small scale, where its media didn't take on a kind of independent life. But since that is not the way it has developed, we are forced to deal with the question of appropriate media for the conduct of academic life. And that brings us to the possibilities of the new media.

THE NEW MEDIA OF ACADEMIA

The Internet and related technologies hold a great deal of promise for academic work. How can new media help professors carry out their tasks of research, peer review, and information dissemination? The first steps are easy and obvious and are already being pursued by academics of all sorts. But in a field like academics where information is king, blogs and new media hold much greater promise than is currently realized. We have spent considerable space here describing the fundamental tasks of academic work in a formal, content-free way because stripping them down to their essential elements makes it obvious that they can be carried out in a variety of media.

Research itself is the area where it is most difficult to see an imminent new media revolution. Identifying a research problem requires human creativity and thoughtful analysis, and so far the new media have not significantly changed the basic structure of research itself. Certainly electronic storage and retrieval have eliminated whole regions of scholarship that were unduly labor-intensive. A few decades ago, a scholar could earn a doctorate for being the person who looked up every occurrence of a particular word in a specified body of literature—"justice" in Plato or "grace" in the earliest church fathers, for instance—and writing up a thoughtful description of the word's usage. What took months of patient labor and a nearly superhuman attention span back then can now be accomplished effortlessly using databases, even publicly available Internet databases. The whole idea of a concordance, which was an astonishingly powerful study aid for biblical scholars, may now be relegated to the status of a curious relic made necessary by the print age itself.

Time-intensive tasks have been eliminated, but has new media technology opened up any new possibilities in research itself? So far, in the humanities at least, there have not been any breakthroughs. There are visionary committees promising breathlessly that "qualitatively different" forms of research and scholarship are about to become possible, if only the "cyberinfrastructure" will make this new "cyberscholarship" a reality. So far the results are as gimmicky as the names suggest. But at the heart of the research task is the need to share information with other practitioners, and it does seem likely that new media will deliver some goods here eventually. The ease of use offered by blogging, for instance, may make researchers more comfortable with sharing their early results and hypotheses openly with each other rather than putting off all sharing until their ideas have matured to the level of formal publication. If scholars can let each other have access to the creative process in an earlier phase, then it may be that truly new forms of sharing and refining will become possible.

New Testament scholar Michael Bird (http://euangelizomai.blogspot.com) calls this "going live" with ideas in biblical research. "Researchers and teachers can think aloud in a global context that gives the entire world immediate access to what they are thinking and doing." Theologian Peter Leithart (http://www.leithart.com) agrees: "Obviously, blogging speeds up exchanges of ideas in the academy. Bloggers can go public with hypotheses that would not pass a peer review process but which might be valuable. And, the hypothesis can be critiqued, revised, qualified, and so on very rapidly." Critics might label as half-baked this sort of early blog-publication of "hypotheses that would not pass a peer review process," but early publication of ideas not yet fully formed is the whole point. It lets a little bit of critique creep back into the earlier part of the research itself.

The coming crisis in academic publishing is centered on the expense of printing and distributing scholarly works with an extremely narrow focus. Electronic publishing is the obvious source of a solution to this problem. The current editorial systems could stay in place just as they are, with the cost of production dropping to a fraction of the current system. It may be a long time before paperless publication is desirable for all users, but in academia it seems like an obvious need. The current system, enmeshed in the ambiguities of inadequate peer review and the blurred line between subvention and vanity publishing, must find a way out of its deadlock.

It is easier to see how peer review will benefit from new media. Scholars can interact critically with each other in online forums much more easily and rapidly than through media such as print publications. As leading academic bloggers begin to establish themselves as worthwhile sources to read on a regular basis, electronic communities of readers will form that can provide detailed feedback on ideas and arguments. A few such forums are already beginning to appear, where important arguments are being launched, criticized, and refined in a very rapid and fluid exchange of expert opinion. The traditional book review is likely to retain its basic structure, but the speed with which qualified reviewers can now respond is remarkable. New Testament scholar Scot McKnight (http://www.jesuscreed.org) describes how the book reviewing process has changed: "I get a book and the review is out before many even know the book is released. Instantaneous reviews, interaction, and often the author weighs in as well . . . that is a huge improvement on the current system of reviewing, which often takes at least a year."

In addition to getting responses from the acknowledged experts, new media book reviewing is also more open to a wide range of readers whose voices are never heard in the academic conversation. New Testament scholar Michael Bird describes a situation where a scholar posting on a specific topic can draw "instant feedback from a pastor in Iowa, a post-grad researcher in Oxford, another New Testament lecturer in Wisconsin, or a lay-person in Kenya who can seriously engage him through comments or through another blog." Not only has the "publish, review, response" cycle dropped from months to minutes, but it now reaches a more diverse audience. Theologian Peter Leithart writes from a North American context but reports that his blog has picked up a large number of international readers. For no reason that Leithart can identify, his blog is especially popular in Poland. Leithart blogs extensively on his current reading and notes that "blogging allows non-academics to have access to ideas and theories that would be hidden from most of them. The Poles I know can't afford theological journals, but can read my summaries of articles on my blog." The faster rate and broader range of peer review is an area where new media yield an obvious improvement.

Blogging and other forms of web publication have been especially attractive for academics who want to teach a broader public. There are professors who would like to extend their reach not only to other students beyond the ones enrolled in their courses but would like to provide information to the public at large. In this case, they are not using new media to improve what they once did through old media; they are taking up a new kind of public ministry that they would not have pursued using old media. Christian academic bloggers have been especially prominent in this regard and express themselves with a strong sense of mission.

New Testament scholar Andreas Köstenberger (http://biblicalfoundations.org) says that blogging fits perfectly well with his academic project: "My primary goal is to disseminate some of my scholarship in a format that reaches a wider audience: by presenting a digest of my scholarly work; by simplifying it; by excerpting it and directing people to my full research in form of books, periodical articles, etc." Blogging lets him reach a new audience. Michael Bird also describes his goal as "disseminating my research, writing, and theological/spiritual reflection to the widest possible audience. I also aim to stand between the academy and the church as a mediator so as to show the relevance of academic debates for the life of the church. Blogging is a superb medium to do those two tasks." Scot McKnight is one of the best examples of a professor whose blog has a large group of regular readers and commenters, forming a new virtual community for extended conversations in response to McKnight's posts. McKnight says, "I blog in order to speak to and interact with the church at large." He adds that one of the great benefits of blogging is that it "makes academics more accountable to the church and to the opinion of the average person who can simply jot down his or her ideas without any credentials whatsoever."

The next question will be what kind of online peer review will count for things like publication and promotion. The established systems of academia still have a tendency to view the new media as a source of problems. Every professor with a blog has been haunted by the stories of academics who have been reprimanded or terminated for blogging in a way that put them at odds with their schools. These cases raise interesting questions about whether the meaning of academic freedom has changed in the age of the Internet, with the blurring of traditional lines between academic and public discourse. Every would-be professor who has a blog but can't get a job wonders whether he or she has perhaps been too outspoken in posting opinions for all the world and all its search committees to see.

Though these widely publicized negative implications of academic blogging have garnered the most attention, the more important indicator to keep an eye on is the coming recognition of academic blogging as legitimate scholarly activity in its own right. When the Google search "hired for blogging" finally returns more hits than "fired for blogging," we will know that the walls have come down and new media have rushed in to fill the void left by old media. Currently, the most successful academic bloggers tend to be highly productive in old media venues as well. The test cases that will show up in the near future are cases where a professor's main contribution to his field and his public takes the form of electronic publication or some form of blogging. Already we are seeing strange discrepancies in what counts as legitimate scholarly work: a substantive article self-published online is worth nothing, but when the identical article appears in print in a recognized journal, it instantly acquires academic seriousness and prestige. One minute it is not worth putting on a curriculum vitae, and the next minute it is. This distinction might be defensible if the peer review system of old media were really in good order, but it is not. Just as in journalistic old media, academic old media rely far too heavily on their prestige and reputation, along with the fact that they have not faced real competition in a long time. This is an area where the move to new media for academia will run fairly parallel to the move to new media for journalism.

The credibility of old media systems is drastically overextended. New media such as blogs have not yet evolved credible systems for accountability, peer review, quality control, and academic reputation. Publishing in an online journal is still widely considered to be inferior to publishing in a print journal. But the phrase "widely considered" gives the game away, revealing that what is at work here is a sociology of knowledge and reputation rather than a hard, definable criterion of quality. As soon as promotion and tenure committees have to ask these questions about their colleagues, it will be up to them to establish some criteria for saying which publications should be rewarded and which should be discouraged. Those decisions are being made right now in college after college. In the academic world, the question is not "Does blogging pay?" but "Is blogging tenurable activity?" As soon as there are enough publicized cases of scholars being hired for blogging, promoted for blogging, and tenured for blogging, the incentive system will be in place, the inertial weight of academic decision-making will swing around, and the work of scholars will surge forward across the new media frontier. In the meantime, blogging may also be able to establish itself as a viable form of academic self-promotion, giving professors a higher profile and drawing students to come and study with the academic blogger who is already so well known through his work online. Blogs can publicize a professor's academic interests more thoroughly than any marketing department could possibly do, and reach the right audience. As institutions begin to see this kind of academic publicity pay off, academic blogging will probably buy its way into academic respectability through the marketing and admissions departments.

There is a great deal of work to be done before the Internet is a hospitable place for academic virtues such as peer critique, accountability, deliberative discourse, and editorial credibility. But that is precisely the kind of work academics are eager to do and have been trying to do under the restraints of the old media systems. The move to new media might well bring the solution to the entrenched problems of the old media.

12

VIRTUAL CLASSROOMS, REAL LEARNING

Jason D. Baker

www.BakersGuide.com

THE INTERNET HAS SIGNIFICANTLY CHANGED education in the past decade. A recent study by the Sloan Consortium revealed that three and a half million higher education students in the United States were enrolled in at least one online course. This represents almost 20 percent of college students and doesn't include those taking blended or web-enhanced classes or the many homeschoolers and K-12 students using the Internet in education.

More than two-thirds of all colleges and universities currently offer some type of online instruction with the majority of those offering fully online courses and programs as part of their educational catalog. Clearly these institutions are responding to a demand in the marketplace since online enrollment is growing at over six times the rate of the overall higher education student population. Furthermore, the largest accredited private university in the United States is the for-profit University of Phoenix, with approximately half of its 250,000 students attending their online campus. Online learning is also growing rapidly in the K-12 arena, particularly with the development of virtual charter schools, online homeschooling academies, and web-based curriculum supplements used in public, private, and homeschools.

Given the global mission of the church, it's not surprising that Christians have employed the latest technologies to promote learning.

Christians have been in the forefront of distance education, with such milestones as circular letters written by the apostle Paul in the first century, the use of the printing press to spread sermons and writings during the Reformation, the Moody Bible Institute's development of Bible correspondence courses in 1901, and Regent University's launch of online graduate programs in 1995. There are currently Christian education programs offered online from kindergarten through the doctoral level, offering instruction to students who wouldn't otherwise be able to attend classes on campus. Such rapid growth obviously raises a number of questions that are worthy of consideration, not the least of which is whether online learning actually works and if it's consistent with a biblical perspective of education. Since personal relationships are central to the biblical model of training and equipping, can online learners actually develop real relationships, form communities, and engage in *koinonia*, or is this merely an individualized and decontextualized approach to sate a consumer-driven culture?

This chapter will consider this growing online learning phenomenon. In particular, the chapter will highlight how the Internet is used to teach online and blended courses, what faculty and students report about their experiences, and how to select a suitable program. Since not all Christians are in favor of using the Internet for education, particularly the practice of fully-online instruction, the chapter will conclude with a critique of this phenomenon and recommendations for enhancing the online learning experience.

ONLINE LEARNING BASICS

Distance education has been traditionally defined as planned learning that occurs where the students are geographically (and often chronologically) separated from the instructor. Distance education can incorporate a variety of media including printed workbooks, audiotapes or compact discs, videotapes or DVDs, telephone conferences, cable or satellite television, videoconferencing, e-mail, or the World Wide Web to deliver the instruction or facilitate student interaction. Distance education is actually not a new field—American universities have run correspondence and distance degree programs for over one hundred years. But with the emergence of the Internet, online learning has become the dominant delivery model, and the practice has moved into the mainstream of education.

Rather than engaging in self-paced independent study, most online courses involve regular class schedules, online student discussions, and plenty of deadlines. Some even include group projects, online presentations, and live chat sessions to help develop a sense of academic community among participating students. Courses are generally developed in online course management systems, computer software designed to support virtual online classrooms, with Blackboard and Moodle being two of the more popular. Such systems enable instructors and learners to post content, participate in discussions, maintain a gradebook, keep a roster, track participation, and generally engage in learning activities in an online environment.

Despite the variety of technologies available, most online courses have adopted a seminar-style approach. Content traditionally presented in a classroom lecture is generally delivered through a combination of printed online materials (such as PowerPoint presentations or text-laden web pages) and audio or video podcasts. Where online learning separates itself from previous types of distance and correspondence courses is the use of online discussions to engage students with the instructor and with each other. In most online courses, these topical discussion boards form the heart of the online learning experience. Students congregate in the online course site and, after reviewing the week's lecture and reading materials, participate in a bulletin-board-style conversation about weekly discussion questions. Typically the instructor interjects comments throughout the week, but the core interaction is among the students themselves. Course assignments are generally written, such as research papers, case studies, and discussion question responses, and are submitted to the instructor in the CMS (course management system) or via e-mail. The instructor then provides general class feedback by posting to the class discussion board while one-on-one communication occurs through e-mail.

Let's highlight typical online learning activities to gain a sense of the dynamics of an online class. Some courses may follow a traditional semester schedule, while others may start every few weeks throughout the year. What they probably have in common is that they lack a set class meeting time; so instead of meeting for class three mornings a week, you're expected to log into the course management system regularly throughout the week to read, watch, or listen to new material from the instructor and engage in online discussion. After registering for the course (probably online), you're likely directed to a virtual bookstore where you order your textbooks and other supplemental reading materials. When the materials arrive, you'll likely notice that the enclosed syllabus outlines the entire course (which is divided into weeks rather than class sessions), including weekly readings, discussion questions, group projects, and major papers, so you can map out your schedule for the duration of the course. On the first day of class, you'll be expected to log into the course site and read various messages posted by the instructor such as an introduction to the class, a podcast commentary on the week's reading, instructions for how to use the discussion forum, and your first week's assignments.

As with traditional classes, the first week is often a time to get acclimated to the course content and participants; so you'll probably be asked to post a brief biographical sketch to the discussion forum as a way to introduce yourself to the class. Throughout the week you'll get to know your classmates through the online discussions and begin to engage in dialogue based on the interaction questions that your instructor posted. Perhaps you'll have to summarize the required readings for the week, answer a reflective question based on the instructor's podcast, participate in a group debate, take an online quiz, or share ideas for a future writing assignment. Regardless of the specifics, you'll find that these regular online discussions help set the tone for the remainder of the course.

Web 2.0 and newer technologies such as blogs, wikis, podcasts, vodcasts, social networking, and virtual worlds are beginning to change the dynamics of online courses. In addition to asynchronous faculty and student interaction in the virtual classroom space, more synchronous collaboration is occurring in online courses. Additionally, students and faculty alike are using blogs, podcasts, and other content creation tools to reflect on the course content and engage with others outside the classroom. Where the emergence of online learning adds interaction and collaboration to the distance education experience, these new technologies are extending the learning experience outside even the virtual classroom into the professional and personal contexts of the instructors and learners.

ONLINE LEARNING EFFECTIVENESS

It's probably not too surprising that the first question many ask when considering online learning is, is it as effective as face-to-face education? It seems this question is asked every time an educational approach differs from the norm. It was asked with early distance education efforts, it was asked with homeschooling, and it is now being asked about online learning. The answer is a resounding yes. Now let's be clear about what's being asked—does this mean that all online instruction is as effective as all face-to-face instruction? No. Does this mean that online instruction is the ideal mode for all students? Of course not. However, numerous studies have demonstrated that alternative educational experiences, such as online learning, can produce outcomes similar to face-to-face instruction, provided that the method and technologies used are appropriate to the instructional tasks, there is student-to-student interaction, and there is timely teacher-to-student feedback.

The vast majority of research indicates that online students learn and retain information as well as, if not better than, those in traditional classes. Furthermore, the use of the Internet for class discussion makes many distance courses more interactive than face-to-face courses (at least the large, lecture-hall types). In addition, unlike the stereotypical correspondence courses, online courses are generally not easier than their campus equivalents. Sometimes online courses are virtually identical to their campus counterparts including lectures recorded during an actual class (although delivered via podcast rather than in person), while at other times they involve increased reading, group projects, and class participation, thus actually making them harder. Additionally, there has been increased scrutiny of online courses, which makes it more difficult for an institution to achieve accreditation with low-quality online offerings.

One famous research review identified over 350 research reports, summaries, and papers from 1928 to the present that demonstrated no significant learning difference between distance and face-to-face courses. This has been termed "the no significant difference phenomenon." In other words, the research indicates that media or delivery method is not the determining factor in educational effectiveness. However, a more recent examination of 232 comparative studies concluded that while there is no average difference in achievement between distance and classroom courses, the results demonstrate wide variability. In other words, while the average results are the same, a large number of online courses are significantly better, and a large number are significantly worse. This is analogous to having one foot in a fire and another on ice and noting that on average you're comfortable. These findings suggest that the central issue isn't whether a course is taught online or face-to-face but rather the effectiveness of the instructor, the course design and content, and the appropriateness of the course to the student. This shouldn't be surprising—after all, most of us have experienced both excellent and awful courses in our academic lifetimes—but while we have had years of experience in traditional education, few have had similar breadth of online classes.

ONLINE LEARNING EXPERIENCES

Studies into student perceptions of online learning regularly reveal three benefits of the experience: convenience, interaction, and community. One researcher at a large state university frequently notes that the top three reasons that students enroll in online courses are convenience, convenience, and convenience. This is consistent with how institutions regularly market themselves. An informal survey of promotional materials reveals that many institutions tout convenience, not learning, as the centerpiece of online distance programs. Prospective students are told that they can take courses anywhere, anytime, and without significant disruption to life. Similarly, student surveys regularly reveal increased satisfaction with the opportunity to pursue coursework or a degree that wouldn't otherwise be available. If convenience were the only benefit of online learning, one would have to wonder whether educational quality and rigor were being sacrificed in the process. However, increased interaction and community are also highlights of online learning reports.

Online classes offer many possibilities for student interaction— that is, interpersonal and group discussion among students within a particular class. Such interaction can broadly be divided into synchronous and asynchronous discussion. Synchronous communication occurs when multiple students are online simultaneously and communicating with one another, such as with Skype or Instant Messaging. Some schools require all students to log into an online conference room for weekly lecture and discussion, thus simulating the traditional classroom dynamic. Asynchronous communication is conversation that doesn't occur in real time, such as with e-mail or threaded discussion boards, and is even more popular in online courses. Such asynchronous communication enables students to participate at times personally convenient, which makes it possible to offer online classes with students scattered throughout the country or around the world. Proponents of asynchronous discussion list numerous benefits: shy students may be less intimidated to participate, quick-thinking students cannot dominate discussions, student writing skills are improved through online discussion, and the additional time for reflection and research has the potential to increase the quality of student discussions.

The growing popularity of online learning has resulted in an interest in the application of virtual groups and teams within the educational process. This has been consistent with the continued promotion of collaborative and cooperative learning within higher education. The resulting studies have found that students can indeed develop a sense of classroom community with both task and social components. Furthermore, such community has been found to positively impact cognitive learning, affective learning, student satisfaction, and overall learning effectiveness. This is particularly interesting since the stereotype of online learners is that they're isolated individuals, and yet the research findings are exactly opposite.

SELECTING AN ONLINE PROGRAM

Given the growing number of online programs, how can you ensure that you're selecting a quality program rather than an inferior one? The first step is to choose a program offered by an accredited institution. Within the United States, accreditation from a recognized agency such as one of the six regional accreditors or the Association of Theological Schools is the generally accepted standard of academic quality for colleges, universities, and seminaries. This standard is generally what colleges use to determine whether your undergraduate degree is acceptable for graduate school, what companies use to determine tuition remission, and what student loan programs use to determine eligibility. When considering an online undergraduate or graduate program, such accreditation is essential to ensure the educational quality and marketability of your degree. This is why Baker's Guide to Christian Distance Education (www.BakersGuide.com) only lists accredited institutions in the directory of online degree programs. On the K-12 level, the issue gets more nuanced, especially since some parents choose online courses to supplement their homeschooling, while others enroll their children in virtual public or private schools. In this case, resources from the Home School Legal Defense Association, the Association of Christian Schools International, and BakersGuide.com can help parents select reputable online programs.

Once you know you're dealing with an accredited institution, the next step is to determine whether the program fits your needs and learning style. It's important to consider whether the courses match your area of interest, how long the program will take, how much it costs, the possibility of transfer credits, and whether you need to participate in any on-campus residency sessions. You should note that while it is possible to apply a virtually unlimited number of transfer credits (or credits for prior learning, portfolios, and the like) to most undergraduate programs, graduate programs generally accept a minimal number of transfer credits (six to nine is typically the maximum) and no prior learning or portfolio credits. Furthermore, some online programs (usually graduate degrees) require some on-campus residency time, often in the form of modular courses or seminars. On the K-12 level, some courses require the parents to serve as co-teachers, while others have online instructors tutor the students directly. Such options should be weighed when selecting courses and programs.

It's also helpful to consider whether the program matches your learning style preferences. There are a variety of online delivery methods including book reading, podcast lectures, online video lectures, synchronous (live) interaction, asynchronous discussion boards, independent study, collaborative group learning, and more. If you know, for instance, that you prefer listening to reading, then you might want to seek out a program that uses podcasts or iTunesU for regular lectures rather than one that delivers the content exclusively through articles, books, and web pages. Similarly, if you're an introvert who prefers reflection over rapid discussion, then courses that use threaded discussions would be more beneficial than live online classes. One of the potential benefits of online learning is that you can not only fit courses into your life context, but you can select ones that will maximize your learning.

CRITIQUE OF ONLINE LEARNING

One of the critiques of online learning, regardless of the associated technologies or instructional design, is that the very act of separating learners from their instructor and one another deprives students (and faculty, for that matter) from developing a complete relationship. As God created man as an integral body-mind/soul/spirit being, any attempt to educate without engaging both the body and the mind, soul, and spirit is necessarily limited. An extensive body of empirical research has demonstrated that online students can develop a strong sense of community. Similar research has revealed that students in a Christian learning cohort develop an even stronger sense of community than students in a secular learning cohort, although the face-to-face courses still exceed the online courses in such levels.

Clearly the biblical precedent for both divine communication (e.g., Hebrews 1) and human communication (e.g., Philippians 2) is incarnational, and so the question is whether incarnational communication can occur in an online learning environment. Can students who are not located in the same place, who cannot share meals together, who cannot touch one another, actually develop real relationships and thus fulfill the biblical model of incarnation? Additionally, numerous models of distinctly Christian education incorporate the concept of community, often using the biblical term *koinonia*. One leading Christian education author notes the centrality of nurturing relationships within the learning process and uses the metaphor of pilgrimage to highlight the relational dynamic between teacher and student.

If a learning community is essential to a biblical model of education, and it cannot be cultivated in an online learning environment, then Christians must reject distance education as a viable model for education. If such a community can be developed, however, then Christian educators need to seek ways of fostering it within online courses. Clearly online learning can result in isolation and detachment as a result of the physical separation of students. Not only can isolation adversely influence a student's attitude toward learning, and arguably learning outcomes as well, but the concept of learning exclusively in isolation runs counter to biblical themes. As evidenced in 1 Corinthians 12, God gives his people different gifts that are to be manifested for the common good. This can best occur in a strong community environment where people love and edify each other and where excessive individualism is avoided; hence the analogy of the parts of the body in that same passage. Such a caring environment should counter student feelings of isolation and detachment.

The apostle Paul offers an interesting case study in distance education. On the one hand, his circular letters were a primitive form of distance learning. On the other hand, he clearly indicated his preference for being physically present with his churches, and his separation was usually a result of imprisonment rather than inconvenience. Arguably, one can view the Pauline model as a form of blended learning, where instruction occurs both face-to-face and at a distance.

Online learners don't live, move, and have their being with their classmates, which is a disadvantage for Christian education since believers rightly value the extra-cognitive aspects of the educational experience. Missing from many online learning programs are the personal connections formed between students and among students, professors, and staff during meals and ministry activities, in socializing while waiting for class to start or during course breaks, in personal exchanges that take place during visits to the offices of faculty and staff, and in numerous other seemingly insignificant encounters on and off campus.

IMPROVING ONLINE LEARNING

There is a flip side to this discussion, however, and that raises the possibility that Christian online learning can actually be a uniquely beneficial model of instruction. The advantage of access (distance education makes formal instruction accessible to those who would otherwise not be able to attend a school, college, or seminary) is the most obvious benefit but not necessarily the most profound. Arguably one of the most significant results of the growth in online education is the recognition that the educational experience extends outside of the classroom. In other words, there's more to Christian education than textbooks and lectures and classrooms, and the distance model has the potential of offering an alternative approach than that taken by most Christian schools.

In weighing the concerns of the critics concerning the diminished learning community experienced by distance learners, there would appear to be at least four responses: accept the trade-off, enhance institutional engagement, blend the online learning experience, or extend the learning community.

The first option is simply to accept the difference as a consequence of teaching online and chalking it up as a logical trade-off—online learning extends access to students who would otherwise not be able to take classes on campus, but they necessarily give up the larger social experiences that they would receive online. This is not an unreasonable solution; after all, millions of students are voluntarily accepting such a trade-off and enrolling in online courses. Given the increased availability of Christian education made possible by online learning, perhaps Voltaire's declaration that "the better is the enemy of the good" would rightly apply in this case.

A second option is to enhance the institutional engagement with the online learner. Rather than limiting the experience to online or offline distance courses, perhaps an institution could make additional resources and opportunities available to the distance students. Faculty might consider real-time opportunities for students such as virtual office hours, telephone conference calls, instant messaging availability, or streaming campus classes over the Internet using real-time videoconferencing. Opportunities for brief residential experiences such as residency sessions, modular classes, special event weekends, and other face-to-face activities could also serve to enhance the overall community experience for online learners.

Blended course designs represent a third approach. Such a distance education model is broadly similar to the blended model used by the apostle Paul that included both face-to-face and correspondence components. This blended approach is particularly appropriate for Christian education since believers are part of a larger invisible church and have a shared identity that can be harnessed even in limited gatherings.

A fourth option is to extend the campus community beyond the physical campus and the virtual classroom. Rather than seeking ways to draw the online learners into the campus community, campus leaders can seek ways of enriching the distance learners' existing community connections. By arranging mentoring relationships, experiential learning activities, internships, professional networking events, and similar experiences, an institution can increase the online learners' local sense of community. While this may seem to be an inverted approach to fostering community, it has the potential of putting the institution in a position to positively affect the students' larger culture, which is not inconsistent with a Christian philosophy of education.

Much of the research into virtual community has focused on the relational dynamics that appear in synchronous chat rooms, asynchronous discussion boards, e-mail, and other mediated environments. Such community experiences are then compared to their face-to-face counterparts and, not surprisingly, criticized as shallow imitations of the ideal. Such approaches fail to consider that the learner, regardless of geographic location, is simultaneously a member of multiple communities—academic, vocational, familial, social, and others—and these communities exert influence even when they're not in focus.

CONCLUSION

One significant problem with many of these critiques is that they accept an institutional model of education as the basis of evaluation rather than considering other models of education and training, such as those found in the Bible. (This isn't to say that schools are not biblical; they appear at least as far back as the post-exilic period.) Scripture is full of a variety of instructional techniques (including oral, written, and interactive teaching, formal repetition and memorization, as well as on-the-job training, formal and informal learning, etc.) while not exalting any particular technique as exclusive. It's interesting to see that even God communicates with his people using a variety of methods throughout history.

Clearly different communication media may be better suited to different applications within the educational endeavor. For all of the benefits of the Internet, for example, there are many valuable characteristics of print. While teachers harness some of these in online courses (since the written word is a significant component of most online courses), there may be times when books are more appropriate for instructional communication than web sites. Similarly, the use of audio or video can be far more effective than print for certain educational ends and should be used accordingly regardless of whether the class is taught online or face-to-face. This isn't to say that technologies (or media) are value-free but that there needs to be appropriate consideration when matching the media and mode to the learning environment.

Marshall McLuhan, famous for his quote "the medium is the message," proposed a tetrad as a means of examining the various patterns embedded within a medium. His tetrad asks four questions about a particular communication technology: What does it enhance? What does it obsolesce? What does it recover (that had previously been made obsolete)? What will it reverse into when it reaches its own limits? When considering online learning, one could say that online learning enhances learning communities by abolishing time and distance as a hindrance to collaborative learning, obsolesces centralized and edited control of information as anyone can produce or consume instructional content, and retrieves writing as a major form of instructional communication for both teachers and students. And while some would probably say that the current online classroom would reverse or flip into virtual reality (such as Second Life and beyond) when the limits of the medium are reached, I'm inclined to think that the greater change will be a systematic acknowledgment of knowledge and competencies rather than institutional educational processes. While I'm no futurist, I suspect that just as homeschooling has produced scores of well-educated students apart from the institutional school system, so will future online education elevate personalized education apart from the institutional establishment.

Rather than considering a model where the school, university, or seminary classroom is the center of learning, consider a contextual model where the primary learning environment is the student's existing home, church, or workplace. By harnessing the locality of the students rather than ignoring or minimizing it, such online education pedagogy offers the potential of a rich complement to traditional campus experiences rather than an inferior substitute.

13

POLITICS AND JOURNALISM

Scott Ott

www.ScrappleFace.com

RETIRED LT. GENERAL RICARDO SANCHEZ gave a speech in October 2007 to a convention of journalists who cover the military in general and the war in Iraq specifically. The speech had two parts.

(1) A scathing attack on reporters who twist the truth, fail to report the good news in the U.S. war effort, have no regard for the reputations of people who sacrifice their lives to defend the country, and therefore who literally become accomplices in the slaughter of U.S. troops.

(2) The second half of the speech addressed what Sanchez felt were the shortcomings of, mostly, the State Department in failing to develop a "grand plan" for Iraq, incorporating the military, economic, and diplomatic elements of a holistic victory. During the course of those remarks, he said that for the American people Iraq had become a "nightmare with no end in sight." He went on to make the case that the U.S. must stay and fight and work in a variety of ways to solve this seemingly insoluble problem.

Predictably, headlines on all the major national news web sites for the next several days trumpeted the phrase "nightmare with no end in sight."

Neglected in all mainstream media reports was even a passing mention of the fact that the former commander of U.S. forces in Iraq had lambasted the journalists and their employers. The first half of his speech was entirely ignored.

At ScrappleFace.com, my satirical news blog, I posted a story that

SCOTT OTT

included a Top 10 list of "least newsworthy remarks" from the Sanchez speech. Here are the best of them:

> 3. "In my business, one of our fundamental truths is that 'the first report is always wrong'. Unfortunately, in your business 'the first report' gives Americans who rely on the snippets of CNN, if you will, their 'truths' and perspectives on an issue."
>
> 2. "When you assume that you are correct and on the moral high ground on a story, because we have not responded to questions you provided, is [*sic*] the ultimate arrogance and distortion of ethics. One of your highly-respected fellow journalists once told me that there are some amongst you who 'feed from a pig's trough'. If that is who I am dealing with, then I will never respond, otherwise we will both get dirty, and the pig will love it. This does not mean your story is accurate."
>
> 1. "All are victims of the massive agenda-driven competition for economic or political supremacy. The death knell of your ethics has been enabled by your parent organizations who have chosen to align themselves with political agendas. What is clear to me is that you are perpetuating the corrosive partisan politics that is destroying our country and killing our service members who are at war. . . . For some of you, just like some of our politicians, the truth is of little-to-no value if it does not fit your own pre-conceived notions, biases and agendas."

I harvested those Sanchez quotes from a verbatim transcript that appeared on a web site within hours of the speech. I linked to the transcript so ScrappleFace readers could determine the context of the quotes. I was not alone. Dozens, if not hundreds, of political bloggers posted excerpts from the speech, linked to the full transcript, and noted how mainstream media sources had ignored the harsh critique of their own trade while magnifying the rebuke of the Bush administration's management of the war. As a result, millions of blog readers learned what Lt. Gen. Sanchez actually said that day, while those whose news diet came exclusively from the kitchens of the mainstream media received only the appetizer.

The new media have utterly changed the world of politics and journalism in ways never imagined by A. J. Liebling, the journalist and press critic who wrote, "Freedom of the press is guaranteed only to those who own one."[1] Liebling would be delighted that today literally every American has access to a distribution channel for his views with a potentially global reach.

CREDIBILITY

In 1984, as a cub reporter for *The Centre Daily Times*, a Knight-Ridder paper that then boasted twenty-five thousand daily readers, I attended a gathering of journalists in Harrisburg, Pennsylvania. In the midst of a roundtable discussion on the "profession" of journalism, my colleagues from around the Commonwealth bemoaned the lack of public respect for our trade and for the stalwart professionals who ply it. One veteran scribe suggested that if we had a professional certification process, people would trust us more, like they trust doctors and lawyers.

It was all I could take. With more passion than wisdom, I spoke up in the presence of my elders.

The last thing in the world I want, said I, is for people to increase their trust in what appears in my newspaper or to put their skepticism on hold because I'm a certified doctor of credibility. We all know what a sausage factory the newsroom is. Speed trumps accuracy. Clever beats comprehensive. Bias lurks behind the thin veil of quotes from experts. I don't want people to trust me more. I want them to trust me less. I want them to have access to multiple reports of any news event. I want them to critically compare what the various journalists recorded. If anything, I want a certification process for news readers and watchers, so they're trained to notice the subtle ways we steer the story—not wherever the facts may lead but to our own predetermined destinations. Even the best of us, with the highest integrity, find ourselves involuntarily hobbled by our humanity and our skewed view of reality.

Of course, that's what I recall saying twenty-three years ago. I didn't take notes.

That twenty-three-year-old small-town reporter could not have imagined what would happen in his lifetime.

As a result of the new media, primarily bloggers on the Internet and user-generated video sites like YouTube.com, readers are no longer hostage to one eyewitness account of events.

---

[1]A. J. Liebling, "Do You Belong in Journalism?," *The New Yorker*, May 14, 1960.

RADICAL TRANSFORMATION IN COMMUNICATION

Cheap, user-friendly technology and a pervasive global communication network have combined to radically transform the world in which we live. Today many people know more on a daily basis about the lives of Buddhist monks in Burma than they do about their relatives in Philadelphia or Kansas City.

The implications for politics may be self-evident. Journalists and politicians have enjoyed a symbiotic relationship for years, each feeding off the other for their mutual benefit. Message control was the chief currency in the relationship. There was a continual balancing act between the need for the politician to present himself in a certain way to the public and the need of reporters to get interesting stories. If the reporter pressed too hard, he would lose access to the politician. If the politician treated the reporter like a PR flack, the journalist could cut off his access to his constituency.

The essence of politics has not changed, but the relationship has. The reporter's role has become far less significant because the candidate now has ways of getting his message out through myriad blogs, YouTube, social networking sites, and his own web site. Because no single journalist controls content distribution, theoretically the political candidate is free to shop the marketplace of distribution channels and choose those that best suit him. However, the reality is more complex.

Today a politician can "go direct" by posting text, audio, or video on his own site or on user-generated content sites like YouTube. However, this is blatantly self-promotional and therefore lacks credibility.

He can also tap the power of the information network by doing or saying something that intrigues bloggers, thus inspiring them to write about him.

To match the reach of, say, *The New York Times*, you have to get hundreds of bloggers, or a few big ones, to write about you. Human nature being what it is, the best way to get people to write about you is to say something stupid or do something scandalous. But of course this won't advance your cause in the way you had hoped.

The alternative strategy, though much harder to pull off, can result in hundreds of positive posts in the blogosphere (a widely accepted term coined by Bill Quick of DailyPundit.com, to describe the world of blogs).

Here's the three-part strategy for a politician to attract the attention of the blogosphere:

1. Be yourself.
2. Say what you mean.
3. Do what you say.

Of course, bloggers would also appreciate it if you would treat them with respect, or at least as much respect as you accord to reporters in the mainstream media—not that most bloggers aspire to be part of what many of them call the LSM—Lame Stream Media (aka "the Dinosaur Media" or in radio host Rush Limbaugh's memorable phrase "the drive-by media").

It's a simple strategy, yet rare. Politicians illogically continue to employ "old school" tactics crafted by image makers, honed by non-stop opinion polls. As the influence of the new media grows, politicians and journalists alike will pay an increasingly heavy price for their failure to acknowledge the new reality.

The barbarians are at the gate of the once unassailable politico-journalistic fortress.

Once dismissed as cranky people in pajamas spewing unvarnished, and unedited, opinion based on hearsay and innuendo, many bloggers have attained respectability through the sheer dint of their skill, solid research, and prodigious production. Some of the best political writing in the world now appears on blogs run by people who have no aspiration to wear press credentials on a lanyard around their necks.

These barbarians come from a broad spectrum of professions. In addition, they have passions and expertise in areas beyond their professional skills.

When CBS news anchor Dan Rather produced a story in autumn 2004 about President George Bush's Texas Air National Guard service, alleging that the future Commander-in-Chief had received preferential treatment, bloggers raised questions about the provenance of a 1972 memo used in the story. The font used in the memo had proportional letter spacing, most likely produced with word processing software not available in an era when every office hummed and clacked with electric and manual typewriters. Instead of shattering Mr. Bush's political future, as some said Mr. Rather had tried to do, the story brought an end to the career of the news anchor whose reputation was second only to that of his predecessor, the revered Walter Cronkite. Apparently Mr. Rather and his staff had either failed to notice the flaw in the memo or simply didn't care. However, once CBS posted the memo on its news web site, bloggers debunked it within hours.

THE NEW SYMBIOSIS

Now, oddly enough, bloggers have a symbiotic relationship with political reporters. The "real" journalists gather the primary source data and write their stories for "legitimate" publications and networks. The bloggers then comb through their stories looking for nits—inaccuracies, misrepresentations, bias, and the like. They're not only scrutinizing the subject of the story—the politician, for example—they hold the journalist accountable to the truth, or at least to the facts, in a realm where truth can be what you make it. The journalist who ignores the rebukes of the blogosphere does so at his own peril.

For the blogger's part, he often provides the journalist with fodder for stories, advance word on news that's about to break, and even expertise not available in the mainstream newsroom. As a bonus, the blogger does all this for free.

Publications as exalted as the agenda-setting *New York Times* now quote bloggers with some frequency and even link to their sites. (It's about time they return the favor. Much of the traffic to sites like NYTimes.com in recent years has come via links from blogs.)

Within just a few months in 2007, most mainstream media web sites began proactively strengthening their ties to the blogosphere by providing links next to their news stories to services like Digg, Techorati, Del.icio.us, Newsvine, StumbleUpon, Reddit, and Facebook.

These sites allow users to bookmark and comment on stories they read and to share the links with their friends and with anyone who visits those sites. This way readers help each other find stories of interest. A story that in the past might have gone unnoticed can get elevated to prominence through these social bookmarking sites. Essentially readers vote, and popular stories rise to the top.

This is a big step for the likes of *The New York Times*, the

Washington Post, and CNN. In the past they treated their sites like information silos, with few links to outside sources. Any links to other stories were limited to their own domain. Now they're immersing themselves in the blogosphere. Some of them even allow reader comments. At this writing, CNN provides a link under each story that pulls up a list of related blog postings. The *Washington Post* displays related blog headlines next to the story.

For the political process, all of this means that the era of controlling the message is dead. In a time of limited distribution and few gatekeepers, a political strategist could play the system to his advantage, thanks to a small number of known variables. Now there are innumerable distribution channels and virtually no gatekeepers, or rather millions of them. In this kind of world secrets rarely remain. The market controls the message. Adam Smith's "invisible hand" has reached from the world of economics into the realm of politics and journalism.

If this new media paradigm intrigues you, let's take a brief walk through my daily process of preparing stories for my satirical site, ScrappleFace.com, to give you a sense of the process and the potential of these new tools.

A DAY IN THE NEW MEDIA LIFE

After my morning devotional time, reading the Bible and praying, I sit down at my iMac in a spare bedroom. I literally pray each morning that the Lord will help me to write something that is true, that glorifies him, and that's entertaining enough to reach a lot of people. That may seem silly to some. After all, does God really answer the prayers of a satirist?

I think so.

In fact, in the Scriptures we read that when important people exalt themselves, God laughs—he holds them in derision (Psalm 2:4; 37:13). And what is satire if not holding in derision the ideas and statements of those who consider themselves important?

During these pre-dawn moments, I often also pray for the people in the news, our leaders and our enemies. Frequently I pray that Jesus will save Osama bin Laden, Kim Jong Il, Sheik Hassan Nasrallah, Ayman al-Zawahiri, Mahmoud Ahmadinejad, and others. I also pray for those on the other side of the political fence.

Once online, I first visit my iGoogle page. I have set it up to pull in the five to seven most recent headlines from mainstream media sources like *The New York Times*, the *Washington Post*, CNN, Fox News, ABC News, the Drudge Report, and *USA Today*. It saves me a lot of time I would have spent visiting each of these web sites. Anyone can do this. Just go to iGoogle.com, create a free account, and then follow the simple directions.

I skim the headlines. If I see a story that interests me, I open it as a tab in the background of my Firefox browser for later viewing.

Next I visit the Drudge Report. In many ways Matt Drudge has stolen the role of agenda-setter from *The New York Times*.

DrudgeReport.com is just a bunch of headlines linked to stories, usually at mainstream media sites. Drudge gets millions of visitors each day; so if he thinks a story is important, it's usually a self-fulfilling prophecy because his attention to it makes it important. By the way, Drudge does not want you to call him a blogger. He's just Drudge, and there's really no one like him.

Once I have eight or ten tabs open in my browser, I begin weeding out the ones I know I won't write about. I read a paragraph or two and make a quick decision. This is very much like what my editors at the *Centre Daily Times* did with the Associated Press newswire.

Sometimes I get an idea for a satirical story right away. If that happens, I copy the URL (the web address) of the page, and then I open another tab and go to the administration panel of my blog, ScrappleFace.com, and write the post. Within the story I will create a link to the "real" story that sparked my idea. Usually I read several stories on the subject and sometimes do more in-depth research to assure that I have my facts straight. Often it seems I do more research to write "fake" stories than mainstream journalists do to write "real" stories. The links help my readers better understand what I'm trying to lampoon and the point that I'm making.

More typically, I don't get an idea for a story right away, but I find some news stories more interesting than others.

However, when I find one I'd like to write about, I save it through a social bookmarking site called Del.icio.us. I put it in a category called Today. After I'm done reading through the news, I go to my Del.icio.us page and review the headlines I've saved.

Meanwhile, there are some interesting things going on behind the scenes. Each time I save a headline to Del.icio.us, it automatically appears on my Facebook page.

Facebook has become one of the top social networking sites, and you can do so many things with it that it would take a book to describe it. I have configured my Facebook to automatically display links to my ScrappleFace stories, as well as to the news stories I have bookmarked through Del.icio.us.

Of course, this all sounds rather confusing when you try to describe it in a book. (It's rich and delightful irony that you're now reading a good old-fashioned book about the new media.)

Don't worry if you don't understand all the technology—neither do I. Just learn enough to use it, and let the geeks of the world worry about how it works. I do know that all of this stuff allows people in every region on earth to read my daily writings.

Because my news satire depends heavily on readers understanding what I'm lampooning, I confine my news browsing to the most widely read sources in the mainstream media. However, there are two other sites I visit regularly.

FreeRepublic.com provides a wealth of user-posted links to stories. A lot of them are useless to me, but I browse the Freeper links daily because they often give me a heads-up on stories that are about to break on the national or global scene.

I also use Google Reader to skim a few blogs that regularly take the lead in breaking, or at least brokering, significant news stories: MichelleMalkin.com, InstaPundit.com, PajamasMedia.com, and PowerlineBlog.com.

As a result of all of this, I'm no longer at the mercy of distant gatekeepers who would determine what I read and watch, as well as when. I have now become a gatekeeper, not only for myself but for others, through the links I post at ScrappleFace, Del.icio.us, and Facebook.

Gone is the 6 o'clock evening news. I don't watch TV. I don't subscribe to a single newspaper or news magazine. Instead I read all of the major American news sources, as well as several British and French sites, and an occasional al-Jazeera (based in Qatar) or Pravda (in Russia) story. I focus only on the news that interests me, and I do it whenever I want. Thanks to my MacBook and iPhone, I also read the news wherever I want.

The gates are gone. The walls are gone. I am the barbarian, and so are you. Now we're on the inside.

BUT HOW DO YOU KNOW IT'S TRUE?

When you try to describe the blogosphere to the uninitiated, the question that arises most frequently is one of credibility. In an untrammeled marketplace of ideas, how can a reader discern what's true?

Of course, the question assumes that the old model provided an accurate picture of reality. But the more we peek behind the veil of the news business, the more we see that the newsroom was not so much a truth factory as a sausage factory. As Lt. Gen. Sanchez indicated in his critique of journalists, what we read is often shaped by less noble aspirations than a selfless pursuit of the truth. The news business has always been a mixed bag. Some reporters allowed their integrity to guide them; others were steered by their ambition. Usually it was a bit of both. In a free marketplace of ideas, the best way to determine the facts is to shop around. Just as you can establish the current market value of an item by surfing eBay.com and shopping dealers, so you can get closer than ever to the actual facts of an incident by comparing and contrasting the various portrayals of that event among the mainstream media, the blogosphere, YouTube, and other primary and secondary sources.

Here's a political example. For a few days in October 2007, Sen. Barack Obama, D-IL, made news and sent ripples through the blogosphere thanks to a photo of him and several other Democrat presidential candidates standing for the playing of our national anthem. While the other three on stage appropriately placed their right hand over their heart, Sen. Obama stood with his hands in front of him, fingers interlaced. I first saw the photo at FreeRepublic.com.

Immediately I suspected that it had been PhotoShopped (altered). I didn't write anything about it at ScrappleFace. I felt that I didn't have enough information. Later, through a blog, I found a video of the incident on YouTube. Now it became clear that the photo had not been altered. However, I noticed something else. Even though Sen. Obama had violated flag protocol by not saluting by placing his hand over his heart, he appeared to be the only person on the platform singing "The Star-Spangled Banner." Reading his lips, it seemed that he actually knew the words, which is always a bonus for a senator who seeks to be President.

In the days when the dinosaur media stalked the earth unchallenged, this photo never would have appeared in public. If it had, it might have elicited a letter to the editor or two from veterans who fought to defend that flag, but that would be the end of it.

But in the new media age, the photo rapidly began cropping up on blogs. In light of the senator's previous remarks that he no longer wears an American flag lapel pin because he thinks it trivializes patriotism, this failure to salute the flag forced the candidate and his staff to answer more questions about his peculiar brand of patriotism.

THE NEW MEDIA REFORM POLITICS, JOURNALISM

The new media revolution affects politics at its core by demanding greater transparency from candidates and elected officials and faster responses to allegations and events, as well as constant awareness of the socially networked world in which we now live.

Journalists and politicians must now contend with what überblogger Glenn Reynolds calls "An Army of Davids," a reference to the classic mismatched battle in which the giant warrior wound up flat on his back and headless at the hands of a diminutive opponent.

Every politician must now assume that every person with whom he comes in contact is recording the moment on video or audio or least blogging it through a mobile device. This ought to force him to behave with integrity and authenticity in every setting.

Every reporter must now assume that each sentence she writes will receive intense scrutiny, with every flaw highlighted and trumpeted throughout the blogosphere. This should force the reporter to do the research, triple-check the facts, withhold uncorroborated information, and restrain the urge to inject her bias into the story.

In other words, the new media have the potential to force a reformation of politics and journalism. This could become the fabled sunshine that is the best detergent. The potential for public shame just might drive politicians to tell the truth and journalists to tell it like it is.

THE NEW MEDIA CALLING

If you're a Christian who sees the new media as a way to have an impact in the world of politics, first consider your calling. You literally need a calling from God to engage in this arena persistently and effectively. If I *had to* get up each morning and read the often-tragic news of the day, I would become depressed. If not for my knowledge of God's sovereignty and my confidence in his calling, I couldn't bear it.

In fact, many ScrappleFace readers have told me that they enjoy the site because it keeps them from despairing about the news—either through humor or through illustrating that finite man does not have the ultimate word in history.

Technically speaking, blogging doesn't make anyone's list of spiritual gifts. Yet without a sense of calling from God, you'll quickly burn out. I can remember one prominent blogger telling me in the first few months of ScrappleFace that I should slow down because no one could maintain my pace over the long haul. Well, six years and more than 3,000 stories later I'm still going. It's not work for me. It's literally a joy and a calling.

So, whether you want to affect your local political scene or make an impact on a statewide, national, or global level, start with prayer and a sense of calling from God.

Next, realize that blogging takes passionate persistence and prodigious production. To develop a nucleus of regular readers you must provide regular content. You don't have to crank out new posts daily, but several times a week seems a reasonable minimum.

Blogging is a personal medium, so write in your own voice. You can quite literally do that by posting audio or video clips along with or instead of text.

If you're going to write about political, cultural, and moral issues, then it helps to have a discernible point of view (or at least a lame shtick like ScrappleFace) and a distinctive voice with which you express it.

Some bloggers have a specific niche based on who they are, what they do, or perhaps what they're passionate about. La Shawn Barber has become a go-to guest for cable news channels as a conservative, evangelical, African-American, female blogger. You can try to fit in that niche if you wish, but La Shawn owns it. Lores Rizkalla is a daughter of Egyptian-born parents who fled jihad and moved to America. She's a Christian, conservative, female blogger who has also done great work as a radio talk show host. Lores speaks with authority and yet with grace against Islamo-Fascist terrorism as she fights what she calls "the September 10 mentality" among politicians and pundits. You can read Lores at JustaWoman.org as well as hear her KRLA radio program and even see an online video talk show she does. She's a new media master.

You can use new media tools to highlight your cause, goad your peers to action, challenge your opponents to debate, or just express your opinion. Remember, the new media frontier guarantees you a channel but not an audience. You have to earn the audience day by day, one post at a time.

LIMITATIONS AND HAZARDS

The new media are not inherently good or bad. They make up another part of God's fallen creation that can be redeemed by those who trust in Christ.

Keep in mind that as a participant in the new media revolution, you have no immunity from criticism. If you decide to allow readers to comment on your blog, for example, you'll have to decide whether to edit them before they appear on the site, or you might allow direct posting and clean up any messes later. You'll also have to decide whether to interact with those who comment or simply provide a platform for readers to express themselves while you remain above the fray. The Internet is a rough-and-tumble world, and the language can be harsh. Some blog platforms provide ways to automatically weed out obscenities, but no system is perfect.

You'll also quickly discover that church-speak and Christianese are not spoken outside of church buildings and seminaries. Authenticity communicates most effectively. That may sound odd coming from a guy who makes up news stories every day. But even satire can be done with authenticity, integrity, and in a way that conveys truth.

Warning: Keep in mind that every word you write could remain online after you've gone on to be with the Lord in paradise. Cached (preserved) copies of your writings last longer than the half-life of plutonium-238. If you're pleased with your writing, you may enjoy leaving this legacy. If you post something that later embarrasses you, it's impossible to completely purge it from the public record.

THE REACH

When I checked this morning, in a single moment ScrappleFace.com had readers in twelve time zones around the world, including Europe and the Far East. There have been times when someone was reading ScrappleFace in every inhabitable time zone in the world. Most of the day, at any given time, more than a hundred people are on the site. During a typical twenty-four-hour period, ScrappleFace.com will entertain and inform two thousand to four thousand visitors, with frequent spikes to eight thousand or ten thousand. In a single day the site once had more than thirty thousand visitors. In the six years since I started ScrappleFace.com, more than twelve million people have stopped by. Many blogs have much more traffic than that.

When I was at Penn State in Journalism 101, tapping away on a typewriter, I could not envision this kind of power. The ability of a single person, from a spare bedroom, to reach a global audience was unthinkable by all but a few restless geeks back then.

Thanks to this technology, ScrappleFace has been mentioned by the likes of talk show hosts Rush Limbaugh, Glenn Beck, Mark Levin, Hugh Hewitt, Roger Hedgecock, Michael Medved, and Mike Gallagher. ScrappleFace has been quoted by Michelle Malkin, James Taranto, David Limbaugh, and many other pundits, not to mention literally thousands of bloggers, including some who write in French, German, Russian, and even Farsi. ScrappleFace material has appeared, with attribution, on web sites or in print editions of *The Wall Street Journal*, *The Philadelphia Inquirer*, *The Weekly Standard*, National Review Online, *World Magazine*, *The Kansas City Star*, the BBC, and even *Sports Illustrated*.

I don't tell you this to brag or show you how I'm living out my dream of *fama sine opulentia*—"fame without wealth." The reason I rattle off that list is to demonstrate how the world has fundamentally changed in the brief twenty-five years since I left Penn State.

I want to suggest that this technology opens a door for the proclamation of the gospel (or at least for the communication of a Christian worldview) that is unparalleled in history.

THE GOSPEL ACCORDING TO SCRAPPLEFACE

Before I launched ScrappleFace, I had intended to start a web site called something like Atheist.com. My idea was that I would attract those who are hostile to God, engage them in reasonable discussion, provide them with biblical wisdom, and so, I hoped, win them to Christ. Of course, I didn't really think it through. Who but the most committed atheists would even visit Atheist.com? By definition atheism is unlikely to attract such devotees. Nevertheless, as that idea was stewing in my head, I read a *Time* magazine story about a new phenomenon called blogging. Apparently there were thousands of weblogs online, and people were essentially writing things online that they used to trust only to a diary stuffed under a mattress. Now anonymous Japanese men could read about your life, loves, and failed diets.

Of course, I had no interest in baring my soul to the world, but the technology intrigued me. Here was a gizmo that made it simple to create a web site and write new stuff on it anytime you felt like it, without being a pathetic geek who lived on Pixie Stix and Mountain Dew and who wrote computer code at 3 A.M.

Instead of pursuing an overtly evangelistic or apologetic web strategy, I decided to use the gifts and passions that God has given me to make an impact in a sector of society about which I care deeply. Together with thousands of other citizen-journalists, we have created a force with which politicians and journalists alike must reckon.

The new media revolution provides a platform from which a Christian can demonstrate the sovereignty of God in every cranny of creation.

14

BLOGGING AND BIOETHICS

Joe Carter and Matthew Eppinette

www.EvangelicalOutpost.com; http://blog.aul.org

INTRODUCTION

In response to very real human suffering, the past quarter-century has seen unprecedented advancement in science, technology, and medicine. The result is both great opportunities for what it means to be human (longer life, greater health) as well as great threats to what it means to be human (using the weakest members of our human family for the health benefit of others). The harsh reality is that while bioethical issues such as cloning, stem cell research, reproductive technologies, abortion, euthanasia, and assisted suicide are increasingly confronting us in the media, in the public square, and in our personal lives, few people grasp the science involved in the *bio* or the moral dilemmas involved in the *ethics* of bioethics. No issue in our new century will have more of an effect on the way we live than biotechnology. Yet few Americans have reflected on how these advances will change their lives.

This chapter explores reasons why Christians have a particular responsibility to understand and be involved in bioethics, ways that blogging can be a means of informing Christians about bioethics, and practical tips for and examples of blogging to impact bioethics in the public square.

WHAT IS BIOETHICS, AND WHY SHOULD I CARE?

Questions regarding appropriate ways of acting in medical, human, life-and-death decisions are bioethical questions. One source defines bioethics as "The application of ethics to the fields of biological science, including medicine, genetics and related areas."[1] Bioethics involves medicine broadly, whereas traditionally medical ethics has focused more on the doctor-patient relationship and interaction.[2] In sum, "Bioethics involves distinguishing between what we should and should not pursue in matters of life and health."[3] The need for this discipline arises out of what H. Tristram Engelhardt calls "an embarrassment of riches; now that one can treat such [defects], *must* one treat them?"[4]

Bioethics is interdisciplinary in an age of hyper-specialization. It brings together philosophers, doctors, nurses, theologians, lawyers, and other specialists in order to make decisions and evaluate decision-making across a broad spectrum of interrelated fields. Bioethics is also unique in that it is committed to the idea of objective reality in an age of relativism. Underlying the quest for proper decision-making in this realm is the idea that an identifiable, correct way of acting exists and can be discovered.

There are at least five reasons that Christians should be involved in bioethics. First is what we'd call the "it can't happen to me" syndrome. The situations that arise in bioethics are often considered to be classic examples of situations that affect other people but have no bearing on our own lives. Other people must make painful decisions about the dying process; other people suffer from the problems associated with infertility; other people must make decisions about "spare" embryos. These are not problems that will touch our own lives, we think.

Yet even if we are not personally affected, our role as "neighbors" to people in a fallen world will lead us to face these concerns. Given the fact of human frailty and the current state of medical technology, it is likely that bioethics will touch our lives or a life very near ours at some point in the near future. A friend may experience an unexpected pregnancy and seek our advice. A parent's health may deteriorate to the point where decisions must be made about feeding tubes or respira-

---

[1]Stanley J. Grenz and Jay T. Smith, *Pocket Dictionary of Ethics* (Downers Grove, IL: InterVarsity Press, 2003), 13.
[2]See the entry for "Medical Ethics," in ibid., 74.
[3]John F. Kilner and C. Ben Mitchell, *Does God Need Our Help? Cloning, Assisted Suicide, & Other Challenges in Bioethics* (Wheaton, IL: Tyndale House, 2003), xii-xiii.
[4]H. Tristram Engelhardt Jr., "Ethical Issues in Aiding the Death of Young Children," in Ronald Munson, *Intervention and Reflection: Basic Issues in Medical Ethics*, sixth edition (Belmont, CA: Wadsworth/Thomson Learning, 2000), 158.

tors. Friends may find they are unable to have children and will seek technological solutions to cure their infertility.

The pace and proliferation of biomedical advancement also compels our involvement in bioethics. Nearly every week the media trumpet a new discovery, treatment, or advance in medicine. How are we to respond as Christians? In *Brave New Church: What the Future Holds*, Richard Kew says, "It would appear that research is advancing at such a pace that our ethical understanding of its consequences is unable to keep up with the moral outcome of our actions."[5] Science's outpacing of ethics places a burden on "the Christian community to step in and become society's conscience in some way or another."[6]

A third reason for our necessary involvement in bioethical issues relates to our rights and responsibilities as citizens. As Americans, we have a right to participate in the political processes of our country and the corresponding responsibility to inform ourselves on the issues. This is a responsibility not to be taken lightly. Notre Dame philosopher David Solomon says, "The political realm has replaced the ethical realm in our society."[7] George Annas, Boston University professor of health law, notes, "Ethics is generally taken seriously by physicians and scientists only when it either fosters their agenda or does not interfere with it."[8] University of Texas philosopher J. Budziszewski links our participation in politics to the biblical mandate to submit to authorities.[9]

Additionally, our responsibilities as citizens have bearing on our involvement in bioethics. Bioethics affects us not only on the personal level as individuals but also on the corporate level as members of the body of Christ. Richard Kew identifies "an array of impossible moral dilemmas" as a key trend that will have an effect on the church in the twenty-first century.[10] Bioethics touches areas of our lives that are deeply personal, often when we are physically and emotionally vulnerable. Many of our brothers and sisters in Christ are currently struggling

---

[5]Richard Kew, *Brave New Church: What the Future Holds* (Harrisburg, PA: Morehouse, 2001), 92.
[6]Ibid., 96.
[7]David Solomon, "An Ethics Presentation: Morality, Medicine and the New Millennium," lecture presented at the Diocese of Shreveport, Louisiana, sponsored by the Slattery Library and the University of Notre Dame Club of Northern Louisiana on April 16, 2002.
[8]George J. Annas, "Who's Afraid of the Human Genome?" *Hastings Center Report* (1989): 21. As cited in Kilner and Mitchell, *Does God Need Our Help?*, 157.
[9]J. Budziszewski, "The Problem with Liberalism," *First Things* 61 (March 1996): 20–26; http://www.firstthings.com/article.php3?id_article=3834.
[10]Kew, *Brave New Church*, 86.

with bioethical issues in their lives. Even more of our neighbors outside the church are in need of our counsel. In times of personal bioethical crisis, they tend to seek out communities of faith for objective, reasoned, biblically sound guidance. As the body of Christ, we must be ready to respond to those who are hurting, to reach out to them, and to point them to Christ, whether by providing prayer, encouragement, or ethical advice.

Finally, wisdom demands that we be prepared, that we develop a carefully reasoned, biblically based approach to bioethics before it is needed. Bioethical quandaries often arise suddenly and in the midst of personal crises. If we have not taken the time to prepare a godly response, we can easily slip into the popular medical ethos of our time, which "has been reduced to the measure of its *utilitarian* and *emotive* value, according to whether the options are *practically* and *emotionally* satisfying."[11] As Christians, we must reject this individual utilitarian approach by providing a God-centered alternative.

Let us turn our attention to the various issues that bioethics addresses. Here we will use three headings that capture many of the high-profile bioethics issues: Taking Life, Making Life, and Faking Life.

TAKING LIFE

In the fourth century B.C., a Greek physician named Hippocrates included in his oath a pledge to forbid the taking of life: "I will neither give a deadly drug to anybody who asked for it, nor will I make a suggestion to this effect. Similarly I will not give to a woman an abortive remedy." Two thousand years later, the profession Hippocrates helped create is in danger of completely abandoning these prohibitions. This first category of bioethics addresses the issues that were once common in the pagan days before Hippocrates: abortion (including "abortive remedies" such as abortifacient drugs), infanticide (i.e., partial-birth abortion), euthanasia (both voluntary and involuntary), and physician-assisted suicide.

Taking life progressed as individuals began to expect complete autonomy and control over their bodies. When disease has progressed

---

[11]Richard C. Eyer, *Holy People, Holy Lives: Law and Gospel in Bioethics* (St. Louis: Concordia, 2000), 13.

to the point where we can no longer control our health, we choose euthanasia—"good death." When we want to regain control over our bodies after becoming pregnant, we choose abortion. When we lose control over our will to live, we expect physicians to assist in our suicide. We are willing to kill ourselves or our children in a desperate attempt to regain one last measure of control.

MAKING LIFE

Until the 1970s, there was only one way for humans to make a baby— the sexual bonding of a man and a woman. Today there are at least thirty-eight ways, almost all of which can be done without sexual intercourse. In an attempt to conquer infertility we've developed dozens of methods, a veritable alphabet soup of acronyms, to create a child: IVF, IUI, ICSI, DI, AI, ET, etc.

The growing number of reproductive technologies has undoubtedly been a blessing to thousands of infertile couples. Yet the methods raise an equal number of ethical concerns. For instance, a number of the reproductive technologies violate God's ideal for the family by involving a third party (i.e., surrogacy, egg, or sperm donation). Other problems arise from the creation of "spare" embryos that will either be discarded or donated for "research" in which they are destroyed and harvested for their parts. The technology has also paved the way for new evils such as human cloning, the creation of "designer" babies, and the individualistic eugenics of preimplantation genetic diagnosis (PGD).

FAKING LIFE

Think of this third category like the third act of a story. However, this third act does not resolve the story. Instead, like a postmodern tale, this third act of bioethics only complicates the situation further by, as Chuck Colson and Nigel Cameron point out, faking life: "'disintegrating' the biological human and melding him with other species or machines."[12]

The issues in this category will be familiar to science fiction aficionados: genetic engineering (the creation of designer humans);

---

[12]Charles W. Colson and Nigel M. de S. Cameron, *Human Dignity in the Biotech Century: A Christian Vision for Public Policy* (Downers Grove, IL: InterVarsity, 2004), 137.

neuroethics (such as the use of psychotropic "enhancement" drugs or implantable brain chips); nanotechnology (the manufacture of molecular machines); cybernetics; and transhumanism (merging of man and machine to create a new form of existence).

All of these concerns seem fantastic and bizarre. Yet they are all being considered, debated, and pursued by biotechnologists.

The controversies in each of these categories—taking life, making life, faking life—raise serious challenges for the Christian community. How should we respond as Christians? Two bioethicists who have explored that question in detail are John Kilner and C. Ben Mitchell. They offer a model for addressing bioethics from a Christian perspective that is God-centered, reality-bounded, and love-impelled.

GOD-CENTERED

Our radical dependence on God must be our primary point of reference (Leviticus 19:18; Deuteronomy 6:5; Matthew 22:37–40). Because of our fallenness, our human reason is inadequate. A God-centered model, however, acknowledges that inadequacy and recognizes that God is more than adequate for the task (Psalm 14:3; 16:7; Proverbs 12:15; Luke 10:29–37; Romans 3:12; 8:7; 12:2; Galatians 5:22–23; Colossians 3:12–13; 1 Thessalonians 4:7–8; Hebrews 1:3).

REALITY-BOUNDED

To be realistic is to understand reality—the way things really are—and to live accordingly. Because God alone sees all of the reality that exists, we must put our trust in him and what he has revealed, both in creation and in Scripture. Indicators of God's intentions serve as guides or principles for moral living. Past and present realities include that God is the author of all creation (Genesis 1:1; Psalm 89), including humans who are made in the image of God (Genesis 9:6; James 3:9) and yet are fallen and sinful (Romans 3:23). The most important future reality is that Christ will return (1 Thessalonians 4:13–5:11) and will restore all of creation (Revelation 21:1).

By reflecting on these realities we can gain a better understanding of the legitimate boundaries. We will gain a better grasp of the forms, freedoms, and limits of autonomy, control, and technology.

LOVE-IMPELLED

All of life is to be directed by love for God and love for neighbor. We are to seek the greatest possible well-being of all persons within the bounds of reality as God has created and intended it. Love considers the consequences of our decisions (Matthew 22:34–40; John 13:34; 15:12; Romans 13:8–9; 1 Corinthians 10:24; Galatians 5:14; 1 John 3:16–17) and the motives for our actions (1 Corinthians 13:1–3; 2 Corinthians 9:7). Jesus shows us what love looks like in the face of suffering, whether from infertility or from impending death, and calls us to live in the same way (Mark 16:18; Luke 16:19–31).

Note the hierarchy in the layers of this model. An action that is not God-centered will not be consistent with reality, and actions that are not reality-bounded—particularly bounded by the realities of Scripture—will not be love-impelled. Furthermore, this model is unidirectional: decisions must accord with the layers above it in order to be ethical and consistent with a Christian worldview.

Because bioethics is an unfamiliar topic for most Christians, we've spent the bulk of this essay on explaining and defining bioethics, noting the challenges, and providing a basic model for responding as Christians. We believe that once these areas are established, most bloggers will be able to find creative ways (including methods outlined in the other chapters of this book) for incorporating the subject in their work.

Nevertheless, we do have a number of suggestions on how to use new media in a way that will enable you to inform yourself, educate your readers, and work toward bringing a Christian perspective to bear on issues of bioethics. Although there are numerous ways to approach this task, we've chosen to emphasize a narrative approach—using story, metaphors, books, and movies—to illuminate the Christian perspective on bioethics.

Raise Awareness

The single greatest contribution most bloggers can make in regard to bioethics is simply to help raise awareness of specific issues, particularly those that threaten human dignity. We often find that Christians are completely unaware of the challenges that arise, particularly from the emerging field of biotechnology. For example, when we speak or write about the creation of chimeras—hybrid creatures that are part human, part animal—many people assume we are talking about futuristic scenarios of science fiction rather than experiments that are taking place in university laboratories today. They are often shocked to learn about the professor at the University of Nevada who created the world's first human-sheep chimera—a creature that has 15 percent human cells and 85 percent animal cells.[13] Although the research was reported in the British press, it received very little attention by the U.S. media.

Even when the stories are covered by the mainstream media, they often pass from the public's attention before the underlying questions can even be examined. By helping draw attention to such articles, bloggers provide the invaluable awareness that is needed for the community of believers to provide an adequate response.

Shape the Language

The preservation of human dignity requires us to fight for the hearts and souls of our fellow man. One of the key ways in which bloggers can aid in this struggle is to reclaim the linguistic high ground. Language not only shapes the thought processes of individuals but molds the public discourse about bioethical issues. Dr. Leon Kass, former Chairman of the President's Council on Bioethics, provides a stark example:

> Consider the views of life and the world reflected in the following different expressions to describe the process of generating new life. Ancient Israel, impressed with the phenomenon of transmission of life from father to son, used a word we translate as "begetting" or "siring." The Greeks, impressed with the springing forth of new life in the cyclical processes of generation and decay, called it genesis, from a root meaning "to come into being." . . . The premodern Christian English-speaking world, impressed with the world as given by a Creator, used the term "pro-creation." We, impressed with the machine and the gross national product (our own work of creation), employ a metaphor of the factory, "re-production."[14]

When you stop to consider the differences between such phrases as "methods of procreation" and "reproductive technology," it begins to become clear why Christians are losing ground in the fight to preserve

---

[13]Claudia Joseph, "Now Scientists Create a Sheep That's 15% Human," *The Daily Mail*, March 27, 2007.

[14]Leon Kass, *Toward a More Natural Science* (New York: Free Press, 1988), 48.

the concept of human dignity. Any attempt to argue that embryonic human life is deserving of a particular moral status is undercut when we are using such phrases as "blastocysts produced by the technological advances of in vitro fertilization." The language of the factory and the language of human dignity are as incompatible as would be the interchangeability of machine and life. Such degradation of language only leads to linguistic confusion and muddy thinking.

Shape the Narrative

When commenting on news articles that touch on bioethical debates, Christian bloggers should "translate" the terms used in a way that does not allow the technical jargon to obscure the issues.

For example, Ernest Hemingway's shortest work of fiction is also one of his most haunting:

For sale: baby shoes, never worn.

This powerful story is a marvel of economy. In a mere six words and three punctuation marks, Hemingway is able to convey a sense of tragic loss without ever introducing a single character. Compare this to a story with a similar theme from an anonymous author:

Infant mortality rate: 6.9 deaths per 1,000 live births.

Although it lacks the emotional impact, this too is a model of brevity. Seven words, two numbers, a colon, a comma, and two periods are used to express—albeit rather dryly—an important fact about the human condition. Indeed, if Hemingway's story was not fictional, it could be considered a singular instance of the second story, a particular example of a more general phenomenon. This is a useful model for bloggers.

Often in bioethics the focus on science and technology tends to obscure the fact that we are dealing with human problems. But as the late media critic Neil Postman noted in an essay titled "Social Science as Moral Theology," "there is a measure of cultural self-delusion in the prevalent belief that psychologists, sociologists, anthropologists, and other moral theologians are doing something different from storytelling."[15]

---

[15]Neil Postman, *Conscientious Objections: Stirring Up Trouble About Language, Technology and Education* (New York: Vintage, 1992), 3.

Postman rejected the very idea that what "social scientists" (which includes bioethicists) *do* should even be considered empirical science. He used the distinctions made by philosopher Michael Oakeshott between processes (events that are bound by the laws of nature) and practices (events that result from human practices and decisions):

> I believe with Oakeshott that there is an irrevocable difference between a blink and a wink. A blink can be classified as a process, meaning it has physiological causes which can be understood and explained within the context of established postulates and theories; but a wink must be classified as a practice, filled with personal and to some extent unknowable meaning and in any case, quite impossible to explain or predict in terms of causal relations.[16]

Processes ("blinks") and practices ("winks") are easily confused when they use the language of numbers and quantification. As Postman explains, the scientist uses mathematics to assist in uncovering and describing the structure of nature, while the social scientist uses quantification merely to give precision to his ideas.

Blogging is often about the "winks," the practices and meanings of human behavior, which makes it a form of storytelling. At its best, blogging can even fill the role that Postman ascribes to social science: contributing to human understanding and decency. Bloggers who want to become deliberate bioethical storytellers, therefore, should learn how to incorporate the tools of social science in ways that help them create metaphors, illuminate archetypes, and "tell tales."

Engage Popular Culture

When Leon Kass took the helm of the newly created President's Council on Bioethics in 2002, he opened the council's first session in a peculiar way: he asked the other members to read Nathaniel Hawthorne's story "The Birthmark." Dr. Kass understood the irreplaceable role that narrative plays in developing a "richer understanding and deeper appreciation of our humanity."[17]

On almost every issue in bioethics, our initial introduction comes not through medical journals or scholarly articles but from stories and

[16]Ibid., 7.
[17]President's Council on Bioethics, *Being Human: Readings from the President's Council on Bioethics*; http://www.bioethics.gov/bookshelf.

narrative forms. Most of us first learn about infertility and surrogacy through the story of the biblical patriarch Abraham, his wife Sarah, and their servant Hagar. We are exposed to the themes of reproductive technology and genetic engineering through high school book reports on Aldous Huxley's *Brave New World*. Many of our fellow citizens recently gained their initial exposure to voluntary euthanasia from watching Clint Eastwood's Oscar-winning film, *Million Dollar Baby*.

In fact, movies are one of the primary media in which bioethical issues are most commonly presented. Just a few of the movies that have included bioethical concerns as primary to central plot are *Bella* (2006), *The Island* (2005), *Eternal Sunshine of the Spotless Mind* (2004), *Godsend* (2004), *Vera Drake* (2004), *Code 46* (2003), *Minority Report* (2002), *AI* (2001), *The 6th Day* (2000), *Bicentennial Man* (1999), *The Cider House Rules* (1999), *Gattaca* (1997), and *Citizen Ruth* (1996). Novels are also a key form for raising questions about medical ethics and biotechnology. Some of the most prominent in the last few years include Jodi Picoult's *My Sister's Keeper*, Kazuo Ishiguro's *Never Let Me Go*, and Margaret Atwood's *Oryx and Crake*.

Most people will react emotionally to such narratives—as the authors and directors intended—but few will examine their intellectual content. Bloggers can help illuminate the discussion of these issues by reviewing such films, books, plays, and stories from a Christian world-view. Exploring how reproductive and genetic freedom is addressed in *Gattaca* or pondering the implications of manipulating the human brain in *Eternal Sunshine* can help guide your readers in thinking Christianly about these issues.

CONCLUSION

Abortion. Euthanasia. Embryonic stem cell research. Some of the most contentious and disputed issues of our day are matters of bioethics. The lines are sharply drawn, and each side presents their arguments on the issues that touch on the very core of our humanity—dignity and worth, sickness and health, life and death.

Eventually either the Christian perspective on bioethics will achieve a dominant level of acceptance or the secularist view will win, slowly but assuredly, by default. Each path will lead to sharply different results. The Christian approach—God-centered, reality-bounded, and love-impelled—leads to freedom, equality, and respect for all humanity. Basing bioethics on utilitarian and emotive values, however, results in the degradation of human dignity. Which path we choose will determine the fate of bioethics. And the fate of bioethics will determine the fate of our future.

Examples

A number of blogs are devoted exclusively to bioethics, while many others address bioethical topics. Among the blogs that focus on bioethics, perhaps the most notable is the blog from the *American Journal of Bioethics* (*AJOB*) (http://blog.bioethics.net), which is written from an entirely secularist/utilitarian perspective. *AJOB* is regarded as the most high-impact scholarly journal for bioethics, and the *AJOB* blog is arguably in the same category.

Attorney and author Wesley J. Smith blogs on bioethics at Second Hand Smoke (http://www.wesleyjsmith.com). While Smith's views are in line with a Christian worldview, he does not argue in Christian terms or categories (e.g., the image of God). Similarly, the bloggers at bioethics.com—a site on which we were frequent contributors—address the issues of bioethics in a way that is consonant with a Christian worldview, yet use language that is common to the public square.

Joe has used the narrative approach to engage the issues of bioethics in a few posts on his blog. Examples include "She's Having a Fetus" (http://www.evangelicaloutpost.com/archives/003211.html), "Four Reasons You Might Be Aborted: An Open Letter to Fetal Humans" (http://www.evangelicaloutpost.com/archives/003669.html), and "Sex and Desire: The Role of Parental Aspiration in Gender Selection" (http://www.evangelicaloutpost.com/archives/001080.html).

Matthew has addressed the intersection of bioethics and fiction (both movies and books) in reviews and commentaries (which would be perfectly suitable blog entries) that he's written for a number of web sites. The Center for Bioethics & Human Dignity has several of Matthew's reviews (along with those of several others) archived on their web site (http://www.cbhd.org/resources/movies/index.html).

What these few examples reveal is the pressing need for bloggers who will engage the issues of bioethics from an explicitly Christian worldview.

Recommended Resources

John F. Kilner and C. Ben Mitchell, *Does God Need Our Help? Cloning, Assisted Suicide, & Other Challenges in Bioethics.*

The Center for Bioethics & Human Dignity (http://www.cbhd.org)— CBHD's primary web site, containing a wealth of original bioethics material written over the past decade.

Bioethics.com—a blog dedicated to news and commentary on bioethics issues.

Bioethics.gov—The web site of The President's Council on Bioethics, which contains the full text of all of the Council's reports.

Cloninginformation.org—the web site for the coalition Americans to Ban Cloning, which consists mainly of Washington-based organizations and lobbyists working on life and family issues.

Stemcellresearch.org—DoNoHarm: The Coalition of Americans for Research Ethics is the banner site for the debate over the destructive use of embryonic stem cells in research. Stemcellresearch.org is a clearinghouse of information on alternatives to embryonic stem cells, particularly information on research with adult and cord blood stem cells.

Americans United for Life (http://www.aul.org and http://blog.aul.org)— AUL is a nonprofit, public-interest law and policy organization whose vision is a nation in which every human being is welcomed in life and protected in law. The first national pro-life organization in America, AUL has been committed to defending human life through vigorous judicial, legislative, and educational efforts at both the federal and state levels since 1971.

15

SOCIAL JUSTICE, SOCIAL RELIEF, AND NEW MEDIA

Stephen Shields

http://faithmaps.wordpress.com

INTRODUCTION

It is a popular misconception that evangelicals have only recently begun to be involved in social justice and relief issues. In fact, evangelicals have been involved in such practical efforts since the very beginning of the movement, with stalwarts such as the great eighteenth-century British evangelist George Whitefield working to start orphanages while in the midst of his Great Awakening campaigns in America.[1] That being said, evangelicals do seem to be working harder to ramp up their efforts in these areas than they have been in the last several decades.

A shift seems to be taking place as more and more congregations extend their interest beyond eternal concerns and address practical issues of the here and now. Yet even to phrase these new concerns as somehow being in tension with the gospel and evangelism is to miss the heart of those churches moving in this new direction. For many of the leaders of these churches are simply following Jesus as he leads them to care for widow and orphan, to clothe those without covering, to feed those who are hungry, to shelter those who have no protection, and, yes, to call those they serve to believe in the Lord Jesus Christ as

---

[1]Mark A. Noll, *The Rise of Evangelicalism: The Age of Edwards, Whitefield and the Wesleys* (Downers Grove, IL: InterVarsity Press, 2003), 103ff.

their Lord and Savior. These churches are serving the whole man with a focus on his eternal and temporal needs. Many are using the term *missional churches* to describe local spiritual communities who take a more holistic approach to serving those around them.

This shift toward *missionality* also has a cultural motivation. Tim Keller, pastor of Redeemer Presbyterian Church in New York City (http://www.redeemer.com), sees this change as one that is necessary in the West because its popular culture is moving away from the predominantly Judeo-Christian-influenced culture of the past. He says that even some years ago as the culture was changing, "the church still ran its ministries assuming that a stream of 'Christianized,' traditional/ moral people would simply show up in services." In speaking of the new missional church that's needed, Keller notes, "In general, a church must be more deeply and practically committed to deeds of compassion and social justice than traditional liberal churches and more deeply and practically committed to evangelism and conversion than traditional fundamentalist churches. This kind of church is profoundly 'counterintuitive' to American observers. It breaks their ability to categorize (and dismiss) it as liberal or conservative. Only this kind of church has any chance in the non-Christian west."[2]

Along with this move toward missionality, many churches are also beginning to transition from an *attractional* model where their *modus operandi* is to incentivize their neighbors to visit their church building for the purpose of evangelism to a more *incarnational* approach where, like Jesus as he entered our world as a man, they move toward those they are seeking to love within their own communities.[3] These churches go to their neighbors where they live rather than just trying to get their neighbors to come visit their church buildings. As these churches go, they seek to meet *all* of their neighbors' needs, whether physical, financial, emotional, spiritual, etc. New media are helping these churches move in these new directions.

Through the lowered cost of interaction and information precipitated by the rise of new media, evangelicals are more resourced than they've ever been to involve themselves in social justice and relief min-

[2]Tim Keller, "The Missional Church," Redeemer Presbyterian Church; http://www.redeemer2.com/resources/papers/missional.pdf.
[3]Michael Frost and Alan Hirsch write about the *attractional* and *incarnational* churches in their 2003 work *The Shaping of Things to Come* (Peabody, MA: Hendrickson Publishers, 2003).

istries. Online discussion groups, e-mail, instant messaging, and other technologies allow more spontaneous communication that is less tied to participants' calendars or locations than ever before. These capabilities allow local church communities to strategize, organize, and execute more quickly. Web sites can be quickly set up to act as portals to and repositories of the most critical information relevant to the specific task at hand. And these online tools enable local church communities to quickly inform their constituents of updates under changing conditions.

DELAY IN THE USE OF NEW MEDIA

In technology, hardware development precedes software development. The most efficient uses of such development generally lag way behind. This phenomenon is a function of users simply not knowing what's available technologically and of the natural human tendency to keep doing things in ways they've always been done. Another complicating factor that can inhibit technological adoption is the exponential growth of technical innovations. It can be very difficult for any individual or organization simply to keep up with all the opportunities to interact with others online, particularly as various applications come in and go out of vogue.

Anecdotal evidence indicates that most churches are either in the early stages of adopting new media for most church functions, including social justice/compassion ministries, or they haven't begun at all. Most applications within the churches that are using new media have to do with the recruitment, education, organization, and strategizing associated with the execution of these social relief and social justice activities. Churches are not typically using new media to directly serve folks in need because these individuals do not typically have as much discretionary time and income to invest in new media activities such as listening to podcasts, spending time on social network sites, viewing web sites, etc. This is even truer in developing countries, though it is becoming less true in the developed world as the cost of entry to the online world declines.

AN IMPORTANT DISTINCTION: SOCIAL JUSTICE AND SOCIAL RELIEF

In considering new media efforts in these areas of service, it's helpful to underline the difference between *social justice* and *social relief*.

Social relief involves service to individuals and communities to directly meet their immediate specific needs. *Social justice* efforts, on the other hand, address the underlying causes that precipitate those needs. So, for example, my wife Beth and I lead a ministry called KatrinaGrace (http://katrinagrace.blogspot.com) in the Baltimore area through Grace Community Church (http://gcconline.org) that sends work teams to the New Orleans area to do manual labor. This is strictly *social relief* work. If, however, KatrinaGrace were to begin advocacy work in Washington, DC in an attempt to influence the passing of legislation that would, say, mandate federal guidelines for emergency response procedures of municipalities, that would be working in the area of *social justice*.

Kirsten Strand, who leads Community 4:12 (http://www.communitychristian.org/ministries/community412/) at Community Christian Church (CCC) in the Chicago area, elaborates on the differences between social justice and social relief ministries. She says that social relief work is "focused on providing 'relief' or 'hand-outs' to alleviate suffering." She continues, "Food drives, food pantries, homeless shelters, free clothes, etc. are examples of social relief efforts. There are absolutely times when relief ministries are needed; however, they tend not to address the 'justice' issues that keep people living in poverty. 'Hand-outs' are great in crisis situations, but 'hand-ups' are needed to break the cycle of poverty." Kirsten also notes, however, that sometimes individuals and organizations might stop at social relief efforts rather than digging into the underlying causes, because relief is easier and can help salve a person's conscience. She explains, "To be frank, at times, relief ministries can benefit the givers more than the receivers. They make givers/donators feel good. It feels good (and is relatively easy) to drop off a bag of food at a food drive. It is much harder to help set up or participate in a food co-op that helps employ low-income people and allows people the dignity of purchasing food (or volunteering at the co-op in exchange for food) instead of just showing up at a pantry and getting a free bag of food. It is easier and provides more instant gratification to send money to a relief organization than to be a part of an advocacy effort like the ONE Campaign to try and influence systems and structures that can really help impact world poverty/AIDS."[4]

---

[4]Kirsten Strand, interview with author, August 1, 2007.

Churches are using new media in a number of ways to support their social justice and relief strategies.

COMMUNITY 4:12

Kirsten Strand founded the ministry in 2004. "I started Community 4:12," Kirsten says, "because personally I am deeply passionate about justice and development issues." Community 4:12 provides members of the Chicago area multi-site church opportunities to both work for *social justice* and to provide *social relief*. The ministry expresses its purpose in its page on CCC's web site (http://www.communitychristian. org/connect/ccrc412.html):

> Community 4:12 brings compassion, social justice, and community development ministries to under-resourced communities. We bring together CCC attenders and others who feel called to impact communities that are culturally and economically different from our own. Compelled by Jesus' example, we are committed to bringing hope, resources and restoration to struggling communities . . . one neighborhood at a time. We roll up our sleeves and collaborate with community leaders in schools, government, social services agencies and businesses, to address the specific needs of each focus community. Our efforts can extend to many aspects of community life: housing, transportation, education, employment, business development, life skill training, health care and spiritual growth.

In December 2006, Kirsten also started a blog—http://community412.typepad.com—to support Community 4:12's efforts. She sees the blog as one way to help CCC congregants get a clearer understanding of the deeper *social justice* issues that leads to situations requiring *social relief*. Kirsten says that her blog helps her "to make community development and social justice issues 'real' for people through our experience of working and recently moving to an under-resourced community."[5] But Kirsten has discovered a number of other benefits since she began blogging. She has also found that her blog has helped her develop contacts and relationships with like-minded individuals outside of CCC. She comments, "It has put me in touch with people around the world that are interested in his issue."[6] One of Kirsten's

---

[5]Ibid.
[6]Ibid.

primary motivations for starting the blog was simply to create a place where she could chronicle her thoughts. Kirsten sees this as a valuable resource for when she might wish to chronicle Community 4:12's activities in a future article or book. The blog has also exposed Community 4:12 to a wider audience within CCC as folks have clicked on links to the Community 4:12 blog from the site of CCC's senior pastor, Dave Ferguson (http://daveferguson.typepad.com), and from the blogs of other staff members. As a result of the CCC members visiting her blog, Kirsten has had the opportunity to engage them in conversation about Community 4:12 activities and purposes.

Another new media tool that Kirsten believes has been even more helpful than her blog has been a newsletter that she e-mails out to around five hundred individuals every week. She uses this publication to inform her volunteer community of various Community 4:12 service opportunities.

While Kirsten has definitely seen some good results from her new media efforts, she comments, "I'm pretty much in the infancy stage of using this technology."

THE DREAM CENTER

The Dream Center (http://www.dreamcenter.org) was a Los Angeles church founded in 1994 by the father and son team of Matthew and Tommy Barnett.[7] The church moved into the old Queen of Angels Hospital, which had been dormant since the eighties, in 1996. After merging with the famous Angelus Temple in 2001, the local church community was free to devote the substantial Queen of Angel facility entirely to outreach ministry. The 360,000-square-foot facility with over a thousand rooms provides the ministry with ample space to headquarter their over two hundred ministry outreaches to their community.[8] However, while the church has established a headquarters at the former hospital, Jodi Anderson, who's been on staff with The Dream Center since 2000, shares, "Most of [these ministries] don't take place on campus. They take place out on the streets because that's where the people are."

---

[7]"The Dream Center—The Beginning," The Dream Center; http://www.dreamcenter.org/the_beginning.shtml.
[8]"The Dream Center—Queen of Angels," The Dream Center; http://www.dreamcenter.org/the_q_o_a.shtml.

The Dream Center's outreach ministries serve local families struggling with poverty in a number of tangible ways. Jodi comments, "We have multiple food trucks that go out and feed about 35,000 people a week." The Center runs a free clothing store with new or gently used items supplied by local companies from their overruns or through generous individual donations. They also supply families with furniture or even appliances. Other ministries in which The Dream Center is involved include a medical outreach to homeless who are afraid of visiting shelters and an orphan/foster care ministry.

Within the last two years, The Dream Center has discovered that increasingly people are beginning their involvement in the church's outreach ministries *through online channels*. Jodi relates, "We have a lot of people come to us to get information about finding purpose in their lives." Individuals from their local communities use The Dream Center's web site to explore both volunteer opportunities and the chance to get involved financially with the church's impact on the region. Folks who are already part of the church are looking online to get information. "It's right there; it's immediate; it's live; it can be updated at any point," Jodi says.

The convenience of the church's information being available 24/7 and the ease with which people can sign up online draws potential volunteers to this way of interacting with The Dream Center. The church has also found that volunteers who connect with The Dream Center online tend to be more likely to volunteer than individuals who connect with them through other media. Perhaps more significantly, they've discovered that the people whom the church actually wishes to help are also going online to see what the church offers. Jodi comments, "A lot of people come to find us and find how we can help them through the Internet. It's no longer something that only people with means have access to."

Jodi talks about how especially crucial the online connection is for those who travel from all over the United States and the world to The Dream Center as they reach out to Los Angeles as a part of their short-term mission program:

"The vast majority of our short-term mission teams go online, check us out, and then set up their short-term mission trip online. They start with their initial contact online; they actually come out, and then their online connection continues to be the way that they stay in contact and involved. It really becomes their main source of interaction and communication with The Dream Center in addition to the people we serve and the other people whom they met from other churches."

The over five thousand individuals who participate every year in short-term missions at the church are able to continue their involvement with each other through the guestbook function on The Dream Center's web site.

The Dream Center is currently pursuing some new online initiatives. Jodi says they're trying to determine "how to truly maximize the use of this medium to make a world impact—to meet people's needs without losing that personal touch."

SADDLEBACK CHURCH

Rick Warren, pastor of Saddleback Church (http://www.saddleback.com) in Lake Forest, California, launched the church's P.E.A.C.E. Plan in November 2003. P.E.A.C.E. stands for

- Planting Churches
- Equipping Leaders
- Assisting the Poor
- Caring for the Sick
- Educating the Next Generation[9]

Rick addresses his vision this way: "There are thousands of villages in the world that have no school, no clinic, no business, no government—but they have a church. What would happen if we could mobilize churches to address those five global giants?"[10] Toward executing this vision, as of this writing Saddleback has deployed over 7,400 people on international mission trips with future visits planned for Rwanda, Kenya, Uganda, North Africa, the Middle East, Argentina, Mexico, Central Asia, East Asia, Thailand, Sri Lanka, the Philippines, the Ukraine, and the Fiji Islands.[11]

---

[9]Lauri Arnold, "Saddleback Launches History-making P.E.A.C.E Campaign," Pastors.com; http://www.pastors.com/RWMT/article.asp?ID=228&ArtID=8747.
[10]Mark Kelly, "P.E.A.C.E. Plan a Worldwide Revolution, Warren tells Angel Stadium Crowd," PurposeDriven.com; http://www.purposedriven.com/en-US/AboutUs/PDintheNews/Archives/25th_Celebration.htm.
[11]"Global Opportunities, "Saddlebackfamily.com; http://www.saddlebackfamily.com/peace/global_opps.asp.

To support people within the church who are planning a P.E.A.C.E. trip, Saddleback has launched an internal web site that they call their P.E.A.C.E. System. Those planning to go can use the system to find others also going and form teams. On this site, team members can track their trip funds, complete required trip training, and find out about immunizations, how to get visas, passports, etc. The tool also allows trip participants to track themselves as they progress through the steps they need to go through to plan a P.E.A.C.E. trip. P.E.A.C.E. team members can also use the system to research the part of the world they are planning to visit. Jeremiah Goley, who serves Saddleback as a Global Coordinator for the P.E.A.C.E. Plan, says that Saddleback has been using some version of this tool for over three years. He explains that the system has helped them enormously in mobilizing their members to reach out globally.

Current plans are for the site to include a global mapping component, areas for interactive discussion with past P.E.A.C.E. team members, and a feedback-gathering component that participants can use after their trips.[12] Saddleback also plans to offer streaming audio and video of their trip training through this system in addition to integrating it with their church member database and even their General Ledger.

Saddleback's leaders, under Rick Warren's direction, have come to understand that to complete the vision of the P.E.A.C.E. Plan they will have to take advantage of every tool available. Jeremiah Goley explains, "In order for P.E.A.C.E. to be what God wants it to be, technology has to have a role in it. New technology makes distance irrelevant. It is a critical part of the vision of P.E.A.C.E.; a vision of mobilizing God's Church to share Christ's message of hope to the hurting and oppressed peoples of the world." Pastor Rick says, "Every time God's word is put in a new technology, there's a spiritual awakening. We are in a very exciting age where technology is allowing the church to have a far greater impact because it shrinks distance and time, and it multiplies the message. That's good news when you're trying to share good news."[13]

---

[12]"Summary of the P.E.A.C.E. Briefing for Mission Agencies," Catalyst Services; http://www.catalystservices.org/bm~doc/peace1-2.pdf.

[13]Gwendolyn Driscoll, "New-media Missionaries," *The Orange County Register*; http://www.ocregister.com/ocregister/news/local/article_1336884.php.

NATIONAL COMMUNITY CHURCH

National Community Church (http://theaterchurch.com), whose lead
pastor is Mark Batterson, is involved in both social justice and social
relief. The Washington, DC multi-site church launched a homeless
ministry in 2005 called InService. That ministry's two groups meet
weekly on Sundays to hand out lunches and perform other acts of
service at their Union Station and Ballston campuses. NCCers and
folks directly served by InService gather weekly in an associated small
group called The Living Room. The church's *Discipleship Atlas* says
about the group, "During our time together we enjoy a good meal and
dinner conversation, studying the Word of God, discussing the Sunday
sermon, praying together and building community and fellowship."[14]
Another group within the church is called Living out Social Justice, and
that group also meets weekly to discuss "God's heart for justice," in
addition to participating in practical service projects.

John Hasler has been attending NCC since September 2004
and was very involved with the formal beginnings of the church's
initial efforts in the areas of social justice and relief. He started a
blog (http://in-service.blogspot.com) in March 2005 that helped him
easily communicate to interested NCCers specifics about upcoming
events and service opportunities. The blog also provided John and
others the opportunity to share their thoughts and experiences about
these ministries. NCC groups in this ministry space also utilize online
discussion groups such as Google Groups (http://groups.google.com)
and Yahoo Groups (http://groups.yahoo.com) for announcements and
online community.

John shared that the church uses Xanga to set up blog sites to support their Week of Justice events (see, for example, http://www.xanga.
com/weekofjustice2). This site allows them to quickly and easily set
up a specific URL where they can post the schedule for that week's
various events.

InService also distributes a simple weekly newsletter via e-mail to
keep members up-to-date on upcoming events and sign-up information.

John suggests that it's important for ministry leaders not to be
discouraged if they don't get a lot of traffic or feedback from their
online efforts. He says, "I still think that it's important to get it out

---

[14]*Discipleship Atlas*, National Community Church, 9.

there because there are always people online and you never know who's going to come across your blog or your discussion group and who's going to be affected."

John also believes that it's important for evangelical churches working in this area of ministry to let their light shine online because of the belief that such churches don't do much in terms of social justice and practical social relief work. He says, "It's a stigma that we have to fight against."

ONLINE MICROFINANCE

While most online efforts related to social justice and relief ministries are primarily designed to provide resources for those providing services, there is one striking exception to this general rule. That exception is in the area of online microfinance. Microfinance is one area where people can *directly* impact the lives of those in need through online media.

The World Bank on their YouThink web site (http://youthink.worldbank.org) defines *microfinance* as "small loans to start or expand small businesses given to poor people who are usually not able to borrow money from commercial banks because the amount of money is too small."[15] Online microfinance allows participants to directly make small loans—called *microloans*—online to individuals and small businesses in developing companies. Perhaps the most famous online microfinance site is Kiva (http://www.kiva.org). MSNBC reports that over 94,000 microfinanciers through Kiva have made over fifteen thousand loans with a total amount of over ten million dollars.[16] The amount that these small businesses request for a loan averages about 650 dollars, and the average lender on Kiva is providing three loans for twenty-five dollars. Ninety-nine percent of borrowers repay their loans. No money from loans goes toward Kiva operational costs; those costs are all provided by donations.[17]

One lender named Keri from Nashville says, "I've helped people to buy rice to plant and flowers to grow, and I've given money for sewing

---

[15]"Microfinance," YouThink Glossary; http://youthink.worldbank.org/glossary.php#mmm.
[16]Jen Brown, "Changing the World One Loan at a Time," MSNBC; http://www.msnbc.msn.com/id/20534002 (accessed 9/18/07).
[17]"The $10 Million Giveaway?", People of the Web—Yahoo News; http://potw.news.yahoo.com/s/potw/37837/the-10-million-giveaway;_ylt=Aowt8JsFPfGUKgZm9keDJ0cKwId4.

machines and fabric and even cows. It makes me happy that I can see exactly where my 'charity' is going. I have a portfolio of people I've loaned to. It's almost like you know them personally."[18]

Kiva's model for working with entrepreneurs in developing countries is suggestive for how churches in developed countries might get more deeply involved with the communities of developing countries. On their Partners page (http://www.kiva.org/about/partners), Kiva says:

> Kiva partners with quality microfinance institutions. To partner with Kiva your organization must be registered with your government, and must have regular internet access. Kiva prefers to partner with organizations that have a long history of lending to the poor.[19]

The online access of the partnering institution allows Kiva to communicate more easily with local entrepreneurs and to provide them with loans. Similarly, churches could establish relationships in providing funding and other resources to the local communities of other countries.

CONCLUSION

Whereas just a few years ago it was a novelty for churches to have their own web sites, today online tools are increasingly becoming an integral part of the church's approach to various ministerial endeavors. As evangelical churches are getting more and more involved in social justice and relief, they are taking what they've learned about new media and applying it to these areas of service as well. Ministry web sites provide easily accessible resources where volunteers and church staff can get information specific to social justice and relief concerns. Online discussion groups and chat rooms, in addition to e-mail, provide individuals within the church with an easy way to communicate and strategize approaches together. Podcasts, streaming video, and other downloads enable ministry leaders to cast their vision to their constituents and provide critical education. And the ability to execute

---

[18]M. P. Dunleavey, "7 Ways to Buy Happiness," MSN Money; http://articles.moneycentral.msn.com/SavingandDebt/SaveMoney/7WaysToBuyHappiness.aspx.
[19]"Kiva's Field Partners"; http://www.kiva.org/about/partners (accessed November 2007).

online monetary transactions provides churches with a powerful tool for serving targeted communities in very tangible ways.

As Westerners increasingly live a portion of their lives online and as the cost of entry to the virtual world declines, new media will provide missional churches seeking to use more incarnational approaches a valuable channel for education, strategizing, and, for some, a means of communicating directly with those they wish to serve.

We are in the early days of online community; so churches will need to vigilantly pay attention to what's working and what needs to be abandoned. As church leaders become increasingly comfortable with online tools and strategies, they will be able to focus more on the people they are targeting to serve and less on the tools themselves. What's truly exciting is that these tools are making it easier for local churches to get practically involved with the people to whom they wish to show Christ's love.

ABOUT THE CONTRIBUTORS

Roger Overton (BA, California State University Long Beach) is currently a graduate student at Talbot School of Theology. He has taught apologetics classes and workshops at several churches, schools, and youth camps in Southern California. Originally a solo-blogger, Roger currently blogs with some of his friends at www.AteamBlog.com.

John Mark Reynolds is the founder and director of the Torrey Honors Institute and associate professor of philosophy at Biola University. In 1996 he received his PhD in philosophy from the University of Rochester. Reynolds's first book, *Maker of Heaven and Earth: Three Views on the Creation and Evolution Debate*, was coauthored with J. P. Moreland. His latest book, *Towards a Unified Platonic Human Psychology*, is a close examination of Plato's view of the soul as seen in the *Timaeus*. Several of his technical articles have been published on philosophy of religion as well as popular articles in journals such as the *New Oxford Review* and *Touchstone*. Reynolds lectures frequently on ancient philosophy, philosophy of science, homeschooling, and cultural trends. He regularly appears on radio talk shows, including the *Hugh Hewitt Show*, and actively blogs on cultural issues (www.johnmarkreynolds.com). Dr. Reynolds and his wife, Hope, have four homeschooled children—L.D., Mary Kate, Ian, and Jane.

Matthew Anderson graduated summa cum laude from Biola University in 2004, where he is also a Perpetual Member of the Torrey Honors Institute. After graduation, while starting and maintaining his blog, he began working as a high school teacher. In 2005 he not only married his beautiful wife, Charity, but was also heavily involved in the planning of the first ever GodBlogCon. Since then he has continued to work with high schoolers while pursuing a writing and speaking career.

Joe Carter is the director of web communications for the Family Research Council and the author of the award-winning blog, Evangelical Outpost (http://www.EvangelicalOutpost.com).

Matthew Eppinette, MBA, MA, is communications director at Americans United for Life (Chicago) and an associate fellow at The Center for Bioethics & Human Dignity (Bannockburn, Illinois). A chapter authored by him appears in *Everyday Theology: How to Read Texts and Interpret Trends* (Baker Academic, 2007). In addition, he has been published in *Ethics & Medicine: An International Journal of Bioethics* and in *Industrial Management and Data Systems*. Conferences at which Matthew has made presentations include the St. Louis Conference on Biblical Discernment, the Humanities and Technology Association's Technology and Religion conference, and The Center for Bioethics & Human Dignity's Neuroethics: The New Frontier. He and his wife, Ginger, live in Chicago.

Terence Armentano is the assistant director of distance education at Bowling Green State University. He is a lead instructional designer and has designed, developed, implemented, and regularly facilitates BGSU's three-week Online Faculty Training Program. He also develops multimedia courseware and provides technological and pedagogical support to assist administrators and staff, campus program directors, and individual faculty in the planning, design, development, and implementation of distance courses for various campus curricula and degree programs. In addition, he has taught graduate courses online in curriculum and instruction with an emphasis in technology for Grand Canyon University. He received a Bachelor of Science in technology in visual communication technology and a Master of Education in career and technology education from Bowling Green State University. He is also the webmaster and youth pastor for Bowling Green Covenant Church in Bowling Green, Ohio.

David Wayne is a graduate of the University of Florida and Reformed Theological Seminary and has done additional graduate studies at Columbia Biblical Seminary and Graduate School of Missions. He has served as a youth minister and senior pastor at two churches in Florida and since 2002 has been the senior pastor of Glen Burnie Evangelical Presbyterian Church (PCA) in Glen Burnie, Maryland. David has been blogging at the Jollyblogger (http://

jollyblogger.typepad.com) since 2004 and was a plenary panelist and workshop speaker at the first GodBlogCon in 2005.

Tod Bolsinger came to San Clemente Presbyterian Church (www. scpres.org) in 1997 after serving for ten years at First Presbyterian Church of Hollywood. He earned a PhD in theology and Master of Divinity from Fuller Theological Seminary, where he teaches as an adjunct assistant professor of practical theology. He has been married to Beth since 1989. Beth is a marriage and family counselor in private practice. They have two children, Brooks and Alison.

The Rev. Dr. Mark D. Roberts is the senior director and scholar-in-residence for Laity Lodge, a multifaceted ministry in the Hill Country of Texas. Before taking on this position in 2007, he was for sixteen years the senior pastor of Irvine Presbyterian Church in Irvine, California (a city in Orange County about forty miles south of Los Angeles). He studied at Harvard University, receiving a BA in philosophy, an MA in the study of religion, and a PhD in New Testament and Christian origins. He has taught classes in New Testament for Fuller Theological Seminary. He has written several books, including *No Holds Barred: Wrestling with God in Prayer* (WaterBrook, 2005), *Dare to Be True* (WaterBrook, 2003), *Jesus Revealed* (WaterBrook, 2002), *After "I Believe"* (Baker, 2002), and *Ezra, Nehemiah, Esther* (Word, 1993). His most recent book is *Can We Trust the Gospels?* (Crossway, 2007). He serves on the editorial board of *Worship Leader* magazine, where he publishes articles and reviews, including his regular column "Lyrical Poetry." Most of his writing these days appears on his blog, www.markdroberts.com. He also writes a daily devotional that appears at www.thehighcalling.org. He often speaks for churches and other Christian groups and has been interviewed on over eighty radio programs nationwide. Mark is married to Linda, and they have two children.

Rhett Smith has been involved in college ministry for the last thirteen years and most recently launched the online college ministry network Collective Muse (www.collectivemuse.org) as a way to collaboratively explore innovative ways of doing college ministry. He graduated from Fuller Theological Seminary with an MDiv in 2003 and an MSMFT in 2007. He is passionate about working with college students and emerging adults, especially as they face the many issues

related to the transition from one life stage to the next. You can find
his writing at his blog www.rhettsmith.com, the youth ministry blog
Collection of Crumbs (www.collectionofcrumbs.wordpress.com), and
Leadership Network's book blog (http://books.leadnet.org). He lives in
Dallas with his wife and baby daughter.

Fred Sanders (fredfredfred.com) is associate professor of theology
at Biola University's Torrey Honors Institute. He blogs with a team of
friends at Scriptorium Daily (http://www.ScriptoriumDaily.com). He
has a PhD in systematic theology from the Graduate Theological Union
in Berkeley and an MDiv from Asbury Theological Seminary. He has
written a book on the doctrine of the triune God entitled *The Image of
the Immanent Trinity* and is also the cartoonist behind *Dr. Doctrine's
Christian Comix*, considered the best theological comic books ever
made. He lives in Southern California with his wife, Susan, and their
two children (Freddy and Phoebe).

Jason D. Baker is an associate professor of education at Regent
University where he teaches and conducts research about online
distance education. He has advised and trained faculty in the use of
educational technology, has consulted with institutions developing
online learning programs, and has been an active online instructor and
distance learner for the past decade. On the forefront of educational
technology and online learning, he has authored numerous articles
and books in the field, including *Christian Cyberspace Companion*,
Baker's Guide to Christian Distance Education, and *The Student
Guide to Successful Online Learning*. He manages the Baker's Guide
to Christian Distance Education web site (www.BakersGuide.com),
which contains over five hundred Christian distance education programs from kindergarten through graduate school. He earned a BS in
electrical engineering from Bucknell University, an MA in education
from The George Washington University, and a PhD in communications from Regent University. Jason and his wife, Julianne, currently
live in Chesapeake, Virginia and homeschool their three children.

Scott Ott is editor-in-chief, senior reporter, and the entire "vast editorial staff" of ScrappleFace.com, the family-friendly daily news satire
site that he started in July 2002. He writes a non-satirical column at
ScottOtt.Townhall.com. Father of four and husband of Stephanie, he
holds a BA in journalism from Pennsylvania State University and serves

as executive director of Victory Valley Camp, a children's ministry of the Bible Fellowship Church.

Stephen Shields is the founder of faithmaps.org, a manager with *USA Today*, a freelance writer, and a consultant. Stephen also serves on the Leadership Development Team of Grace Community Church in Fulton, Maryland. In addition, Stephen and Beth co-lead a ministry serving folks in Louisiana that survived Katrina and Rita called KatrinaGrace. Stephen received an MDiv from Grace Theological Seminary and lives with his wife and three daughters—Michaela Siobhan, Skye Teresa, and Alia Noelle—in the Baltimore-Washington corridor.

GLOSSARY

AdSense: An ad serving program run by Google. Web site owners can enroll in this program to enable text, image, and/or video advertisements on their sites. These ads are administered by Google and generate revenue on either a per-click or per-thousand-impressions basis.

Bandwidth: In web site hosting, the term *bandwidth* is often used metaphorically to describe the amount of data that can be transferred to or from the web site or server, measured in bytes transferred over a prescribed period of time. This can be more accurately described as "monthly data transfer." Web hosting companies often quote a monthly bandwidth limit for a web site—for example, 500 gigabytes per month. If visitors to the web site download a total greater than 500 gigabytes in one month, the bandwidth limit will have been exceeded.

Blog: A web site where entries are written in chronological order and commonly displayed in reverse chronological order. The term *blog* can also be used as a verb, meaning to maintain or add content to a blog. Many blogs provide commentary or news on a particular subject; others function as personal online diaries. A typical blog combines text, images, and links to other blogs, web pages, and other media related to its topic. The ability for readers to leave comments in an interactive format is an important part of many blogs.

Blogger: Person who runs or posts on a blog. Also blogger.com, a popular blog hosting web site.

Blogosphere: All blogs, or the blogging community. The term is sometimes used to refer to a subsection of the entire blogosphere, such as all religious or all political bloggers.

Blogroll: A listing of links to other blogs that is used to relate the site owner's interest in or affiliation with other bloggers. Blogrolls are typically found on the sidebar of a blog's template.

Categories: A method of organizing blog entries by assigning each entry to a predetermined topic. Each category topic will link to a list of entries, all with related content.

Comment spam: Similar to e-mail spam; robot "spambots" flood a blog with advertising in the form of fake comments.

Content Management System (CMS): Software that facilitates tasks required to publish web content to web sites. Some of the most popular for bloggers are Blogger, MovableType, TypePad, and WordPress.

Feed aggregator: Also known as a feed reader or simply as an aggregator, this is client software or a web application that aggregates syndicated web content such as news headlines, blogs, podcasts, and vlogs in a single location for easy viewing.

Fisking: Blogosphere slang describing detailed point-by-point criticism that highlights perceived errors, disputes the analysis of presented facts, or highlights other problems in a statement, article, or essay. Named after Robert Fisk, a British journalist who was a frequent early target of such treatment.

Flaming: Hostile and insulting interaction between Internet users. Flaming usually occurs in the social context of a discussion board, blogs, or even e-mail. A series of such interactions is known as a flamewar.

Godblog: A nickname for blogs that promote or discuss religious, usually Christian, themes.

Hat tip: Sometimes abbreviated as HT; an acknowledgment of the source where a blogger found a noteworthy item or link.

Hit: Unit of site traffic. A hit is generated when any file is served. The page itself is considered a file, but images are also files; thus a page with five images could generate six hits (the five images and the page itself).

Instant message: An electronic message sent via conversational software such as Google Talk or AIM (AOL Instant Messenger). Instant messages (or IMs) are typically brief and often contain acronyms or abbreviations for common phrases such as LOL (laugh out loud), BRB (be right back), or TTYL (talk to you later).

Link: Short for hyperlink, a navigation element in a document to another document, typically to another web site.

Milblog: A contraction of military and blog. Term for blogs written by members or veterans of any branch of service—Army, Navy, Air Force, Marines, etc.

New media: Any digital format that democratizes the production, distribution, or accessibility of information. This includes blogs, podcasts, vlogs, and social networks.

Newsgroup: A discussion group centered around a topic of common interest. Newsgroups are typically accessed through Newsreader software or via e-mail and function like a public bulletin board. Interest in newsgroups has declined as blogging has gained popularity.

Page view: Unit of site traffic. A page view is generated when a visitor requests any page within the web site. A visitor will always generate at least one page view (the main page) but could generate many more.

Permalink: Permanent link, the unique URL of a single post. Used when a blogger wants to link directly to a blog entry.

Podcast: An audio or video broadcast that has been converted to an MP3 file or other digital file format for playback in a digital player or computer. "Pod" in podcast was coined from "iPod," the predominant portable, digital music player. Most audio podcasts are primarily verbal, but they may contain music. Using the RSS syndication format, podcasts are made available to subscribers just like news feeds, allowing users to listen to the program at their convenience.

Podcatcher: Client software or a web application that aggregates podcasts for easy viewing.

Post: An entry written and published to a blog.

RSS: Acronym for "Rich Site Summary" or "Really Simple Syndication." *RSS* refers to a family of web feed formats used to publish frequently updated content such as blog entries, news headlines, or podcasts. An RSS document, which is called a "feed," "web feed," or "channel," contains either a summary of content or the full text entry from the associated blog or web site. RSS makes it possible for people to keep up with their favorite blogs or web sites in an automated manner that's easier than checking them manually. RSS content can be read using software called an "RSS reader," "feed reader," or an "aggregator." The user subscribes to a feed by entering the feed's link into the reader or by clicking an RSS icon in a browser that initiates the subscription process. The reader checks the user's subscribed feeds regularly for new content, downloading any updates that it finds.

Second Life: A virtual world in which users can create alternate identities. The software has been used for gaming, business, and developing community among other things. Similar virtual worlds include Active Worlds and There.

Site traffic: The amount of data sent and received by visitors to a web site; used to gauge the popularity of a blog or web site. Web traffic can be analyzed by viewing the traffic statistics found in the web server log file, an automatically generated list of all the pages served. (See also *Hit, Page view*.)

Skype: A program that enables users to make calls from their computer. Fees for the service are usually determined by the type of device receiving the call (computer, cell phone, or telephone).

Social network: An online place where a user can create a profile and build a personal network that connects him or her to other users. Some of the most popular social network sites are MySpace, Facebook, and LinkedIn.

Tag: A keyword or term associated with or assigned to a piece of information (e.g., a picture, geographic map, blog entry, or video clip) that describes the item and enables keyword-based classification and search of information. Tags are usually chosen informally and personally by its author/creator or by consumers/viewers/community.

Template: Similar to a form letter, a web template allows a user to generate multiple web pages using a pre-defined layout or design.

Thread: A series of messages related to a similar topic. Threads are usually developed as replies to a specific post on a message board or newsgroup.

TrackBack: A system that allows a blogger to see who has seen the original post and has written another entry concerning it. The system works by sending a "ping" between the blogs and therefore providing the alert.

Troll: A commenter whose sole purpose is to attack the views expressed on a blog in order to derail the discussion or to start a flamewar.

URL: Abbreviation of "Uniform Resource Locator," the global address of documents and other resources on the Web. The URL includes the Hypertext Transfer Protocol (http://), three w's (www), and the generic top-level domain (i.e., .com, .org, .net). For example, the URL for Google is http://www.google.com.

Viral: An Internet phenomenon such as a blog entry or video clip that becomes popular after having been passed along voluntarily throughout the blogosphere or social networks.

Vlog: Short for "video blog" or video podcast; a blog that contains video content.

Web 2.0: A perceived second generation of web-based communities and hosted services—such as social networking sites, wikis, and folksonomies—that aim to facilitate collaboration and sharing between users. Although the term suggests a new version of the World Wide Web, it does not refer to an update to any technical specifications but to changes in the ways software developers and end-users use the Web.

INDEX

sermons on a web site, 129; and
interactive web sites, 129-130;
and new media devotions, 133;
and pastoral care through the
Internet, 132-133; and pastoring as communication, 127-128;
and pastoring beyond the flock,
135-136; and sermon preparation, 128-129; and talking
with the leadership board of
the church, 131-132; topics
appropriate for pastors' blogs,
130-131
Pearcey, Nancy, 109
Peck, M. Scott, 122
Phaedrus (Plato), 27
Plato, 26-27, 35, 36
Podcast Alley, 86
Podcast Gear Guy, 92
podcasting, 82-83; benefits of,
88; and copyright, 89; cost of,
88; creating a podcast, 89-90;
definition of, 82; podcast directories, 86; podcast examples,
84-86; podcasting tools for
Apple, 83; podcasting tools for
Linux, 83; podcasting tools for
Microsoft Windows, 83; and
podcatchers, 82, 86; publishing
podcasts on a web site, 93-94;
software required for, 91-93;
subscribing to a podcast, 86-87;
why people create podcasts,
87-88; why people subscribe to
podcasts, 88. *See also* Podcasting, hardware required for;
Videopodcasting
podcasting, hardware required for,

desktop stand, 90; microphone,
90; mixing board, 91; Porta
Brace case, 90-91; recorder, 90;
video camera, 91
Podcasting News, 93
Podcast.net, 86
PodcastPeople, 93
Podsafe audio, 89
Podsafe Music Network, 89
poet, task of, 60
political journalism, bloggers
and journalists, 196-197; and
CNN, 197; and credibility, 193;
and the discernment of truth,
200-201; and limitations and
hazards, 203-204; and the new
media, 194-196; and the *New
York Times,* 196; and the reformation of politics and journalism, 201; and the *Washington
Post,* 197
Postman, Neil, 215-216
Pray the Psalms, 133
preserved performance/discourse,
26; and an aristocracy of information and performance, 31-33;
benefits of, 26, 30; Christians'
need for, 33-34; lack of interaction between audience and
performers, 28-29; limitations
of, 30-31; vulnerability of to
misinterpretation or vandalism,
29-30
printing press, 14-15; benefits of,
15; unintended consequences
of, 15
professors. *See* Academia, and the
new media; Academia, old me-